Tearing up the Silk Road

Tearing up the Silk Road

A modern journey from China to Istanbul, through Central Asia, Iran and the Caucasus

Tom Coote

www.tomcoote.net

Visit the author's blog to see many photos from his visit to the Silk Road and read his travelogues. Just scan the QR code above with your QR reader.

Tearing up the Silk Road

A modern journey from China to Istanbul, through Central Asia, Iran and the Caucasus

Published by
Garnet Publishing Limited
8 Southern Court
South Street
Reading
RG1 4QS
UK

www.garnetpublishing.co.uk
www.twitter.com/Garnetpub
www.facebook.com/Garnetpub
blog.garnetpublishing.co.uk

First Edition

ISBN: 978-1-85964-300-6

British Library Cataloguing-in-Publication Data
A catalogue record for this book is available from the British Library

Typeset by Samantha Barden
Jacket design by Sanna Sporrong
Cover images Travel © Bowie15 and Road to Salvation © Wimstime, courtesy of Dreamstime.com

Printed and bound in Lebanon by International Press:
interpress@int-press.com

Contents

Introduction

There is no such thing as *the* Silk Road. There were actually many Silk Roads that shifted and twisted through Asia, Europe and Africa over hundreds of years. The best known starting and end points were Chang'an (Xian), the old capital of China, and Byzantium (Constantinople/Istanbul), but many Silk Roads would bypass those cities all together. They didn't even carry mainly silk. About 30 per cent of the trade was made up of silk but these routes would also carry fruit, plants, paper, art, compasses, jewels, gold, gunpowder and the Black Death. More importantly, they carried ideas, skills and DNA.

Many consider the Silk Road to have been the Information Superhighway of its time. It can be seen as the first real instance of globalization, and to have laid the foundations of the modern world. It acted as a bridge between all the major civilizations – Egypt, China, India, Persia, Arabia, Byzantium and Rome – for over a thousand years and acted as a catalyst in their development. It wouldn't be until the sixteenth century, when new maritime trade routes opened up, that the Silk Road would begin to decline in importance.

Very few traders would ever travel the whole of the Silk Road – they would usually specialize in one particular section before passing their goods on to other merchants with the necessary skills and knowledge to extend the trade. To travel the entire Silk Road would have taken many years and been full of dangers. In 2010 I decided to make this journey from China to Istanbul, through Central Asia, Iran and the Caucasus, using only public transport. I tore through in nine weeks.

Endings and Beginnings

From East to West • Sedentary vs. Nomadic • Isolationism and Expansionism • Imitation and Identity • Love Will Tear Us Apart

It had been her birthday the day before and the clock was ticking. I had bought her a silver bracelet in the night market in Luang Prebang but what she had really wanted was a baby. I probably could have bought her one in Laos for less than the price of a silver bracelet but she wanted to make her own one.

During our last day together I had been ill for the first time in more than six months of travelling. My head was spinning and my stomach was gurgling. She told me that I didn't have to go but I felt like I did. After months of being settled in the East, I would now be taking the long, hard road back to the West. She would travel back down through Laos and Thailand to stay with her family in Krabi, while I would carry on into China and beyond. It was something I had to do. I wasn't sure why.

The sleeper bus from Luang Prebang to Kunming would take twenty-four hours and was due to leave at seven in the morning. I had paid a bit extra to the shop I had bought the bus ticket from to be picked up at 6am from our run-down wooden guest house. We sat at the picnic table outside with our backpacks and waited. Now that it was time to leave, I was surprised to feel a lump rising in my throat. I had never expected to feel this way. After six months of being together every day we had started to snipe and bicker. I thought that it would be a relief to get away but, now that the day had come, it felt like things would never be the same again. At first, she had resisted when I told her of my plans to travel back to Europe overland. I had asked her to come with me but she thought that it would be hard work and that Kazakhstan was a stupid place to go on holiday. And she didn't want me wandering off on my own as she thought I was too buffalo (the Thai equivalent of a silly cow): she worried that I always believed everything everybody told me; it was better for me to stay where she could keep an eye on me. Recently, however, she had warmed to the idea of sending me off on my own and had seemed quite pleased to be getting me out of the way – or at least until today. When a battered pick-up truck reversed into our alley and tooted its horn, we slid out from under the table and hauled in our backpacks and ourselves. We held our bags between our legs and each other's hands as we rattled off down the track. Only a few minutes later we stopped outside a Chinese restaurant that was just opening up and the driver told me to get out. We held each other tight for a few seconds and then she was gone.

After half an hour or so, a few Chinese people started to turn up outside with large hold-alls and suitcases. When the bus eventually turned up I was pleased to find a friendly Swedish couple on board who had got on at the bus station. The bus had bunk beds that were too short to allow you to lie straight down but had too little head space to allow you to sit upright. My heart sank. I was inclined to suffer from a bad back, so this could well be a less-than-comfortable journey (although all the time that I was travelling my back seemed fine; it was only when I was sedentary for most of the day that I seemed to get problems).

I settled into the top bunk in front of Jacob and Elsa, who were due to fly back to Sweden from Beijing in a few weeks. It was awkward to talk as I had to keep turning around from a half lying, half sitting position. As I didn't even have a guidebook for China, Elsa let me have a look through her badly photocopied version of the old *China* Lonely Planet guide. They had bought it second hand in Laos and it wasn't until they had taken off the cellophane wrapping that they had realized many of the pages had been ripped out. Apparently the Chinese border guides would often rip out any pages from these guides that had anything to do with the troublesome provinces of Tibet or Xinxiang.

I tried to prop myself up on the top bunk so that I could read the ropey China guidebook, but, every time we swerved across the mountainous road, I would have to grab hold of something so that I didn't fall out. Spreading out my legs on either side of the bunk and jamming them into the corners kept me wedged in for a while but then I almost crashed head first onto the floor of the bus as we careered around a particularly dramatic switchback. After another couple of near escapes I resigned myself to lying down on my back like everybody else. From the top bunk, I couldn't even see out of the window. I handed Elsa back her guidebook and put on my headphones. It was going to be a long trip.

It wasn't long until we came across the first set of road works. The Chinese were helping to finance the building of greatly improved roads all the way from the Chinese border to Thailand, in order to facilitate more effective trade routes between China and its surrounding countries. China was investing billions in its own and other countries' infrastructure in order to bolster its own long-term economic and political goals. Unfortunately, the work was still going on and looked like it would be for some time. Hordes of local peasants had been dragged out of the fields to slowly and laboriously build the roads virtually stone by stone. They were literally carrying baskets of stones to use as foundations on the existing tracks, and then laying them out one by one. Such a labour intensive approach seemed commendable in areas so deprived of decent paying work but it was causing chaos. At one point we were held up for over an hour before being permitted to crawl past on one side of the semi-demolished track way.

Just as my bladder was about to burst, we pulled into the Laos equivalent of a service station. There were two toilet doors but only a queue for one of them. It might seem obvious that there would be a good reason why nobody was going in but I thought I would have a look anyway. The light inside the wooden shack was dim, but once my eyes adjusted I could make out what looked like a molehill of shit covering the squat toilet. That much shit could never have come out of one human being's bottom and yet its near perfect conical shape suggested that it had emerged from a single anus. Had they been letting large farm animals use the facilities? As I backed out and joined the queue for the other toilet, an old man pushed in past me. I would have advised him to leave it for a few minutes but I don't think he would have understood. A few seconds later he re-emerged with a big grin on his face. He approached two of the local ladies and proudly held up a tortoise in each hand. As they lay upside down in his palms, with their legs wriggling, the two ladies looked on admiringly. They all seemed very pleased.

In hindsight I should never have used the stagnant water in the tank to wash my hands – especially as I then went on to eat with them. There wasn't much on offer but by then we were hungry enough to eat whatever we could find. Jacob and Elsa were planning to go on from Kunming to Dali, one of the most popular tourist towns in the south of China, but I wouldn't have time for that. It had taken quite a while to sort out what visas I could in Bangkok and, if I was going to make it all the way overland to Istanbul in time to fly back to England and start back at work, then it was going to be a bit of a rush. I would come to wish that I had pushed my luck a bit further and asked for even more unpaid leave.

We were all rushed back on to the bus again only to be held up a few minutes later at yet more road works. We started to worry that the Laos–China border might close before we got there, but there was nothing we could do. We lay out on the bunks with our headphones on, and stared at the ceiling of the bus. Every now and again I would catch glimpses of the grand mountain scenery if I leant around at an angle, but most of the views were obscured from my top bunk. Despite all the delays, we eventually rolled in to the rather unattractive border town of Boten and were at the customs point with thirty minutes to spare. We then queued up outside with our bags for about half an hour or so before being told that they would open up again in an hour's time. The customs officials shuttered up the windows and disappeared. I walked around to the side of the building to see what was going on and saw them all crowded around an old TV set. I had been warned about this. Apparently, they would always stop at five to watch their favourite soap. As we had been half an hour early – despite all the road works – I had thought we would be fine, but maybe they hadn't wanted to start letting anybody through in case it took longer than expected and they missed the beginning.

After another hour of waiting around and kicking our heels we were told that only the Chinese would be let through when they reopened. As the bus would then carry on without us and leave us behind, this didn't go down so well. The driver told us that we would just have to get the bus at the same time tomorrow night but we really weren't convinced that the same thing wouldn't just keep on happening for days or that there would even be any spare seats for us on their next buses. Some Chinese let us know that the same thing had been happening almost every day but that that hadn't prevented the travel agents in Luang Prebang from selling the tickets. Elsa turned out to be particularly persuasive and eventually the bus driver gave in to our relentless moaning. The money he eventually returned was more than I had expected and seemed like just about enough to pay for another bus tomorrow morning to Kunming – if we could find one.

The bus left without us while we hauled our backpacks back down to the 'town' in the hope of finding the guest house that we had been assured was down there somewhere. By now it was starting to get dark and it didn't look like a good place to get lost with nowhere to stay. Border towns in Asia are usually pretty dodgy and Boten didn't seem like an exception. They are often centres for gambling, prostitution and smuggling, and not much else. After traipsing all the way across town and all the way back in again, we came across two middle-aged Russians who had been sent over here to set up one of the casinos (like the Chinese, the Russians seemed to be doing 'business' everywhere). They helped us to find the anonymous guest house – despite still being in Laos, all the signs were now in Chinese – and, after some seemingly nonsensical bartering, we settled into a twin-bedded room for the night. Despite being quite happy to share a double bed, it turned out that Elsa and Jacob weren't actually a couple at all. Apparently they had known each other for ages and both used to be in the Cubs together. This seemed a little odd as the Cubs are only for boys up to the age of about eleven. I had got used to seeing plenty of lady-boys in Thailand but I found it difficult to imagine that Elsa ever used to have a willy. It turned out that a better translation from the Swedish would have been the Venture Scouts. I was going to ask them why they weren't together when Elsa mentioned that she couldn't wait to get to Kunming so that she could contact her boyfriend through Skype. They had started going out with each other after the trip with Jacob had been arranged. Jacob seemed to go a bit quiet but I don't think Elsa noticed.

China

Jinghong

Environmental Disaster • The Transposing of Popular Culture
Consumption and Identity • Psychotherapy and Dualism
Bridges between Worlds

We managed to get up early so as to be there when the border opened again. Elsa was feeling kind of woozy from some patches she had applied to her neck to prevent travel sickness – she had had some kind of allergic reaction to them, come up in a rash and had the eyes of someone who was deeply stoned. This wasn't a good look for passing through customs. As it happened, after blowing the remains of our Laos money on biscuits, bottled water and assorted snacks, we passed straight through customs in a matter of minutes and soon found another long-distance sleeper bus that was heading for Kunming. We eventually managed to get the driver down on price to the same amount that we had gotten back from the first bus, so we handed over the cash and we were on our way. We couldn't believe our luck. We were in China and on our way! Rather than having to lie all day on another top bunk, or attempt to sit upright on it without falling out, I opted to sit on the floor and propped my back against the metal sidebars with some blankets. I had just got myself about as comfortable as I was going to get when the bus pulled into a station a few minutes on from the border and we were all told to get off. We couldn't understand what was happening but one of the other passengers explained that we were going to have a break and that we should come back in six hours. The bus driver had been up all night; he now needed his beauty sleep.

There really wasn't anything to do in the rather dull border town of Mengla but I was glad that I had Jacob and Elsa to share my misfortunes with – at least we could have a good moan and reassure ourselves that we had only done what seemed sensible at the time. I went off to look around the town with Jacob while Elsa slouched in a wicker chair in the bus station waiting room. After a ten-minute or so walk we had seen everything there was to see in Mengla: a few boring shops, and a handful of restaurants and cafés that only seemed to have menus in Chinese. Quite a few tourists might pass through here but not many would stop for very long. After a bit of half-hearted reading – at least I could check out Elsa's guidebook without falling out of my bunk every time we swerved around a sudden bend – we wandered off to a 'coffee shop' that didn't actually have any hot water. Still, after a round of iced black coffee we all felt a bit better, and it made a change from the bus station. It had begun to dawn on us that if we carried on to Kunming on this bus then we would be arriving there at around three in the morning – this didn't seem like a good idea. Unfortunately, as soon as we had gotten off the bus, the driver had driven off with our bags locked up underneath. We would just have to wait – and hope – for him to come back. Eventually we found a decent-looking Thai restaurant with menus that we could understand and a clean toilet (still something of a rarity in much of China). Even by Thai or Laos standards the meal was excellent value, and we all started to feel much better and more optimistic – we would try to get the driver to drop us off somewhere near to Jinghong, the closest main Chinese city, and try to at least get some of our money back. This seemed a bit unlikely, but if Elsa was willing to unleash her full persuasive powers then we might be in with a chance.

Much to my surprise, Elsa *did* manage to get a reasonable amount of our money back from our driver, and a couple of hours after setting off he dropped us at the junction to Jinghong. We didn't have to wait long until a minivan came along and we were able to wave it down and negotiate a fare into the city (this wasn't such a great deal but we weren't exactly in a strong negotiating position). Jinghong is a large polluted city on the Mekong River. Like many huge Chinese cities with no famous tourist attractions, I had never heard of it. A few backpackers end up there when travelling backwards or forwards from Laos, and a few keen trekkers would use it as a base for visiting the tribal Dai people, but that seemed to be about it. The whole of southern China had been suffering from the worst drought ever recorded, and even the city centre seemed dry, dusty and parched (around 18 million at that time were estimated to be without drinking water, and it was costing the government and charities hundreds of millions of dollars in aid – the government was blaming global climate change but many were blaming the government's own ambitious hydroelectric projects). We wandered out of the bus station in search of what Elsa's fake 'Lonely Planet' had called 'The Banana College Hotel'. The map didn't seem to make much sense and nobody had heard of any hotels or colleges named after bananas. We traipsed up and down for ages but just seemed to get more lost. There were actually plenty of large hotels around but they looked expensive and full of Chinese businessmen or government employees on expense accounts (their actual salaries are rubbish but they can wangle a lot through expenses). As each car pulled up in front of the hotel's lavish forecourt, a small army of uniformed porters, assistants and assorted lackeys would rush to their assistance and enthusiastically guide them through to reception. None of them had heard of the Banana Hotel either but the few with some English were keen to help us. Between them, they eventually realized that we must have been looking for the College Hotel in Banna, and sent us off in a taxi with instructions to the driver. When the driver spoke to us in Chinese I was rather surprised to find myself answering him. It then dawned on me that what he had said must have been the same in Thai (I can't really speak Thai properly but I can make out the most-used phrases). Over the next day or so I would quite often be able to pick up on bits of conversation based on this similarity. The Laotian language is more or less the same as the dialect of Thai spoken in the north, but I hadn't expected this part of China to have so much in common linguistically. (As soon as I got into other parts of China I couldn't understand a word of their own language – apart from 'hello' and 'thank you'.)

We eventually checked into another shared room for three, in the College Hotel in Banna, just outside the university gates, and down the road from the botanical gardens. Elsa's main priority was to find an Internet café with webcam so that she could talk to her boyfriend through Skype, but first we needed to sort out our onward bus tickets and get something to eat. This might not seem very adventurous but we were quite pleased to come across a generic-looking fast food restaurant called Dico's. Along with KFCs, I would find these all over the country. When I had first visited China fifteen years previously, the McDonald's next to Tiananmen Square in Beijing had been a real novelty. After far too much green sludge with either rice or noodles on excessively long bus journeys, we had been strangely pleased to find somewhere to eat that was so clean and familiar. (I would avoid places such as McDonald's like the plague if I was at home but weeks of bad and unfamiliar food can play strange tricks with your mind.) The gleaming surfaces and air conditioning lured us into Dico's in search of burgers, fries and other fattening junk. When I first visited the Far East, you would very rarely see overweight people but now they seem to be catching up with the West in terms of excessive wobbliness. American-style fast food still retains a certain amount of glamour there, which has been lost to all but the youngest and poorest in the West. Apart from offering the options of rice and a few spicier sauces, Dico's was pretty much the same as any anonymous fast food restaurant in Europe or America. For the moment, at least, that suited us fine.

Although the city was large and busy there wasn't that much to see except for a few parks and some carved elephants. I was surprised to find a shopping mall with a multiplex cinema showing the latest Hollywood films but they had all been dubbed into Chinese (I found out some time ago that most Hollywood films are watched by more non-English speakers than by native English speakers – this might go some way to explaining why so many of certain types of films still get made). As we shuffled through the slightly tatty mall, bad cover versions of cheesy Western pop music blared out from hidden speakers. Western food and popular culture seemed to be seeping into every part of China but it still had to be transformed and translated into something that was suitable for consumption by the Chinese masses. Any sophistication, subtlety or irony seemed to get lost in the process. After (eventually) booking up the tickets for the overnight buses, we decided to visit one of Jinghong's premier attractions – the supermarket! Tourists often think that they can get a feel for the local people and culture by visiting such 'attractions' as museums and art galleries. This is absolute rubbish. Most such places have about as much to do with the real culture of a country as Morris dancing has to do with the culture of England. It is through the humble supermarket that the real soul of a people is revealed. Their other big advantage is that you can eat the exhibits. We wandered up and down, inspecting the pictures on the packets, and taking a risk on anything that looked interesting but wasn't too expensive. I bought a fake Cornetto for dessert and dripped chocolate down my front.

* * *

The next morning we managed to track down an Internet café with webcam, so Elsa could talk to her boyfriend, but they wouldn't let us use the computers unless we were members and we couldn't become members without a Chinese ID card. Eventually we found another one that was keener to take our money (fifteen years ago we would often come across people who simply couldn't be bothered to do their job if they thought it might possibly be any kind of hassle – I guess this stems from the fact that they would get paid the same pittance whatever they did). The PCs were still running ancient software that nobody had bothered to update and seemed to be riddled with viruses. After updating the browser and downloading Skype, Elsa got through to her boyfriend in Stockholm. He waved enthusiastically at us and we all had to wave back. After a while I left Elsa to her boyfriend and Skype and made my way back to our room – I still had a dodgy stomach and wanted to make use of the decent Western-style bathroom in our room before we had to check out.

After completing my ablutions and packing my bag, I wandered onto the terrace outside our rooms and ended up chatting to an older American guy who had just arrived. He had been teaching English in China for a few years now and had come down here to try to sort out a new job at the university. He had already met some of the students and they were offering to take him along and introduce him to the right people. As the students at the university passed by they would often wave and say hello. They weren't pushy at all but always seemed happy to talk to you and practise their English. It seemed that there were plenty of opportunities for native English speakers to teach in China and that, although the wages were low by Western standards, they were still enough to pay for a reasonable standard of living in most parts of China. Since my first trip here, there were noticeably more young people who could speak some English. While few of the older or middle-aged Chinese had ever had the opportunity or desire to learn, to the younger generation speaking in English seemed to be considered to be quite cool. It might well also have been necessary if they were to land the best jobs at the big international companies. China is set to become a far greater world power and, like it or not, English is still the international language. I had also taught English to Chinese students in England. They were friendly and keen and their parents were rich enough to pay for an international education. They would eventually return to China bringing new skills, ideas and attitudes (some of which might not be compatible with their parents' world view).

Jacob and Elsa came back just in time to pack up their bags before check out. They said it would seem strange to be in China without me. I had only known them for two days but it seemed longer. They hailed down a taxi on the main road and then they were gone. I still had quite a few hours to kill before catching my overnight bus to Kunming. I wandered around on my own back down in the town but couldn't find much of interest apart from some European-style bakeries selling animal-shaped cakes. I still wasn't feeling that great so made do with a chocolate mouse for my tea, and walked back up to the College Hotel. The students held up their arms to wave to me and shouted 'Hello' in English. As the computer in reception was free I sat down to check my emails and do a bit more research on where to stay in Kunming. A girl who worked on reception asked if I could help one of the students search on the Internet for information about psychologists. As I was at something of a loose end I was happy to help. She introduced me to a rather anxious-looking young woman who appeared to speak very little English. What did she want to find out about psychology? Was it actually famous psychotherapists she was interested in, such as Sigmund Freud or Carl Jung or R.D. Laing? None of these names seemed to mean anything to her. The receptionist explained that this shy young woman had problems in her head and needed someone to help her. She had asked at the university but they could only recommend some kind of counsellor or therapist who was far too expensive. I wasn't sure how I could help when we didn't even speak the same language. I tried searching 'psychotherapists in China' but it didn't look as if psychotherapy had ever really caught on there. Then I tried to explain that I wasn't really convinced that just talking about psychological problems would necessarily be enough to resolve them – if this were ever actually possible – but I was just saying words. We couldn't even speak the same language. Psychotherapy itself is deeply rooted in the culture, thoughts and language of the West – it is difficult even to discuss matters of the mind without using terms such as 'neurosis' that are alien to Confucian thought. While Chinese culture places great emphasis on harmony and conflict avoidance, Western thought is rooted in a dualism – from God and the Devil, to the conscious and the unconscious, to thesis and antithesis – in which resolution can only be achieved through conflict. Much in the same way that psychoanalysis professes a faith that psychological suffering can somehow be magically cured through simply talking, Confucianism holds that the desirable qualities of a teacher or other figures of authority will somehow be passed on to the subservient through a process of respect and reverence. It is this rigid hierarchy between the analyst and the analysand that is antithetical to the process of psychotherapy; in order for it to work at all there needs to be honesty, openness and genuine collaboration between the two. The Confucian obsession with not 'losing face' or not facing up to uncomfortable realities will inevitably put up barriers to the 'self' and, if the therapist is then seen as an infallible purveyor of wisdom, then no real dialogue or resolution can ever be achieved.

While I am sceptical about many aspects of psychoanalysis and psychotherapy, I am reasonably convinced that there is a link between the repression of the 'self' and depression. According to the German psychologist and psychoanalyst Anne-Marie Schloesser, there are 250,000 recorded suicides a year in China and another 2 million attempts. The Chinese obsession with not losing face would suggest that the real figures are far higher. The authorities have only recently acknowledged the need to address the issue of mental health, and the study and development of psychology and psychoanalysis in China is in its infancy. During the Cultural Revolution it was, to all intents and purposes, banned. Many Western 'missionaries' of psychotherapy tried in vain to spread the word to China only to find that their words don't translate. I tried my best to talk to the girl with the problems but the few words we shared could never be enough to form a bridge between our worlds. As she resigned herself to isolation and left to walk away, she turned and held up her arms to me – not waving but drowning.

Kunming

Copies of Copies • Babel • Generational Shift • Unity through Art

I had been very silly indeed. For months I had been getting around in just shorts, t-shirts and sandals. This had still been fine in Jinghong. When I emerged from under the stale smelling duvet and crawled down from my cramped bunk to emerge from the bus, I was shocked by the early morning cold in Kunming. Everybody else in the bus station was wearing jackets and scarves and woolly hats, and I was shivering in my shorts and t-shirt. We were still miles from the actual city. I had no idea where to go so just followed some other people with bags who were walking through the main gate. This seemed to be the right thing to do as I ended up in a smaller station where I managed to get a minibus into the city. As we rattled past miles of bland Chinese tower blocks, I covered my bare legs with my backpack in an attempt to repel the cold. I had photocopied some pages from Elsa's (photocopied) fake Lonely Planet but the maps hadn't come out well. I had no idea where we were so, when we passed a large McDonald's in what appeared to be a busy central square, I opted to get off. I tried to figure out where I was but my hands were shaking so much that I couldn't read the map. A beautiful Chinese girl took pity on me and offered to help. She kept waving down taxis for me and attempting to get them to take me to the hostel that I had read about, but none of them seemed to be interested (they probably took one look at me in shorts in this weather and decided that I mustn't be quite right in the head). I was just about to give up and attempt to change into my combat trousers in McDonald's when a nice lady taxi driver agreed to take me for a price that seemed quite reasonable. I squeezed in next to her on the front seat. There was a metal cage around her but she hadn't bothered to lock herself in. Maybe I just seemed mad but not dangerous? She dropped me off at an office block and pointed upstairs. I got out of the lift and was welcomed into a large modern open-plan office. I really wasn't sure what I was doing there but they seemed pleased to see me so I emptied out my backpack and began to dress in some clothes that were more appropriate for the weather (rather than taking my shorts off in front of all the office staff, I opted to put my trousers on over the top of them – I feel that it's important to maintain a certain degree of decorum when dealing with other cultures). I wasn't sure why I was there and they weren't sure what to do with me but at least I was a bit warmer now and they had made me a nice cup of tea. It turned out they had something to do with student accommodation and they tried to explain how to get to the hostel. As I was still being a bit slow, they eventually packed me off into another taxi with instructions to the driver who succeeded in dropping me off outside a YHA (it wasn't until I had checked in that I realized this *wasn't* the hostel I had been trying to find at all, but it was going to have to do).

As it was still quite early the dorms weren't ready yet, but I could go ahead and use the shared bathrooms. This was a relief as, although I'd made it through the night alright, I was still at the mercy of a runny bottom. When I walked into the shared bathrooms, a Chinese guy who was enjoying a quiet smoke nodded to me. He had his trousers around his ankles and was squatting over the toilet. This clearly wasn't one of those posh toilets with cubicle doors. I was tired and felt grotty and really couldn't be bothered with this so I went back down to reception and upgraded from the dorm to my own room with an en suite bathroom and a television (I justified this by thinking that as I had got there early in the morning I was getting two uses of the private bathroom for the cost of one night's sleep). There were some Western programmes being shown on the TV but they had all been dubbed into Chinese. Every now and then as I flicked through, I would think that I had found a channel in English but then some Chinese voice would start talking over the top. I don't know why they didn't just add a new soundtrack altogether rather than just having somebody talk on top – surely the Chinese must find it annoying to hear two people speaking at the same time in two different languages? The television might have been unwatchable but it was worth the extra money to have my own bathroom. After I'd got clean and had a bit of a rest I was finally ready to see what Kunming had to offer the discerning tourist.

Kunming, the capital of Yunnan province, is home to over 5 million people. It was once a gateway to the Silk Road and acted as a crossroads for trade between India, Myanmar and Tibet. According to the tourist brochures, Kunming is also 'the City of Eternal Spring'. I put on two t-shirts, did up my denim jacket and thrust my hands into my pockets before daring to venture back outside. Just around the corner was the popular Green Lake Park. Even on a cold weekday morning, the park was full of people just wandering about. There were pedal boats all around the lake but nobody was using them. They were more interested in eating, chatting, chess and line dancing. In every park in China there always seem to be groups of all ages, and abilities, doing their own kind of choreographed dance routines. It seems similar to US-style country dancing, but like most cultural imports it has been transposed and modified into a uniquely Chinese form of expression. There is none of the inhibition that you find among amateur dancers in the West and neither the dancers themselves nor the crowds that gather to watch them seem particularly concerned about just how good or bad the dancing actually is. It's just something to do and a bit of fun and some exercise. Outside gym equipment is also often found in Chinese parks and you would still see people using it while wrapped up warm in their coats, gloves and scarves. To be honest, they didn't seem to be putting a lot of effort into it but at least they were getting out and about (it must have been better than being stuck in a grey tower block with only rubbish TV as amusement).

Not far from Green Lake Park was Yuantong Si, a Chan (Zen) Buddhist temple that was first built in the late eighth or ninth century. Over the centuries it has been restored and rebuilt a number of times. More recently it was expanded with money from Thailand. Unusually, it lies in a natural depression and you go down steps to the temple, rather than ascending. Such attractions bring in huge amounts of tourists but nearly all of them are Chinese. The Chinese love to be tourists but, for the moment at least, they are mainly restricted to visiting their own country. If China's economy continues to grow at the current rate, then in a few years they will no doubt be getting everywhere. Every tourist attraction in the world will be overflowing with wealthy Chinese consumers, capturing the sights on the latest digital cameras. For the moment, however, they would rather save most of their newfound wealth while the West grows further into their debt (China now owns more US Treasury bonds than Japan and is therefore its principle creditor). In a few years' time the balance of power could have shifted dramatically. On the other hand, China's huge debt-backed property boom could make the Western property bubbles look like inconvenient bumps. If the whole thing comes crashing down, it could bring the rest of the world's economies with it and ruin everybody's holiday plans.

As the only Western tourist in the temple complex, I edged between the incense lighting worshippers and tried to avoid walking into too many holiday snaps. I tried not to make a nuisance of myself and nobody seemed to mind me wandering around their holy place. Not all Western visitors have been so well tolerated. At the beginning of the twentieth century, one of the French engineers who was working on the Kunming to Vietnam railway project set up house in the temple's main building. There weren't many nice places for foreigners to stay in Kunming at the time, so he selected the Yuantong Treasury hall as his place of residence. This didn't go down too well with the locals who still wanted to be able to get into the temple to pray and burn incense sticks. It took a few months, but they eventually managed to chuck him out. It would be difficult to imagine a Chinese engineer coming over to England and setting up house in the nearest cathedral because he couldn't find anywhere else that was up to his standards.

Now that I was in Kunming I would at least be able to get the overnight sleeper trains for most of my trip across China. They were much more comfortable than the buses and only slightly more expensive. As the only way to get my ticket to Chengdu was to go to the train station, I set off with my less-than-satisfactory photocopied map. I couldn't make out the lines of the roads and, although many of the main roads signs did have English translations underneath the Chinese, the spellings varied considerably. A guy who worked at the hostel pointed me in the direction of where to get the buses to the train station and I was moderately surprised that that was where I ended up. Actually buying the ticket didn't prove to be quite so easy. Nobody at the 'international' counter could speak English and I seemed to get waved on from one queue to another. Once I had eventually got hold of a second-class sleeper ticket to Chengdu, I noticed just as I was leaving that the date was for tonight and not for tomorrow. Luckily, I was allowed to change it after going through the whole process all over again. By the time that I had got the bus back to the hostel, the whole ticket-buying expedition had taken up half the day (in contrast, my visit to Yuantong temple had only taken up about ten minutes).

I still didn't feel up to eating a proper meal but as a reward for all my efforts I decided to treat myself to an ice-cream sundae at a trendy-looking café called Just Fruit. It was full of teenagers playing cards, drinking fruit shakes and smoking. Everyone seemed to be smoking everywhere in China. Apparently the cigarettes weren't very good but they were really cheap. Even though smoking in public places in England had been banned very recently, it was surprising how quickly everybody had gotten used to it. So to enter a public place and find it full of cigarette smoke seemed strangely exotic. My main reason for choosing this café had been that the menu outside was partly written in English. The café seemed to be aimed at youngsters, and to them speaking English was 'cool' (even if they couldn't really understand it). I sat down in the corner and leafed my way through the selections of desserts. I was extremely tempted by The Heaven of Ice Snow and Heart Deeply Drank in a Romantic Feeling but eventually opted for Love to get Occulty with Black Forest. It sounded exotic and I thought there might be some chocolate in it (the only decent chocolate I could find in China was called Dove, which is a brand of soap in the UK; it was far more expensive than a similar quality product in England but the cheap stuff was dreadful). My choice of a large ice-cream sundae as a main meal was justified by the existence of some fruit that was covered in sweet sauce and fake cream. I wasn't sure what the fruit was, and it didn't taste particularly good, but at least I was making an effort.

After a few more hours of traipsing around the city I went back to my room and failed to find anything that I could make sense of on the television. I lay down on my bed and searched through the bootlegged rock and metal CDs that I had bought in Bangkok. A few of the copies were a bit ropey but they had been cheap and would help to keep me amused on the long bus and train journeys. I chose a copy of Paramore's 'Brand New Eyes' and lay there on my back with the CD spinning around in the Discman on my gurgling stomach. Paramore have arguably articulated the hunger, melancholy and yearning of youth more successfully than any other rock band of their generation. Their songs bleed with a longing and passion that could only be understood by the young or the young at heart. The final track on the album, 'Decode', had been taken from the soundtrack to the teenage vampire movie *Twilight* and added on to the end. This song, more than any of their others, captures a kind of darkness and desire that is both universal and deeply American. Their world seemed a long way from China as the final lines of 'Decode' rang out ('There is something I see in you. It might kill me. I want it to be true'). The music shuddered to an end and I fell into a long, deep sleep.

* * *

Most of the next day was spent wandering around Kunming getting lost. I tend to get lost a lot at the best of times but my useless photocopied map just made matters worse. I had been trying to find some other temples that were supposedly of interest, but managed to miss them completely. Whenever I got hungry I would walk into somewhere with food and point at things that looked like they might be edible. It usually worked. I eventually managed to make my way back to the hostel to pick up my backpack. As I still had some more time until I had to leave to catch the train, I had a go on one of the PCs that the hostel had set up for Internet use. I had only been logged into my Hotmail account for a few minutes when it started automatically sending out junk emails from me to everybody who had ever sent me an email. I had been warned not to use any of the public PCs in China for any kind of financial transaction but I hadn't expected them to be quite this bad. They could easily have downloaded some free anti-virus software and upgraded the infected software to the newer, free and better-protected versions but nobody could be bothered. While technology was loved by some and cited as the way forward by many, the implementation of technical advancement was patchy to say the least. While many sites such as Facebook or YouTube were banned in China, and around 30,000 people were employed as full-time Internet censors, you still couldn't book your train tickets through the Internet and had to traipse down to the actual station that you were leaving from yourself and queue up for ages. (That said, it is possible to book Chinese train tickets from outside of the country through the Internet but this is done through agencies who you pay directly and who then send one of their staff members out to go and queue up at the station.) Surely the government could have spared a few of those 30,000 from censorship duties and got them to do something more useful like setting up an Internet-based booking system for the national train network? A system like this could literally be set up in a few hours and would save thousands and thousands of man-hours every year. Although it now seems far better than it was when I had first visited China fifteen years earlier, it still appears there are loads of people employed for the sake of it in pointless occupations while useful or necessary tasks are often neglected. I am well aware that the working lives of many in the West are also absurdly pointless but China is still far worse. The inefficiencies or illogicalities of those in authority in China are rarely challenged by those beneath them and it would take a huge cultural shift before China could produce enough innovators and iconoclasts to lead the world in any kind of technological advancement. It may well be that China's system of government will only get it so far in terms of social and economic development and for it ever to really catch up with the West it must become something else completely. This may yet happen when a younger generation takes over but the transition is unlikely to be an easy one. As young Chinese are increasingly exposed to Western culture and ways of thinking, many of the older generations' actions will be called into question and their authority will increasingly be challenged. Less of a gap, and more of a chasm, will open up between the generations. In the end, it will be those who best exploit this new influx of ideas, and harness the inevitable conflict to their own needs, who will come to form the new China.

I walked along the platform and presented my ticket to each new conductor I came across. He would look at the Chinese writing for a few seconds and then wave me on in the right direction. Eventually I made it to the right carriage and the conductor waved me inside and, after presenting my ticket again to a few more random strangers, I eventually found my way to my bed for the night. I've always quite liked sleeping on trains. The rhythm helps me sleep and I like the idea of just going to bed and waking up where I want to be. I hauled my backpack up onto the overhead baggage racks and sat down on a small foldaway seat to read my book on Genghis Khan and listen to my bootlegged CDs.

Not long after we had set off, a uniformed lady came into our carriage and made a very important-sounding announcement. Everybody stopped what they were doing – which admittedly probably wasn't much – and paid her rapt attention. After formally making what seemed to be some great claim, she opened up her bag and proudly held up what appeared to be a brightly coloured, shiny metal sausage. She turned it around so that everybody could see it, then she opened it up to reveal a set of cutlery. The shiny metal chopsticks were held up and unfolded to their full length, much to everybody's amazement. As her presentation rose to its climax, half the carriage scrambled through their bags and pockets to find the necessary cash to purchase such a wonder.

Rather than scrambling through my bag for cash, I searched through for my toiletries and wandered off to the end of the carriage to use the shared bathrooms. One of the signs above the sinks had thoughtfully been translated into English. It read 'Be careful of your treasures'. This seemed like sensible advice. When I climbed into my top bunk bed I took my passport and camera out of my bag, rolled up my lightweight army trousers which had my money in them, and placed them right next to my head and under the pillow. It seemed unlikely that anybody could climb up onto my third-level bunk and steal them without waking me. After a while, I turned off my Discman and put it into the small net that hung just above my bed. I gave up the sounds and the words of the Western world and let them be replaced with the rumble of the train and the faint sound of Chinese pop music that some teenagers in the next carriage were playing to each other on their mobile phones. As I was drawn into sleep, a few familiar notes rang out from a not-too-distant mobile phone. They were playing Paramore. Their world didn't seem so far away as the final lines of 'Decode' rang out ('There is something I see in you. It might kill me. I want it to be true'). The music shuddered to an end and I fell into a long, deep sleep.

Chengdu

International Travelling Culture • Class and Nationalism
Insularity • Sacrifice

In 1279, Genghis Khan arrived in Chengdu and killed 1.4 million people. In 2010 I arrived at Chengdu and promptly got lost. The city eventually recovered from Genghis Khan's brutal sacking and now has a population of more than 11 million. Most of them seemed to be in the queue for taxis and I had no idea what bus to get. It didn't look that far on the map so I decided to start walking. Ten minutes later I was still trying to find somewhere to get across the road from the train station. An old Chinese bloke on a motorbike started following me. Eventually we agreed a price for him to take me to Sim's Cozy Guest House – he seemed to recognize it on the map – and we were soon weaving in and out of the busy traffic. It became apparent early in the journey that he had no idea where he was taking me. When we saw a couple of Australian girls on bicycles, he sped off after them and waved them down. They seemed to think he must have thought that we knew each other. I just thought that, now he had me, he had no idea where to take me. It was quite clear he hadn't gone in the direction of the hostel at all. Like many drivers I came across in China, he didn't seem to get the idea of maps. Surely if you can point out where you are on a road map and where you want to be on it, then you must know more or less what direction to go in? In every other country in the world, pointing and miming are remarkably effective but China seems to be an exception. They would be rubbish at charades. Luckily enough, the two girls were staying at the hostel I was trying to find and gave me a much better promotional map from the hostel itself. This still didn't seem to help; I was eventually dropped off somewhere near the river and waved in the direction of a point slightly beyond. I was now far more lost – at least I would know where I was if I were still back at the train station. I handed over the fare we agreed (even though the bloke hadn't actually taken me where I wanted to go), but put my foot down when he asked for more. I walked up and down for a while trying to find something on the map that would indicate where I was but I didn't seem to getting anywhere. I went back to the big hotel where he had dropped me outside in the hope it might have some staff on reception who spoke English. While standing outside, with my bags between my legs, and attempting to match both my old and new maps, a young Chinese guy came up to me and asked me in excellent English if I needed any help. After a quick glance at the two maps he realized the hostel must have moved – not that the old guy had taken me anywhere near the original location – and asked if I would like a lift. His parents were just checking out of the hotel that we were standing in front of and they ended up dropping me off right outside the front door to Sim's Cozy Guest House.

As soon as I had walked through the doors, I felt as though I was right back on the backtrackers trail. Everything was extraordinarily well organized and efficient for somewhere in China (it had been set up by a couple of well-travelled backpackers from Singapore). It had its own laundry room, bar, restaurant, Internet café (with decent, non-infected PCs), and organized day trips to the panda bears and the Chinese opera; the guest house would even book onward train tickets for you!

Brochures were displayed throughout reception for similar-looking backpacker hostels in other big tourist cities such as Beijing, Shanghai and Xian. They all looked far better than any of the places I had stayed at on my trek across China fifteen years previously. I wondered how many of the most popular hostels were actually run by foreigners. Most of the other backpackers I met there had been going around a fairly well-established circuit from one main tourist centre to another. It was all very easy and convenient but you couldn't help feeling sometimes that you were all just holed up together in an over-protected tourist bubble. Backpacker places all over the world seem pretty much the same. Whether you are in Latin America, Africa or the Far East, they all seem to have Bob Marley posters and banana pancakes. Neither the music, the food or the décor seem to have changed for decades. The only thing that really seems to have changed is the Internet. Every backpacker centre in the world now seems to be full of people who would rather be chatting online to friends in their home countries and researching their next destination than talking to and finding out information from the other guests (let alone bothering to try to communicate with the locals). The world is increasingly connected, and more and more people are travelling further from their homes, but many of those 'international' travellers seem to have little real interest in anything outside of their own culture. It's difficult not to feel at times that 'travel' is just another commodity to be consumed on the way to other rights of passages, such as getting a mortgage and reproducing. Still, at least I could read the menu and they had decent toilets.

I was staying in a dorm room but I was the only occupant; despite being surrounded by other backpackers it was still very much off-season. Each bunk was more like a carved wooden capsule with its own drawers, shelves and wrap around curtains, and it all seemed strangely empty. But that suited me fine, having slept on a train the night before. After a full cooked breakfast – another thing I only seem to have in backpacker places – I went up on the roof to sort out my laundry and met Darren. Darren was a young English electrician on his first big trip around the Far East. Unlike most of the guests, he was on his own and very working class in outlook. When I first visited China fifteen years ago, I couldn't believe how many posh kids I met who all seemed to know each other from Oxford or Cambridge or who seemed to have been 'educated' at expensive boarding schools. What were they doing in China? Why couldn't they just go to Spain like normal people? Despite coming from wealthy, privileged backgrounds they seemed to be incredibly tight with money and thought that all Chinese people were trying to rip them off. It seemed as if the desire to visit China came more from an obligation to the values of their own culture (to acquire a superficial veneer of worldliness and be 'well travelled') than it did from any genuine curiosity or desire for difference. Over the last decade there seems to have been a marked cultural shift within the global backpacking sub-culture. Not only have backpacking and budget travel become increasingly popular among all classes within Western countries, but also they have become more genuinely 'global'. Not very long ago, the only non-Western backpackers you would ever meet were the Japanese but now you regularly meet South Korean, Taiwanese, Singaporean and Malaysian backpackers all over the world. While travelling up to China through Laos, I even met my first backpacking Thai couple. These young oriental backpackers really aren't that different from the backpackers you would meet from any Western country. They have grown up surrounded by Western culture and have absorbed Western values and beliefs in a way that is alien to previous generations. Many might argue that the real change is simply economic and that the real reason they didn't go in for this kind of budget travel before was that they simply didn't have the money. This isn't quite true, however. If most young Thais or Chinese, for example, had the money, they would far rather spend it on luxury consumer goods such as expensive cars so that other people could see how wealthy they were. Although it could be argued that travel can be just as much of a status-related purchase as name brand goods, the choice to spend on 'experience' rather than on things still reflects a cultural shift. Once people rise beyond a certain level of affluence, much of their spending becomes about the acquisition of status. This desire for symbols of status, and a poorly developed ability for critical thinking, has made the less-developed parts of the Far

East easy prey to those marketing luxury name brand products. Once a people reach a higher level of real education and analytical thinking, however, how they choose to spend their money will start to change. Although this cultural shift has started to become apparent among 'the new tigers' of the Far East, China is still a long way behind in many respects. It may be producing new millionaires every few minutes, but these still make up a tiny percentage of the population, and when they do come into money it is often absorbed into the acquisition of status symbols that will quickly lose their real and relative value.

By the time that I had eaten, showered and done my washing, most of the day was over. I ended up in the restaurant upstairs with Darren and another English guy called Theo. Theo had a posh upper-class accent, went to an expensive fee-paying school and hoped to start at Cambridge next year after finding himself in China. He had been in China through most of the winter, which didn't seem like much fun, and loved to show off the Chinese phrases he had learnt. He had started studying Chinese as he thought it would make him look cool. I'm pretty sure that nobody who went to my comprehensive had ever set about learning Chinese in the hope of seeming cool. Darren the electrician must have seemed almost as exotic to him as a Chinese peasant – posh kids like that don't normally talk to those sorts of people. That's one of the benefits of travel. He thought it was splendid that Darren had learned a sensible trade when everybody seemed to go to university these days to do things like sociology and media studies. Darren didn't seem so convinced – he had just been made redundant as an electrician and didn't think it would be that easy to find another job. As somebody who had had loads of crap jobs and then gone to university as a mature student to get a useless degree (Third World Studies) and then ended up in more crap jobs before winning a scholarship to do a Masters in IT before eventually getting a proper job and then being laid off, I wasn't sure what to recommend. I had heard that there was more chance of people moving between classes in the nineteenth century than there was today in modern Britain, and judging by mine and others' experiences I could well believe it. It still pretty much seemed as if most of the people with the best jobs had rich parents who knew all the right people and sent them to the right schools. If you came from the wrong kind of background, having any kind of brain at all was likely to cause far more trouble than it was worth. In many respects, Theo would actually have had more in common with upper class people from other countries than with working class people in his own. Until the beginning of the Industrial Revolution in Europe, it was class that provided the principle distinction between groups of people. European elites from different countries would often share the same language, ideas and beliefs of their contemporaries in other parts of Europe and would have little contact with the peasants who worked on their estates. It was only when the peasants started to move into cities to provide the necessary labour for industrialization that it became a practical necessity for all the people in the same area to speak the same language. National identities were then formed – and later exploited – on that basis. I wondered if an upper class Chinese student from a posh international school would have had more in common with Theo than Darren did.

The next morning I set off on my own to fulfil my duties as a tourist. Not far across the Jinjiang River was a whole pedestrianized tourist complex revolving around the Wenshu Temple. Hordes of Chinese tourists gathered around the souvenir shops and stalls selling the Chinese equivalents of sticks of rock and 'kiss me quick' hats. I found what looked like an entrance to the Wenshu Temple and wandered into the monastery gardens. The Buddhist temple – the biggest and best preserved in Chengdu – is more than a thousand years old. Crowds of Chinese gathered around to burn incense and sacrificial paper money in return for blessings. Around AD 960 Chengdu became the first place to widely use paper money; it also seems to have been something of a trade centre along the easternmost part of the Silk Road. Inside the Scriptures Hall was a white-jade statue of Buddha from Myanmar, incantations on leaves in Sanskrit from India, and gold-plated scripture from Japan. Perhaps the most important import that Chengdu had received along the Silk Road was Buddhism itself. Buddhist missionaries from India first made their way along this route as early as the second century BC but it wasn't until the Tang Dynasty (AD 618–907), when the Wenshu Temple was first constructed, that a uniquely Chinese form of Buddhism began to take root. The monasteries at such temples would act as a haven for the travellers and missionaries who brought with them the ideas and art that would change their world.

When Buddhism was first introduced into China it was largely thought of as a variant of Taoism as Taoist terms were all that could be used in explanation. It wasn't until later on when trade and travel began to increase along the Silk Road that many of the ideas, which had been lost in translation, began to be incorporated into the Chinese conception of Buddhism. Mahayana ('Great Vehicle') was starting to be developed around the same time that Buddhism was taking off in China, and it was this particular branch of Buddhist belief that was most compatible with the Chinese way of thinking. Mahayana Buddhism was far more flexible about incorporating a range of other already recognized deities, as Bodhisattvas, within the spiritual pantheon, and also seemed quite happy to include many existing Chinese rituals in order to keep the locals happy. The Mahayana reverence for Bodhisattvas was also central to Buddhism's mass acceptance in China – it was difficult for those from a Confucian background not to feel that simply striving for your own nirvana was a bit on the selfish side but this difficulty could be overcome through the existence of the less self-centred Bodhisattvas (really deep spiritual beings that postponed entry into Nirvana so that they could help others). Another reason for the success of Mahayana Buddhism was also – like Christianity – its intrinsically syncretic and populist nature; it would absorb and adapt local cultures, rituals and deities into the existing framework of belief and then offer salvation to all. As with Christianity, it was a religion that could be adapted for everybody – including women and poor people – and its fundamentally universal nature made it far more compatible with the early form of globalization that the Silk Road opened up.

After wandering around for a while in the park and the temples, I decided it was time for a nice cup of tea. Along with its spicy Sichuan cuisine – it's the state capital of Sichuan – Chengdu is also famous for its teahouses. People seemed to sit around for hours outside, still all wrapped up in their coats and scarves, while waiters wander around topping up their bowls of tea with boiling water from large thermos flasks. I handed over some money to a middle-aged lady in a booth, who handed me back a large white bowl with what appeared to be a selection of twigs and garden clippings inside of it. She waved me over to a table where I sat and waited for the waterman. I couldn't help feeling they had charged me rather a lot for a bowl of sticks but I found out later that the seating section I was directed to cost ten times more than the section on the other side of the path. I couldn't see any difference. I was quite happy to sit there on my own, sipping at the edges of the bowl so as not to burn my mouth, and trying not to suck up any of the twigs that were left floating around on the top.

I thought that I had seen everything in the temple complex but wasn't sure if I had actually seen the monastery. After leaving the way I came in, I noticed a sign and a ticket booth for the monastery. It seemed strange to pay to see the monastery but not the temple – although these things didn't always have to make sense. I coughed up for the ticket, walked through the elaborately carved entrance and found myself back in the temple complex I had just left. After a quick look around to make sure I hadn't missed anything, I walked out again into the cobbled pedestrianized streets and set off among the stalls of tourist tat.

It wasn't long before I was drawn to a stall by its inquisitive and friendly owner. She was clever enough not to launch straight into a hard sell and after a bit of a chat she showed me how she could write a name or a phrase onto a single grain of rice using an incredibly fine brush without even the assistance of a magnifying glass. The calligraphied rice grains could then be encased into a variety of crystals to form the pendant of a necklace. I don't normally buy these sorts of things but, as I liked her and it was something a bit different and surprisingly cheap, I had one done as a small present for my wife (every day she would send me emails to remind me to wrap up warm so I didn't get a chill, and wondering if I still had that lump on my throat).

I carried on walking towards some more parks and temples and eventually came across what appeared to be a small sushi bar. I picked out some varieties of sushi that I hadn't seen before and was given a clear, plastic, medical-looking glove to eat them with. This seemed, and felt, a little strange but was actually a good idea; as well as keeping a condom-like barrier between my probably very dirty hands and the food, it also prevented the white sticky sauce from oozing out all over my hands. The guy who worked there was keen to practise his English and told me that sushi actually came from China and not from Japan (this sounded a bit unlikely but I looked it up later and China did actually have sushi before Japan, although the original version came from somewhere around Vietnam). I tried out quite a variety of the sushi on sale and it was very different from the Japanese style I had enjoyed all over the world. Maybe Chinese-style sushi will be China's next big culinary export? If I hadn't forgotten where to find it I would definitely have gone back for more.

After a considerable amount of traipsing I eventually ended up in Renmin Park, watching yet more line dancers, pedal boaters and ice-cream lickers. The Lonely Planet had said that there was some kind of ghost train but disappointingly I couldn't find it. On the way back I was surprised to find myself walking past what appeared to be a Catholic cathedral. It turned out to be the Immaculate Conception Cathedral (also known as the Ping'anqiao Catholic Church). It had been unused since the last Bishop died in 1998, but there were still around 120,000 baptized Catholics in the Chengdu diocese. Up until the disastrous earthquake in 2008, there had been fifty-nine Catholic churches in the surrounding area, but twenty-five of these had collapsed and twenty-two had been seriously damaged (central Chengdu fared relatively well in the earthquake but out in the provinces where building regulations were far from rigorously enforced, more than 70,000 people are estimated to have died; the American actress Sharon Stone suggested this was a result of bad karma brought about by China's behaviour towards Tibet).

The Catholic missionaries didn't arrive in Chengdu until around 1740 but China was first introduced to the Nestorian version of Christianity when it was exported along the Silk Road during the time of the Tang Dynasty (618–907) – around the same time that Mahayana Buddhism began to make inroads into Chinese culture. When Marco Polo visited China in the thirteenth century, he commented on the surprisingly large numbers of Nestorian Christians still active in southern China. It wasn't until the fourteenth century that Nestorian Christianity started its rapid decline as the Ming Dynasty, following the fall of the more tolerant Mongols, started to systematically eradicate all foreign influence in China.

* * *

The next morning I wandered down to the reception area of the guest house to join the huddle of backpackers waiting for the trip to the Chengdu Panda Bear Breeding and Research Centre. We were each given a plastic entry pass to hand over and a panda bear key ring as a special gift. I squashed into the back seat of the minivan with Jonny and Jessica from England. They were on a big round-the-world trip and had recently flown into China after completing an overland truck tour through Africa from Nairobi to Cape Town. When I asked them if they'd been through Namibia, they weren't sure. It seemed difficult to believe that they didn't know which countries they had actually been to, but apparently they were kept in the back of the truck and told very little. Whenever they got to a border, the driver would take away their passports and give them back later on. They offered to get out their passports and have a look through the stamps so that I could see where they'd been. I had heard before that groups of backpackers on overland trucks can often feel like they've been cocooned in their own little tourist bubble, but I'm still not sure how this can happen. I have been known to accidently visit countries after getting on the wrong bus and have often ended up in small towns that I didn't know the name of, but how could you not know the names of the countries that you had travelled through? You would think that anyone who had taken the time and saved the money to go travelling would have a bit more curiosity. My wife always complains that I am far too nosy – I ask lots of questions and always want to know what's going on, but I think that that's a good thing. If I ever have kids I'd like to think I would be patient enough to encourage their questions and curiosity – even if it were to become wearing at times – as that kind of nosiness would help them to learn more and understand more. Admittedly, knowing or understanding too much of the wrong kinds of things can make life harder at times, but overall I would still like to think that knowledge and understanding came out on top of ignorance. I probably used to think this too much. I had some vague Gnostic-like idea half-derived from Jung's concept of individuation that striving for knowledge and understanding would in some way lead to a higher state of being.

I no longer think this. My beliefs are now more akin to Homer – that's Simpson, not the old Greek bloke – in that I'm not sure if there's any point in forcing new things into my brain when it's just going to push out the old stuff.

When we arrived at the Panda Centre, I was surprised to see so many tourists all in one place. When wandering around Chengdu the day before, outside of the hostel I had hardly seen any Western tourists. It seemed strange, but shouldn't really have been a surprise as the main reason that most tourists come to Chengdu is to see the pandas. We swarmed around taking pictures of fat giant pandas lying on each other, contentedly munching bamboo. They didn't seem particularly bothered by all the tourists or by anything else. They may be cute but they don't really do much. Like any other animal they basically just eat, sleep, shit and fuck (although it's very rare for giant pandas in captivity to bother with the last activity). Posh Theo had put up enough money to support an extended Chinese family for a few years, in order to 'volunteer' as an assistant at the Panda Centre. It was obvious what the Panda Centre was going to get out of this arrangement but I really wasn't sure what Theo would get out of it, other than something 'interesting' to put on his CV. Every poor country in the world now seems to be full of rich Western youngsters 'volunteering' to do the kind of unskilled work – if it is actually required at all – that could easily be done by the locals for a pittance. The whole 'volunteer' business has become an increasingly popular way of raising fast, easy money from naïve tourists but from what I have seen very little of it seems to end up in the hands of those who most deserve it. The pandas didn't even look like real animals. I half expected some Chinese actor to unzip himself from a bear suit and stand there bowing to applause with a giant panda head under his arm. Disappointingly, this didn't happen. Instead, they just lay there, disinterestedly chomping on yet more bamboo. Nobody seems to agree on what they actually are. They are called panda bears but nobody seems to think they are really bears. They should probably be in some special kind of 'panda' category on their own. This is further confused by the existence of red pandas. They don't even look like panda bears; they're somewhere in size between a cat and a dog and look more like ginger raccoons with a long bushy tail. Some scientists claim that they're closely related to giant pandas, while others quite confidently state they're a completely different species. The fact that they look like completely different animals would seem to lend credence to the latter view.

Once we had taken all the photos that we felt required to, we were herded off to the Research Centre café. The English-only menu proudly displayed cappuccinos and lattes at prices that were higher than you would expect to pay in London or Paris. While we sat there, sipping on decaf double macchiato lattes, we were played an informative video about the Panda Research Centre on a large overhead screen. Jonny unzipped his expensive digital video camera from its padded case and began videoing the video. Jonny and Jessica videoed everything they did and everywhere they went (even if they weren't sure where they'd been). It was proof of what they'd spent their money on. Once their big trip had been consumed they would no doubt get a mortgage and reproduce.

After we had all paid up, we were led through a kind of museum on the way to making more purchases at the gift shop. This featured the worst fake animals I had ever seen. The whole 'museum' looked like it had been put together as some kind of primary school project. We would all take guesses at what kind of animal was being represented before the answer was revealed, to everybody's shock and amazement. While most of the 'animals' were clearly unconvincing models, a few did seem alarmingly realistic. The only problem was that the individual parts of the animal didn't necessarily form a convincing whole – you couldn't help thinking that some kind of veterinarian

Mengele had been involved in some less-than-tasteful animal experiments, with the less-than-successful results being displayed for the tourists' amusement.

Later in the afternoon, I left the comfort and convenience of Sim's Cozy Guest House to board another overnight train – this time to Lanzhou. When I picked up my bag from the store cupboard and said goodbye, one of the girls from reception even took me out to the road and waved down a taxi to the station for me. I thanked her for her kindness and left my fellow tourists behind. It would be some time before everything would be this easy again.

Lanzhou

Degradation and Pollution • Hopeless Propaganda
Aspirations and Dreams • Cappuccino Culture • The Sacred and Profane

Lanzhou, the capital of Gansu province, was once a major stop on the Silk Road. It used to be known as the Golden City but is now one of the most polluted cities in China. Unlike Chengdu, it is not a major tourist attraction and I didn't see any other Western tourists while I was there. There was supposed to be some kind of hostel on the other side of town but I wasn't sure if it was even open at this time of year and really couldn't be bothered to go through all the hassle of trying to find it – especially as I would have to come back to the station again to buy my tickets and to get yet another night train on to Dunhuang. After emerging from the train station, into the crushing midday cold, I quickly retreated to the station's KFC for hot coffee and a chicken burger. Having wrapped up as warm as I could, in my far-from-adequate t-shirts and denim jacket, I readied myself for a long, hard journey in search of suitable accommodation. Two minutes later I had found a nice budget hotel with a decent bathroom and satellite TV for less than the price of a private room in a backpackers' hostel.

It was a relief to settle into my nice, warm hotel room after the long night journey and switch on the TV. I flicked through the usual mix of bad Chinese soaps and badly dubbed-into-Chinese Western imports, and then I came across CCTV 9 – the Chinese government's English language TV channel. This channel boasts of having more than 40 million overseas viewers, but that's not quite accurate. In reality, there are about 40 million overseas TV watchers who could watch CCTV 9 if they were to subscribe to the necessary services and then could actually be bothered to select it from hundreds of other channels. In reality, most of the people who watch it are either foreign tourists on a budget – if they were here on business or staying in the more upmarket hotels they would be able to pick up a whole range of quality English language channels – or Chinese who are trying to learn English (many of their programmes end up being used in colleges and universities as learning aids). The main aim of the channel seems to be to tell everybody how brilliant China is. Anything that might be awkward or difficult to explain is either quickly glossed over or just censored all together, and every section seems to end with an emphasis on China's great achievements. The whole thing seems to be produced on the assumption that millions of foreign viewers will be tuning in to CCTV 9 every day to hear endless tales about just how wealthy, efficient and fair the mighty China really is. Putting aside the fact that the only foreigners who are likely to watch it are a few tourists in economy hotels, what seems most incredible is the idea that anybody would be convinced by such crude and unsophisticated propaganda. No Westerner with the intelligence and initiative to be travelling independently in China would ever be able to view such shameless bragging uncritically. It is far more likely to have the unintended effect of reminding you about all the things they were trying to draw attention away from. While such hopelessly inept propaganda seems laughable to the average Westerner, it is easy to forget that for a long time many Chinese pretty much believed whatever those in power decided to tell them. To ever openly question the honesty, common sense or analytical thinking of a figure in authority was considered to be very bad form indeed. When I first visited China I was amazed at some of the questions I would be asked. On one train journey I was even asked why England wanted to invade China. In *The End of History and the Last Man,* Francis Fukuyama argued that a fundamental failure of Soviet totalitarianism was its failure to control thought. Centuries of Confucianism in China, however, seem to have created an ideal environment for the suppression of independent thought that is essential to the perpetuation of totalitarianism. Although I am sure that critical and analytical thinking will make greater inroads into mainstream Chinese culture over the coming generations, it is still surprising just how unquestioning and uncritical many Chinese are. Such naivety hardly lends itself to the creation of effective distraction, displacement and propaganda through television programmes. Never mind, I don't suppose that it will be that long until they figure out that you hardly need to lie or censor at all if you can just distract enough of the people with the right kind of dream. Rather than sitting through dull propaganda about the rise in manufacturing output, millions of Chinese workers now prefer to tune into the Chinese versions of *The X Factor* and *China's Got Talent*. If they can only convince enough of them that they can be whatever they want to be as long as they want it enough, then the authority of those in power could remain unchallenged for many years to come. All they really need to manufacture is 'The Chinese Dream'.

By the time I had shaved and showered and was back on the streets, it was already the middle of the afternoon and starting to get even colder. I wandered around the station area and bought some snacks and sachets of three-in-one coffee from the supermarket, along with a pot noodle-style polystyrene cup containing bubble milk tea. Flasks of hot water, for everybody's use, are all over the place in China. The hotel had provided me with a teacup and a couple of green tea bags, but I needed a higher dose of caffeine than that would provide, and would be able to reuse the polystyrene cup from the bubble tea on the train.

There were also plenty of Western-style bakeries all over China. I might not have been paying attention fifteen years ago, but I can't remember seeing all those breads, pastries and cakes during my last visit. I bought a couple of huge pastries to take back with me and retreated to my room once the cold had become too much. It wasn't long, however, until the pleasures of CCTV 9 began to pale and I set off in search of an Internet café. Two floors up, in another hotel not far across the street, I found a huge room full of teenagers engrossed in 'shoot 'em up' online gaming. This seemed to be the place to go. I shouted over the sounds of invading aliens and vengeful warriors to the receptionist who eventually figured out what I wanted. After an hour or so I left, and after eventually managing to cross the street returned to my room with my ears ringing from the sounds of online death and destruction. I snuggled up under my nice warm blankets and switched on CCTV 9 again. Apparently, China's manufacturing output was up to record highs. I nodded off.

* * *

If Lanzhou is famous for anything, then it is for its water wheels. Until the 1950s around 250 enormous water wheels were still being used for irrigation along the Yellow River that runs through Lanzhou (the invention of the irrigation water wheel had travelled up the Silk Road from Roman Syria). Not many had survived the Cultural Revolution but some working reproductions had been built for the Water Wheel Garden as a tourist attraction. I had downloaded a bad tourist map from the Internet and there was a picture of somewhere called South Lake Park on it on the way to the water wheels, so I headed off towards it, past the University and in the general direction of the Yellow River. After a longer walk than I had anticipated, a thorough check of my map revealed that I should have been at the entrance to the South Lake Park. Instead, I was apparently in the middle of the Lanzhou bathroom fittings district. Every shop seemed to be selling taps, sinks and shower fittings. Strangely, the shops only seemed to be selling Western-style toilets, and yet outside of hotels you hardly ever saw these in China. I checked my map again but I still couldn't figure it out. Among the stacks of dusty bathroom fittings stood what appeared to be a small temple. I crossed the street to have a look and found myself at the top of some steps leading down to a lake surrounded by pedal boats and children's rides. I had made it. There was a small bridge leading out to a small island in the middle of South Lake with what looked like another small temple on it. It was actually a teahouse. Every city in China seemed to have a park with a lake in it, and pedal boats, and temple-shaped buildings where people hung around drinking hot green tea. But something was missing. Where were the line dancers? It was still quite early but that was no excuse. To make up for my disappointment, a middle-aged woman jogged backwards past me. This didn't seem very sensible at all – she might trip over or fall in the lake. Nobody else seemed particularly concerned that she was running backwards. There were also a few people practising their tai chi stretches and exercises, but they were no match for the line dancers. They weren't even wearing funny hats.

I walked on towards the Yellow River. It seemed more dirty brown than yellow. Sometimes in the summer, tourists would be taken across the river on traditional rafts made from inflated sheepskins. You probably wouldn't drown if you fell out as they made you wear life jackets, but I wouldn't fancy your chances if you accidently swallowed anything. After buying my ticket to the water wheel garden, I took a few photos of some fountains and headed for the museum's waterside café. There was nobody around but three large flasks of hot water had thoughtfully been left out, so I used one of them to fill my polystyrene cup of milk bubble tea then sat down at the edge of the river. To the left of me was a small, partially boarded-up amphitheatre that didn't look like it had seen any performances for a while and behind me were some bronze statues of loyal Chinese workers being productive. Around the sculptures were plonked a few lumps of stone that apparently made up some kind of rock museum. The proper indoor museum was locked up. A handful of Chinese tourists in big heavy coats wandered between the statues and rocks in search of the photogenic. The park extended for another kilometre or so, along the Yellow River, with a scenic line of wooden reproduction water wheels. The few Chinese tourists around all seemed to have come in from the far end of the park where there was nobody to demand an entrance fee. I was probably the only visitor to have tracked down a ticket seller at the dragon-decorated main gates. The few staff on duty clearly lacked the purpose and productiveness of their idealized bronze counterparts.

On the long walk back across town to Five Springs Park, I stopped at a nice-looking bakery and café, which was displaying an impressive range of pastries and cakes. Its expensive-looking coffee bar seemed less popular. In the West, the number and density of coffee shops in an area has become a kind of barometer of affluence and disposable income; all the time that new Starbucks or Costas are opening up, property prices will continue to rise. This association between wealth and expensive coffee seems to have been absorbed by Chinese entrepreneurs but the tea-loving Chinese workers seemed less convinced. Cappuccinos and lattes may be all the rage with young professionals in Hong Kong or Shanghai but there seemed to be more coffee bars than customers in Lanzhou. Apart from any cultural differences, this may have more to do with the fact that a medium cappuccino costs more than many Chinese would earn all day. (Around 25 million people in China still earn less than US$1 a day.)

After crossing over the top of the railway line and queuing up for another entrance ticket, I found myself at the bottom of the hill leading up to Five Springs Park. Like many other parks in China, it was a mixture of ancient temples, elegant gardens and gaudily painted amusement park rides. Groups of bowed-head elders would solemnly light incense sticks and kneel down silently towards their deities as teenagers screamed out in excitement while spinning around on dilapidated roller coasters. Children sipped Coca-Cola in the queue for the ghost train while stooped, wrinkled monks lined up to enter gloomy temples. The old and the fearful prayed for an end to the cycle of life while the young and the brave chose to live it. While the weak reached out for Nirvana, others simply listened to them on their new iPod copies.

I walked off in search of the magic caves. There were plenty of blue signs around in English – even though I was the only foreigner among hundreds of Chinese – but you couldn't be sure that they were necessarily pointing in the right direction. I found myself traipsing up to some temples cut high up into the hillside, and looking down over the smog-ridden city, as far as the Yellow River. By now I had broken into a sweat but the air was still cold. Clouds of my breath emerged from within to join the smoke from the temples and the smog sprawling out far below. Most of the amusements had been abandoned for the winter, but those that were running still drew in crowds. A rusty big wheel ground around down below and screams echoed out from behind a patch of trees. Like the source of the screams, the magic caves remained hidden. I was starting to get stomach cramps. Rather than risking the public toilets at the park, I decided to head back to the hotel, where I had stored my backpack, and used the downstairs facilities there instead. As the hotel was quite nice I thought their public toilets would be OK (although it doesn't always work like that in China). So far, I had been quite lucky with my runny bottom but I had underestimated the distance back to the hotel; there were no other public toilets on the way and my stomach cramps were getting worse. Several times I had to stop walking and wait for the cramps to pass. After a longer and more uncomfortable walk than I had expected I eventually made it back in time (the doors wouldn't shut but the squat toilets were clean, and they had thoughtfully provided a hook on the cubicle door so that my bag didn't get wet on the soaking floor).

In my sleeper section on the night train to Dunhuang, I met Jenny. Her real name sounded something like Jenny in Chinese. Apparently even her parents called her Jenny (a lot of young Chinese would introduce themselves using an Anglicized version of their Chinese name). She spoke good English and worked with a lot of Westerners for the baked beans king, Heinz, in Guangzhou. She had spent two days travelling on the train with a colleague from Heinz, in order to spend three days being a tourist around Dunhuang. She would then have to spend another two days on the train in order to be back for work on Monday morning. Like many Chinese, she only got a couple of weeks holiday a year and wanted to see as much of China as possible. A couple of years ago, Heinz had paid for her to go on a company trip to Sydney and Brisbane, but even with a good job it would have been difficult for her to travel anywhere else abroad on her own.

Jenny and her Heinz colleague had booked an organized three-day tour for when they arrived and asked me if I would like to join them. I probably would have enjoyed it but I only intended to stay a couple of days and was quite surprised at the cost. The different pricing policy for foreigners and the Chinese seemed a long way in the past. Still, they would get picked up at the station and driven around to everywhere from their three-star hotel while I would have to stay in a hostel and attempt to find my own way about.

Dunhuang

Cultural Fusion • The Spread of Religious Ideas • Commodity Fetishism
Lost to Translation • The Importance of Words

The Dunhuang train station was surprisingly grand and modern but around 12 kilometres out of town. It looked like some strange, alien spaceship that had just been abandoned in the desert. As usual, I had no idea where to go, so Jenny found the minibus into town for me and sent me on my way. Dunhuang, in Gansu province, used to be one of most important cities in ancient China. The city was founded by Emperor Wudi of the Han dynasty in 111 BC at the crossroads of two trading routes on the Silk Road. Today, it is best known for the Magao Buddhist temple caves and the huge Gobi Desert sand dunes.

I was dropped off at what seemed to be a central market area of the town and pointed in the direction of Charlie Jhong's Guest House (it had been recommended to me by posh Theo). The people were already starting to look more Central Asian than Han Chinese and there was a large mosque next to the market. Most of the shops around the market were still shuttered up and there were few people on the streets. After about forty minutes of trudging up and down, I decided to ask in Shirley's Café, as I thought someone there might at least speak some English. It turned out that the manager was Charlie Jhong's brother-in-law, and that their own café was just across the road, but still shuttered up. The actual guest house was about 5 kilometres away, right next to the big sand dunes. I sat down for a cooked breakfast and half an hour later Charlie arrived to drop his wife off at the café and give me a lift over to the hostel. Apparently, his wife had had a bit of trouble getting out of bed that morning.

The guest house was right out of town in a parched patch of land with a few small farms scattered around. As we bumped along the dusty camel-shit-splattered track to the hostel, I gazed up past the tree line to the towering sand dunes. The dunes tumbled all the way down to Charlie's back yard. If not for a large metal fence half-way up, you could have walked straight out of the door and up into the Mingsha Shan (or 'Echoing-Sand Mountain') National Park. The facilities were basic but the courtyard was nicely decorated in a traditional Chinese style. Both of the toilet cubicles had Western and Asian-style toilets right next to each other – they obviously thought it was important to offer their guests a choice. If two of you had both been attacked by the runs at the same time then, rather than fighting over who went first, you could always choose to shit in tandem (this might seem distasteful to most Westerners but the Chinese are quite down to earth in these matters).

Nobody else seemed to be staying here so I had the shower room all to myself. The room was divided up by wooden partitions with hooks under plastic sheets so that you could hang your clothes up without them being sprayed. I pushed my worn Reebok trainers out under the ply board half door of my shower section so they wouldn't get wet but they still got soggy as the water from my shower managed to spread out over the whole of the room. Out of the early morning sun it was still really cold so I dried myself as quickly as I could and hastily pulled on my lightweight army trousers and a clean t-shirt (bought cheap in Thailand, like most of my clothes). I hung up my damp towel on a line across the courtyard and laid out the contents of my battered backpack across the bed that I had selected at the end of my shared room. All the other beds remained unoccupied. While I waited for my long hair to dry before venturing out into the freezing desert, I emptied a Nescafé 3-in-1 sachet into the lidded polystyrene cup that had formerly contained bubble milk tea. Most of the other passengers on the train had their own mini Thermos flasks that they would regularly top up from the boiler in the corridor, but my polystyrene cup would serve me just as well (as long as it didn't get squashed). I filled up my precious cup with hot water from one of the three large Thermos flasks in the corner of the courtyard, and sat down at a bench in the early morning sunlight to warm my aching bones and dry my dripping hair.

After plaiting my still damp hair, I set off from the guest house to catch a minibus from the main road into town where I could get another local bus to the Thousand Buddha Caves of Magao. The buses to and from the town terminated at the end of the main road, just down from the entrance to the Mingsha Shan National Park. It was easy enough to get the minibus going back to the town and then find another one that was heading for the caves. Most of the seats had already been taken by an extended Chinese family who seemed to be enjoying their vacation. Unlike Lanzhou, Dunhuang had plenty of relatively expensive tourist hotels and would probably attract plenty of family groups from all over China during the summer season. The different generations of the family seemed to have covered between them almost every type of clothes and hairstyle going. The teenage girl's mixture of Chinese and Western styles seemed least successful. Their hair was badly bleached and their frilly white blouses clashed badly with their cheap tracksuit trousers. While some young Chinese seemed to effortlessly merge the attitudes and stylings of East and West, many others would stumble and crash down the crevices in between.

After it was made clear to me that the last bus would leave at 5pm, we were let out in the car park and I crossed over to buy my surprisingly expensive ticket. I didn't have that much time to see everything, so I bypassed the museum and went straight to the caves themselves. According to local legend, the temple caves were first dug out in AD 366 by a Buddhist monk called Le Zen who had a vision of a thousand Buddhas. The eventual number of the temples eventually rose to more than a thousand, many of which were painted with elaborate murals by pilgrims passing along the Silk Road. In 1987, the Magao Caves became one of the UNESCO World Heritage Sites; they are still being excavated today. I handed over my ticket and walked through the security gates towards the rock face. The doors to the caves were all locked. I followed a group of Chinese into one of the caves that their guide had opened up with a huge bundle of keys, and wriggled through to get a glance of some dimly illuminated murals but I couldn't understand a word their guide was saying. They seemed to be nearing the end of their guided tour and after they had all poured back out into the sunlight, the doors were locked up again. I wandered down to the other end to see if any of the other caves would be left open for me to look at but all of the entrances were securely bolted shut. When I stepped into the small museum the staff seemed a bit surprised and asked me if I needed a guide. The price turned out to be the same as I had already paid to get in, so I really didn't want to have to pay out again. They should have told me I had to pay again for a guide so I would be allowed in anywhere! By now, I was feeling a bit frustrated and annoyed. While trying to find somewhere that I would be allowed into, Jenny from the train called out to me from the other side of the security fence. They had already been to both the sand dunes and all around the Magao Caves, while I still hadn't really seen anything. I reluctantly resigned myself to having to cough up again for an English-speaking guide and they helped to find one for me. Five minutes later, Judy came over and introduced herself as my guide. She was young and beautiful and spoke near perfect English. She explained that her services were actually included in the price of the admission ticket and that as I was their only foreign guest, I would have her all to myself.

Judy selected one of the many keys hanging from a heavy metal ring, and led me through into the dark coolness of the caves. Faded ancient murals adorned the walls and ceilings.

They had been intended as aids to meditation and as mnemonic devices but, perhaps more importantly, they had acted as teaching tools to inform illiterate Chinese of the ideas and philosophy of the Buddhism that had spread into China along the Silk Road. Of course, the spread of religious ideas and iconography wasn't just one way; the beliefs and symbolism of China would also come to influence the West. For example, many of the Buddhas depicted in the Magao Caves were shown with the halos that would later become a symbol of sanctity and holiness in Christian art.

Judy led me into another cave with some garishly incongruous sculptures – they looked like larger versions of the figures that would line the walls of gift shops. She explained that the Chinese government in the 1950s had added these 'sculptures'. In another of the cave temples, I was shown into a smaller cave that had remained a secret for hundreds of years. In the early 1900s, a Chinese Taoist called Wang Yuanlu had broken through a hidden wall to discover hundreds of valuable manuscripts dating from AD 406 to 1002. As well as the expected Buddhist scriptures, they also contained Confucian, Taoist and Nestorian Christian works, along with many government documents. Most of these were sold in 1907 to the Hungarian archaeologist Aurel Stein for just £220. Other caves, further on, contained huge multi-storey Buddhas that only revealed themselves as you emerged from the narrow, stone passages. After thanking Judy for her time, I rushed back to the car park to make sure that I caught the last bus back into Dunhuang.

While I'd been out, some Chinese backpackers had arrived at Charlie Jhong's. They all seemed to have enormous digital cameras permanently hanging from their necks. One of my new room-mates had two black, padded bags full of equipment and a selection of tripods. I asked him if he was a professional but he said he just liked taking photos. I wouldn't have wanted to stay in hostel accommodation with so much expensive equipment, but then maybe that was why they all seemed to keep their cameras on them. Either that or they just wanted to show them off.

As soon as the sun went down, it started to get really cold again. I asked to have a look at the guest house's menu and was recommended to try the Laghman noodles. These are something of a speciality in western China and Central Asia and are usually served in a bowl with a beef or mutton-flavoured soup. Sometimes they are stir fried with a few chillies thrown in. But the ones I was served were disgusting. They seemed to have nothing else that was on their menu except for pancakes, so I ordered some with honey in an attempt to remove the taste of congealed mutton fat that was clinging to the roof of my mouth. By now, I had moved into the lounge area in an attempt to stop shivering. There was a range of bootleg Western DVDs available but I couldn't get any of them to play with an English soundtrack. I fumbled around in the cold, trying to navigate my way through the symbols on the screen, and trying to make it come out with something I could understand. It was all lost to translation. I gave in to the babble and retreated to my shared room to turn on the electric blanket that I had been handed earlier in the day. Once my bed had warmed up enough to stop my shivering from under the sheets, I made sure the electric blanket was both turned off and unplugged. I already had some experiences with Far Eastern electricity and I didn't want to wake up dead.

* * *

The next morning I set out to visit the Mingsha Shan National Park, see the Crescent Moon Lake and ride through the massive Gobi sand dunes, the Echoing-Sand Mountains, on Bactrian camels. On the way to the park entrance, I sat down on a wooden bench while an old lady helped to pull bright orange coverings up over my trainers and then tied them tight at the top of my calves. It had seemed like a good idea to rent them for the day – you wouldn't want loads of sand in your shoes. I waddled off towards the entrance to the towering dunes in my brightly coloured leg attire. At least if I got lost in the desert it would be easy to find me – I could just stand on my head and wave my legs about. After paying for my entrance ticket – again, surprisingly expensive for what is still quite a poor country – I was presented with some magnificent desert scenery and dozens of bored-looking camels. I didn't take it personally – camels always look bored. I said hello to one of them but it just ignored me. Fortunately, the man looking after them seemed keener to talk. I agreed to join with a group going up to the top of the nearby dunes and then across to Crescent Moon Lake, and was allocated a reasonably friendly but slightly mangy-looking camel. He didn't seem to be particularly bothered about having to kneel down awkwardly so that I could sit on top of him, but he grumbled a bit as he shakily rose to his feet. I held on tight to the saddle and tried not to drop my camera. Once raised and settled, he returned to exuding his usual aura of resignation (traipsing up and down sand dunes all day with a tourist taking pictures from your back would probably do that to you). A short while later I was joined by a young Chinese couple who spoke very little English and a youngish woman on her own who spoke no English at all. She seemed to be dressed more for going to a nightclub than for riding camels on sand dunes.

Our camels were soon trudging upwards in a snaking line across the dunes. Further up, another posse of tourists was slowly lurching its way back down another side of the Echoing-Sand Mountain. The story goes that the dunes got their name after an army that was resting at the Crescent Moon Lake oasis was taken by surprise by a massive sand storm that completely submerged them and that the sound you can sometimes hear echoing from the dunes is the screams from the still-buried soldiers. Others think that the sound has something to do with the wind and the shifting sand dunes but I prefer the first explanation.

Once we had reached the ridge, I was surprised to find that a series of large, brightly coloured sculptures were laid out for sale. Some of them must have been seven or eight feet tall. Did the camels have to drag them up here so they could be sold to the tourists? How would the tourists ever get them home? Not surprisingly, they didn't seem to be doing any business, despite their enthusiastic invitations to us to come and have a look around.

Leading up from there to an even higher peak were some half-covered wooded steps. At the top was a man renting out sand sleds. While the young couple stayed behind, the nightclub girl gestured for me to follow her up to the very top. She clearly wasn't going to let the language barrier get in the way of us being friends for the day. After taking some photos of each other looking down from the very top of the dunes, we exchanged some more *yuan* for the loan of a sled and were soon sliding down the other side.

After another half an hour or so of rhythmic camel trudging we were dropped off at what appeared to be a camel park, just around the corner from Crescent Moon Lake. The lake had been formed by a natural spring in the desert and, even though its depth had now decreased quite significantly, it had still retained its half moon shape. 'Nightclub girl' emptied out some sand from her high-heeled boots, picked up her oversized clutch bag and led me off to the lake and surrounding temples. All the Chinese attempted to replicate the classic postcard picture of the temple and crescent-shaped lake, only with them standing in the foreground to prove they had been there. We did the same with each other's cameras and sat down together to have a drink and a 'chat'. She would talk and gesticulate for a while, then I would take my turn doing the same thing. Neither of us understood a word of what the other was saying but it didn't seem to matter. In fact, we seemed to get on remarkably well. Having bonded so well during our nice long chat, she then led me clambering up the side of the facing dunes to look down on Crescent Moon Lake from above. This was hard work. For every two steps forward you would find yourself sliding back at least another step. Whole families attempted to make it up to the ridge but many gave up halfway before slowly sliding their way back down again. After far more of a struggle than I had anticipated and plenty of rests to catch our breath, we eventually made it to the ridge and the superb views over the temple, the lake and the surrounding dunes. Not far out in front lay Charlie Jhong's Guest House and a few small farms, but behind us just lay sand and more sand as far as you could see.

We carried on along the ridge, looking down on those below. Despite visiting two major tourist attractions in the last couple of days, I still hadn't seen any Western tourists since Chengdu. Down below were just Chinese families racing each other up the dunes and then sliding back down again on rented sleds. On the way back down, 'nightclub girl' decided it would be easier just to slide down the whole way, sometimes diving head first and other times sliding on her bum. She'd have been scraping out sand from her orifices for days to come. Walking back towards the main gate, we bumped into the Chinese family that had shared the minibus with me to Magao Caves. Despite not taking much notice of me the day before, they now greeted me like a long lost friend. I rambled on for a bit in English despite being fairly sure that they couldn't understand me, while 'nightclub girl' just stood there and smiled. After walking back out through the main gates and handing back my orange shoe coverings, I waved goodbye to my new friend as she boarded her bus back into Dunhuang. I felt sad to see her go. We had got on so well.

In order to get the night train to Urumqi, I first needed to get to the train station at Liuyan, which was over an hour's drive from Dunhuang (there wasn't yet a direct link to Urumqi from the new space age desert station for Dunhuang). After picking up my bags, I headed off to Charlie Jhong's café in the town, where Charlie's wife cooked me up an enormous plate of surprisingly good sweet and sour chicken and rice. When her mother came in to visit, she presented me with a gift of some of the heavy local bread to take on the train journey and they wrapped it up in some Clingfilm before packing me into a shared taxi. None of my fellow passengers could speak much English but they all seemed friendly. Once we had managed to locate a final passenger – to make sure that the dilapidated car was as full as it possibly could be – we eventually set off out of town and were soon rattling along through dry, featureless wasteland. By the time we arrived at the train station, over an hour later, it was dark. Fortunately, the single female passenger showed me where everything was on the station and explained that there would be a delay. After a while she wandered off, leaving her bags with me. I wasn't sure what was going on as I couldn't read the signs or understand any of the announcements. She returned a few minutes later and presented me with a bottle of Coke. I was actually quite surprised at how kind so many strangers had been to me as I had struggled across China. When I first visited China, although I had met a lot of nice Chinese, quite a few had seemed rude, abrupt or opportunistic. There seemed to be very different rules – and prices – for dealing with the big-nosed foreign monkeys who had dared to visit. The different reaction I had received from most people this time could partly be explained by the fact that previously I had travelled right across China with two other young guys whom I had met at the Pakistan border. Three young men travelling together would have been far less approachable than a single traveller. However, I suspected it was more than this. Fifteen years ago, many Chinese were still quite wary of foreigners; some would cover up their nervousness with a gruff abruptness when approached, while others would almost run away. This attitude seemed to be particularly noticeable among state employees who couldn't be bothered with anything or anyone that might be problematic when they would be paid the same whatever they did. This time, it all seemed different. Not one person tried to rip me off, everyone I met was polite, and lots of people actually went out of their way to be friendly and help me. Either the Chinese were becoming more open to foreigners and the culture they brought with them, or I was becoming less scary.

Urumqi

Disturbed Environment • Memory Fades • Globalization
Fear of the Dark • Identity and Rebellion • Freedom and Censorship
Alien Invaders • The Spread of DNA

I was woken up by a train guard pulling at my foot. I didn't know why he was so keen to get me down from my bunk when it wasn't even 6am yet and we still had another couple of hours to go. I lay there drowsing while everyone else rushed about. It seemed strange that so many people were lining up in the corridor with their bags. In fact, everybody else on the train was getting ready to leave. Slowly it began to dawn on me that this was Urumqi. By the time I had clambered down from my bunk the other passengers were already pouring out of the nice warm train into the freezing cold station.

Urumqi was the only city on this trip that I had been to before and I was curious to see how it had changed. Previously, I had stayed in one big room in a hotel that had been set aside as a backpackers' dormitory. There were no such luxuries as beds – everybody just spread around over the floor on camping mats. Across the street was another backpackers' place and in between was an outside restaurant that seemed to cater exclusively to budget Western travellers. The thing I remember most was trying to find the showers. From the dorm room I had followed a sign down the corridor and another one down the stairs; I then followed another sign down another corridor and down yet more stairs that ended up in an underground car park; from there I followed another sign up onto the street, down the road and around the corner until I arrived at the entrance to the public baths. This time, I was hoping to stay somewhere with showers in the same building.

As neither of those two hostels was still going I would have to stay at one of the two new ones. I opted for the White

Birch YHA and managed to negotiate a reasonable fare with a taxi driver who seemed to find the road it was in quite easily. Every ten metres or so along the street there was a big pile of dirty-looking shovelled-up snow. Apparently the winter in Urumqi had carried on freakishly late this year, and only the week before they had been experiencing full-on snow storms when normally, by this time, they would have been well into spring. Everywhere in the world seemed to be experiencing freak weather; China had recently been devastated by both the droughts in the South and by murderously cold weather in the North, and it seemed as if the whole global climate had been disturbed. The world might have been heading for environmental disaster but for the moment, at least, I was more concerned with finding somewhere warm to stay. The hostel should have been just across the road from the museum – I never found the entrance to that either – and just in front of the park. When we eventually tracked it down, we could see that the single sign out front had been broken. I wondered if anybody would ever bother to repair it and, if so, how many guests they would lose in the mean time. When I rang the bell and somebody eventually arrived at the single unmarked entrance around the back, they were at least welcoming, if a little surprised to see me. They had no other Western guests so yet again I ended up in a dorm room on my own.

After making use of the not-too-clean facilities I poured another sachet of Nescafé 3-in-1 into my still remarkably unsquashed but much used polystyrene cup from Lanzhou, and asked for directions to the Kyrgyzstan Embassy. I had managed to sort out most of my visas in advance in Bangkok but there hadn't been any consulates for either Kyrgyzstan or Turkmenistan anywhere in South East Asia, so I was going to have to sort these ones out on the way. They reckoned it was about 7 kilometres away so advised me to get the bus that passed by outside. I did this easily enough but it really would have been much quicker and easier to just walk. The convoluted one-way system meant that I probably did go about 7 kilometres backwards and forwards by the bus but it would only have been about 2 kilometres to walk.

I'm really not sure why so many Chinese are so bad with directions. All over China, even those with excellent English still seem to have no sense of direction or scale. You may be thinking that it's probably just me – and admittedly I do spend a lot of time getting lost – but I really do think that this particular kind of ineptitude is something unique to the Chinese. Other people might give you bad directions out of laziness, a fear of losing face or an over-willingness to please you in the short term, but the Chinese will give you terrible directions even when they know exactly where somewhere is and are genuinely keen to help you.

I eventually tracked down the metal door to the embassy, set into the wall next door to the Central Asia Hotel, and joined a small group who were waiting outside to be let in. A Belgian couple soon joined me. After picking up their Kyrgyz visas they were planning to cycle back home through Central Asia. Despite being clearly insane they seemed friendly and harmless (at least to other people). They were staying at the other hostel (also its only guests) and had opted to pick up their visas in a week – giving them a few extra days to visit the surrounding area. But I really didn't have the time, so had to pay over US$100 to get a visa for the next day.

Like Urumqi as a whole, the other visa applicants seemed to be about fifty-fifty Han Chinese to other ethnicities. Some were Kyrgyz Chinese or Tajik Chinese or more commonly Uyghur. The 7.3 million Uyghur in Xinjiang province used to be by far the most dominant ethnic group in China's far West but, as in Tibet, the Chinese government systematically moved in thousands of Han Chinese in a deliberate attempt to change the balance of power.

While we struggled to make sense of the forms, the guy behind the desk shouted at a Chinese woman for answering her phone and simultaneously shook his finger at the 'no mobiles' sign. When the mobile of the one Central Asian-looking guy in a bad suit went off, the embassy man behind the counter almost had a fit. Only after receiving a grovelling apology from the object of his wrath did he finally calm down and resume with the required bureaucracy.

I filled in the form as best as I could, then it was finally my turn to step up to the counter. Just as I did so, yet another mobile rang out. I thought the official was finally going to explode when suddenly something dawned on him. He pulled a mobile from his jacket and answered it.

After sorting out the paperwork and coughing up the required dosh, I walked back towards the city centre with the Belgian couple. Their hostel was not far from the People's Park. I vaguely remembered walking around the lake at People's Park but was surprised to notice some scenic-looking temples and pagodas that overlooked the city from what turned out to be Red Hill. Seeing as these were such an obvious landmark, and really must have been there before, it worried me that I couldn't remember them at all from when I first visited. In fact, as far as I was concerned Urumqi might have been a completely different city; the places where I stayed and ate at previously were no longer there, the People's Park looked pretty much the same as any other large park around a lake in a Chinese city – many of which are also called something like People's Park – and the dry, bright summer sunshine had been usurped by a grey, chilly dampness. The Belgian couple led me into a sports and camping shop in search of warm winter gloves. After trying on several pairs they hesitated over buying any as the imported name brand gloves were actually more expensive than in Europe (even though they had been manufactured in China for Third World wages). As they had only just got off the twenty-four-hour bus from Kashgar before rushing off to get to the Kyrgyzstan Embassy on time, they were keen to get back to the hostel and go to bed for a few hours. (When I had made the same bus trip fifteen years ago it had taken forty hours; the train line still wasn't finished but it sounded as if all the roads were at least now paved).

Having more important things to do than sleep, I set off towards the attractions on Red Hill. After a few wrong turns I eventually found the main gates and began the long trudge up the broad hillside stairway towards the temples and pagodas at the top. As with most of the scenic temple and pagoda sites in China, the usual selection of rickety-looking fairground rides had also been planted into the hillside. If all the reverence and spirituality became a bit tiresome you could always cheer yourself up with a ride on a big wheel or get spun around in a revolving teacup. It would be difficult to visualize this happening in other parts of the world – I really can't imagine a ghost train being run through Canterbury Cathedral or a big dipper being bolted on to the roof of the Blue Mosque. Still, neither the solemn monks nor the excited groups of school children seemed at all concerned about this apparent incongruity – they all just seemed to rub along well enough together and were happy to do their own thing. In China, the sacred and the profane were all just a part of the whole, and the whole made for a good family day out.

The pagoda at the top of the steps featured a decent photography exhibition on Urumqi and provided views over the smog-hazed concrete blocks and motorways running through the city. Not much further up was a small temple complex that almost definitely had 'dragon' somewhere in its name (most of these kinds of temples did seem to have 'dragon' in the name and were all remarkably similar). Taking a more circular root back down through the park, a sign for 'The Underground Palace' caught my eye. I was actually surprised by how many signposts in China included English translations

– especially as in most places at this time of year I seemed to be the only native English speaker around. The translations weren't always very accurate, and often the signposts pointed in the wrong direction, but never the less I appreciated the effort – especially considering that I still hadn't learnt to say anything more than 'hello' or 'thank you' in Chinese.

When I eventually managed to track down the entrance to the Underground Palace I was surprised at what I found. Either side of the ticket booth was a series of demonic-looking life-size statues that I assumed to be evil characters from Chinese folklore. This clearly wasn't going to be the kind of palace where old plates were kept on display in ornate cabinets. On entering the darkness, I was greeted by screams. As my eyes grew accustomed to the gloom, I could make out the figures of numerous tortured souls. They were stretched out in racks and hung from their feet as demons whipped, burned and prodded them. A blood-curdling scream from deep in the dark rang out only to fade to the sound of excited giggling. Even after my eyes had had time to adjust, I still had to reach out my hands in front of me to avoid banging into the stone walls. Each new victim or demon that appeared before me brought a sense of relief; for the moment, at least, my journey into the unknown would be illuminated. As I descended further into this underworld, I was met with depictions of every kind of abomination imaginable; there were boilings, rapes and decapitations at every turn of the narrow passage way. A spider's web brushed past my face and a skeletal hand reached out to grab me. The horrors seemed like they would never end but then they did. I seemed to have been feeling my way ever further and deeper into the darkness for a long, long time without a single other tortured soul for company. I couldn't help feeling that I must have taken a wrong turning and somehow got lost. I really couldn't see that well in the dark. Maybe I had missed a sign and somehow descended into somewhere that I should never have seen?

I thought of retracing my steps in an attempt to resurface, but the path had forked several times behind me. How would I know which way to turn? I began to worry that I would still be lost down here when the park closed down for the night; the gates to the world above would be locked to me and I would be abandoned under Red Hill still searching for some demons and their light. I had no choice but to carry on and to trust to my destiny. After what seemed like an eternity, I began to glimpse the deep red fires of hell. Relief swept over me as another blood-curdling scream echoed through the tainted gloom. I had thought myself lost but the demons had always been there, waiting for me to make my way to them. Not much further on, I caught a glimpse of sunlight. And then I was free, released back into daylight at the bottom of Red Hill.

After a pretty decent meal at an Uyghur restaurant – closer to Turkish in style than to Chinese – I returned to the White Birch YHA. As no further guests had arrived I ended up chatting to a new guy who had just taken over at reception. Like many of the staff there, he was a student who was keen to practise and improve his English while earning some extra cash. From what he told me, it sounded very much as if the kind of English teaching they received at school mainly consisted of learning lists of vocabulary and being drilled in verbs and standard phrases. Having previously worked as an English teacher at government schools in Thailand, I could easily imagine what it would have been like – they would often be drilled into mindlessly repeating incorrect sentences or phrases as either the teachers couldn't really understand spoken English or they didn't think that the students would be able to pronounce the English properly anyway. If they spoke better English than their teachers and dared to question their methods they could be beaten with a stick. Apparently, it was the only way they would learn.

The hostel had two PCs but you could only use them to view selected government websites as the rest of the Internet had been blocked from the entire Xinjiang province following the Uyghur uprising the year before. My new friend at reception seemed to think this was entirely reasonable as apparently some Uyghur separatists had been using the Internet to spread their divisive ideas and generally stir up trouble. He argued that the Internet would also have been banned by the governments in England or America if it had been used to spread ideas that the government disapproved off. When I explained this wasn't true, he looked remarkably taken aback. It wasn't just that direct contradiction is so unexpected in China but also, I think, that it had never occurred to him that what his government had told him might not actually be true. He was Han Chinese and had only moved to Urumqi so that he could get a student grant. This sounded like another of the ways in which the central government had been trying to boost the relative number of Han Chinese based in Xinxiang province. According to him, the Uyghur also had a much lower level of educational achievement than the Han Chinese, despite being given all kinds of grants and subsidies, so it was easier to get a place at a good university in Urumqi. The Uyghur may have done less well statistically in the national exams, but what he didn't mention was that all the exams had to be taken in Mandarin rather than in the native Uyghur language. Various initiatives had been set up to promote the inclusion of Uyghur into local government and higher education but their best chance of getting on was still to become less Uyghur and more Han. The recent rise in Uyghur nationalism and the demand for an independent state of Uyghurstan, or East Turkestan, was considered a great threat to the Chinese state. Apart from anything else, Xinjiang is rich in natural resources such as oil and natural gas that have yet to be anything like fully exploited by the national government.

Following the riots in Urumqi in July 2009, in which around 150 people were killed, the government has cracked down heavily on Uyghur separatists. My Chinese friend at reception put much of the blame for the recent uprisings on the exiled Human Rights leader Rebiya Kadeer. She is a self-made millionaire who has been president of the World Uyghur Congress since November 2006. After spending two years in solitary confinement for criticizing the government, she was eventually released early – nominally on medical grounds – into United States' custody in advance of a visit by US Secretary of State Condoleezza Rice. In return for her release, the United States agreed to drop a resolution against China in the United Nations Commission on Human Rights. The Chinese government states that the World Uyghur Congress had orchestrated the 2009 riots and that Kadeer had masterminded it. It has also been alleged that she has close links with the East Turkistan Islamic Movement, which is classed as a terrorist organization by both China and the United States. She denies all of these charges and believes that all Uyghur organizations fight peacefully. Whatever you choose to believe about Kadeer's level of involvement in 'terrorism', the Chinese government's attempts to limit her influence and discredit her have been almost as immoral as they have been inept; when the government wasn't trying to get at her by imprisoning and persecuting her children, it was sending out fake letters from her children – using the kind of language that only government employees would ever use – pleading for her to bring an end to her activities.

If China is ever to become a credible world power then it will need to change. Whether or not it will need to change in any fundamental way, in order to continue to grow as an economic power, is another matter. While many, such as Fukuyama, believe that economic growth is intrinsically linked to a process of liberal democratization, others are not so sure. In his book *What Does China Think?*, Mark Leonard argues that Western-style democracy need not be necessary for China to continue its march towards global domination and that China could become an alternative model of development. Leonard suggests that China could still maintain a one-party state as long as private property is protected and appropriate legislation is reliably enforced. Others such as Lee Kuan Yew, the former Prime Minister of Singapore, have gone as far as to argue that a form of paternalistic authoritarianism is more in keeping with Asia's Confucian traditions, and, more importantly, that it is more compatible with consistently high rates of economic growth than liberal democracy. What worked for a small city state like Singapore, however, wouldn't necessarily work for a country the size of China. Fukuyama believes that the growth of the middle classes becomes inevitable with economic development, and that this growing sector of the community will come to demand greater democracy. Perhaps more importantly, he states that a developed economy will demand a greater level of skill and intellectual development that can only really flourish in a more egalitarian environment. If China is truly to become a world leader then it will need to produce the kinds of scientists and artists who are capable of real innovation and whose creativity won't be stifled by what is still essentially a feudal mind-set (it has often been argued that what has really held back much of Asia is that – unlike Europe and Western civilization – there has never really been an equivalent to the 'Enlightenment' movement and the corresponding break with feudalism and 'traditional' thinking). In the end, China may not become more democratic as a way of creating a fairer and more egalitarian society. It may, however, become more democratic as a way of making the rich and powerful even more rich and powerful. Unfortunately for some, but not for others, if China were to become a democracy then it could no longer be the China it is today; just as the Soviet Union disintegrated into smaller parts with the advent of democracy, China would soon become separated from both Tibet and Xinjiang province (and all the unexploited natural resources that lie within those lands).

* * *

The next morning I set off towards the Kyrgyzstan Embassy to pick up my visa. As I attempted to take a shortcut through the large outdoors market, I kept my eye out for anything that might be of interest. I really don't think the market traders had a single thing to sell that I would ever want to buy. It wasn't just me. For every potential punter there were about ten stallholders looking forlornly down on their piles of tat. Hanging high up above the market was an enormous plasma screen showing the film *Avatar*. As it had only just come out at the cinema, you couldn't buy an official copy on DVD (I found out afterwards that *Avatar* had been pulled from screens throughout China for taking in too much money and seizing market share from domestic films). As I weaved between rusty engine parts and misshapen vegetables, alien warriors with long plaited hair span through the sky on the backs of fire-breathing dragons.

Despite turning up at the Kyrgyz Embassy too early, the grumpy telephone guy from the day before let me have my passport back so I could get on and book the night bus to Almaty in Kazakhstan (I had hoped to get the more comfortable, but slightly slower train, but they didn't run every day and I needed to get on if I was ever going to make it all the way to Istanbul in the time I had left). The ticket office for the sleeper buses to Almaty was also in the same building as the Central Asia Hotel. When I asked at reception about the buses no one quite seemed to know what I was talking about but a vaguely European-looking guy who just happened to be walking past told me that he would sell me a ticket. He led me into a small back office where I handed over a wad of cash. In return I received a crumpled piece of paper with some illegible writing on it and was told to come back to the office at six in the evening. He then shut the office and wandered off again.

Back outside it was still cold, damp and grey. The piles of dirty ice and snow were still sat waiting at every street corner like squat, grubby snowmen. On the way back towards the city centre and People's Park I had to make my way through the pedestrian underpasses buried down under the loops of mangled motorway. The tunnels were full of frozen muddy water. I jumped between the hardest bits in the gloomy passages, trying my best not to slip or land in unfrozen mud. Inevitably, one of my stepping stones shattered and my battered trainer filled with cold, icy mud. I emerged closer to the clean, warm shopping centre but carried on towards the People Park. Even in this weather, the line dancers were still out in force. Anybody seemed to dance with anybody. Good dancers with bad dancers, young dancers with old dancers, any sex, any style, any type. It didn't seem to matter what they danced to or who they danced with. It was just something to do. As in so many Chinese parks, the amusement rides and temples stood happily side to side, seemingly incongruous but rubbing along quite well. On the surface, at least, there seemed to be remarkably little conflict among the Chinese themselves. Everybody seemed to know their place and their obligations. Anything – or anybody – that didn't fit into the broader scheme of things would be modified and manipulated until it did. Anything – or anybody – that got broken during this process would be hidden. In Urumqi, at least, some of the cracks were beginning to show.

On the way back to the White Birch YHA, I stopped off at a nearby supermarket to buy some safe-looking food for the bus journey. When I had visited Xinjiang province fifteen years previously, communist party sloganeering had been inflicted on the shoppers in the outside markets, through rusty, distorting speakers nailed to wooden poles. Every time it started up I would cover my ears to block out the loud, distorted ranting. None of the locals even seemed to notice, let alone complain. The speakers in the clean, modern-looking supermarket were a definite step forward. They blared out a substandard Chinese cover version of a Bananarama track that was itself a cover version (copies of copies fading into the background)

Back in the warmth of the hostel, I used up another sachet of Nescafé 3-in-1 and sat around talking to the attractive fur-coated girl at reception. She already had an eight-year-old daughter and wanted to know if I would have children. I drained out the last of my coffee and finally surrendered my polystyrene cup from Lanzhou to the bin – once out of China the plentiful flasks of free hot water would be a thing of the past. Every now and again some of the other staff would wander in and half-heartedly dust something. It would have been nice if they had actually bothered to clean the toilets but as they were all so nice I didn't like to say anything. They probably weren't being lazy. It perhaps just never occurred to them that the toilets were something Westerners might expect to be cleaned occasionally. If I were to come back to visit in a year's time I expect the same skid marks would still be there waiting for me. After packing up the rest of my now-dry laundry, I said my goodbyes and left to get the local bus back to the Central Asia Hotel.

When I arrived at the bus ticket office next to the Central Asia Hotel, there was nobody there. The lights were off and the doors were locked, and all I had as proof of my purchase was a scribbled-on piece of paper that I couldn't even read. There was nobody else around apart from a couple of old guys running small kiosks. One was selling flowers and the other was selling fruit. The latter was clearly bored, so he came over to talk to me as best as he could. It was a bit of a struggle to understand him but I managed to get the gist of what he was saying. After managing to sell me a surprisingly expensive banana – I really hadn't been eating enough healthy food and bananas are always a safe bet as they come wrapped in their own skin – he expressed surprise that I was waiting to get the bus to Almaty. This wasn't very reassuring. I hadn't really understood what the guy who had sold me the ticket had said to me but I was sure that I was supposed to come back here. Just as I was starting to worry, he turned up at the door, gave me a friendly wave and then walked back out again. At least he hadn't forgotten about me. Ten minutes later he hurried back again and rushed me into his car. As I appeared to be the only person that he sold a ticket to that day, he was going to drive me to the bus himself. He looked more European than Chinese so I asked him where he was from. It turned out that his family had been in Urumqi for generations but that he was part Uyghur, part Kazakh and part Kyrgyz. Contrary to the myth that China had developed entirely in isolation from the rest of the world, there had actually been white people in China for thousands of years. Over a hundred well-preserved Caucasian mummies, which were buried over 4,000 years ago (around 2,000 years before the actual 'Silk Road' trade routes were first established), have been excavated from the Takla Makan Desert in Xinjiang province. The mummies have definite European features and were clearly part of a settled culture in western China. Some of the mummies can still be seen to have had blonde hair. These people were known as the Tocharian and had a language that was closely related to Celtic and Germanic tongues. Later on, they would become Buddhists and intermarry with the Uyghur people after they arrived in western China around AD 800. The Chinese government doesn't appear to be too keen on either publicizing the existence of, or allowing, Western scientists access to the Takla Makan mummies, as claims that non-Han Chinese lived there thousands of years ago might undermine their claims to sovereignty over these oil-rich lands.

My ethnically diverse driver's English was pretty good but he was far more fluent in several other languages. As we drove past a burnt-out building he made a 'boom'-type noise and spread his arms in the air. This was one of the sites where the bombs of Uyghur separatist groups had been detonated last year. I can't remember how many people he said had been killed. All the rioting and demonstrations and bombs hadn't been good for his travel business. He hoped that, now that things had calmed down a bit, he would have a better summer. However, many were predicting that ethnic tensions would soon rise again.

The bus station turned out to be the car park of a large Soviet-style hotel on the outskirts of town. Apparently it was known as 'Little Russia'. Nearly everyone was white but hardly anyone spoke English. It turned out that they were actually mainly traders and business people from all over the former Soviet Union. I say 'business people', as many of the small-time traders were actually women with huge canvas bags full of cheap goods they had bought in China and were planning to sell, back in the 'stans. Not surprisingly, my long-distance sleeper bus had yet to arrive. To his credit, my ethnically diverse travel agent and driver didn't just dump me there but led me off for tea and a chat at the bus company office. The office was a converted hotel room with a decent bathroom, which I made use of to brush my teeth and wash my face before the long journey ahead. I suspected that I wouldn't be seeing a nice hotel bathroom like this one for a while. As I sat waiting, unsure of what was going on, Kazakh women wandered in and out. It seemed like they'd been through it all many times before and pretty much expected there to be delays. When the coach eventually turned up a couple of hours later, most of these women would end up arguing with the coach driver over their baggage allowance. Some of them probably had a couple of carloads of canvas bags and cardboard boxes to try to fit in underneath. Everything from flat-screen plasma televisions to flat-packed furniture was getting crammed in there. My battered blue backpack seemed pitifully insignificant in comparison. Each of the bunks inside had a hard, raised, hollow top end that doubled as an encased foot end for the person behind. I shoved my feet and my valuables into the space beneath the head rest in front and tried to arrange the pillows as best as I could. Finally, the driver surrendered to the outraged Kazakh traders' indignation as they somehow managed to cram it all in underneath, and we were finally on our way to Kazakhstan.

KAZAKHSTAN

Almaty

Inequality and Capitalism • The Cost of Progress • Culture and Authenticity • Out of Time • More Mongrel than Mongol Urban Migration • Capturing Culture • Empty Consumption The Global Media • Religion and Identity • High Art and Low Art The American Dream • The Superiority of Youth • Ethnic Diversity Art and Development • Freedom and Slavery • The End of History The Tourism Dream

We emerged from under the heavy, stale blankets to stagger out into a dark, grey car park. We were nearly at the border. Unsure of what was next, I followed some of the other passengers over to a roadside café. I pointed at the hot Chinese tea and a couple of greasy dumplings that apparently were 'meat', then sat down on my own to worry about whether 'meat' dumplings were really a good idea. As I was hungry and I couldn't find anything else, I ate them anyway. Not knowing how long we would be stopping here, I tried to keep an eye on the other passengers to see what was happening. When I walked around to the toilets at the side of the café, it wasn't with high expectations. After paying the attendant, I braced myself and strode manfully in. High-pitched shrieks greeted me, so I walked straight back out again. The next time I opted for the gents. On entering the right toilets I was also tempted to shriek but managed to resist. None of the Chinese seemed particularly bothered about squatting among all the shit while everybody looked on, but I really wasn't up to it. I limited myself to a quick-as-possible piss before escaping to the car park where some of the other Kazakh passengers invited me along for a meal. One of these Kazakh women had been squatting down over the first of a line of holes when I walked into the wrong toilet. She was called Aisha. We both pretended to be meeting for the first time.

I followed them out of the car park and up the street. I was a bit worried about going too far away from our bus but figured that I'd be all right as long as I stuck with some other passengers. Uridin was the only other man in our group and spoke fairly decent English. He was tall and looked European apart from slightly slanted eyes. Like many Kazakhs he was a bit of a mixture. The women all just looked Eastern European apart from one who had a headscarf and a mouth full of gold teeth. Apparently this was a popular look for Kazakh women of a certain class and age. She couldn't speak any English and when she spoke to the others I had to try hard not to keep staring at her teeth. I'm really not sure that having all those gold teeth is a good idea in a poor country. What if you got mugged?

They had all been buying cheap goods in Urumchi to take back to Almaty, and Aisha was their trip organizer. Every week she would take out groups ('all inclusive') from Almaty to Urumchi and back again. She knew all the best places to go and all the right people. She was a modern-day Silk Road trader and tour guide. As well as her customers, she was also taking back a variety of goods that her Almaty contacts had ordered, such as a huge plasma TV. Ina still looked like she was in her twenties; she had her own business selling children's clothes. Every few months she would make the trip to buy new stock. Uridin also dabbled in some trading but had mainly come to buy a new kitchen for his flat in Almaty. Certain luxury goods could still be ridiculously expensive in Kazakhstan and he reckoned he would be saving a lot of money by buying the kitchen himself in China. He also had a sealed-up box with a picture of a gun on it – they must have been cheaper in China as well.

We went into a Chinese restaurant further up the street, where they all seemed to know Aisha, and where they led us into a private room. As I had already eaten the greasy 'meat' dumplings and really wasn't up for what looked like it was going to be a full Chinese banquet for breakfast, I made my excuses and left them to their feast. Because I had been talking all the time I hadn't been paying enough attention as to where we had been going and wasn't sure how to get back. This was worrying enough but when I *did* get back to what I thought was our car park there were no longer any coaches in it. I wandered around a bit trying to find it but it had definitely gone. Eventually, I came across someone who spoke some English who told me that all the coaches had left for the border. My bag was still locked up underneath our coach and all the other passengers had also disappeared. I rushed back towards the Chinese restaurant to try to catch Uridin and Aisha while they were still there but then I couldn't remember where it was. I cursed myself for talking too much rubbish and not paying attention to what was going on around me. When I found them again in a back room of the restaurant they were just finishing off and about to leave. They bundled me into a taxi with them and we were off to the border. Apparently we had to make our own way there and would meet up again with the coach once it had made its way through customs.

We managed to get out through customs quite easily but then, having officially left China, were just left standing on the other side with hundreds of others. I was the only tourist. Everybody else seemed to be from Kazakhstan and be transporting enough Chinese goods to set up a chain of shops. I hadn't realized, but the border post had only just opened up again after a four-day bank holiday in China and as the trains still wouldn't start running for another couple of days the border post was even more crowded. I knew there could often be delays but this didn't look good. We would just have to wait here with the hundreds of other passengers – and the single chemical toilet – until the bus was allowed through. We took turns to rush over to the coffee stall in the rain and buy each other cups of sweet weak instant coffee and whatever snacks remained. Someone got stuck in the Portaloo until someone else hurried through the puddles to release them. The rain made the hot coffee spill out over the edge of my polystyrene cup and burn my fingers. We stood around our bags and chatted, waiting for something to happen. Several hours later we were still all there, waiting. Even Aisha, who seemed to know all the customs officials, couldn't find out what was happening, but she did persuade them to let us go back to our bus for a 'business lunch'.

Aisha led us into the back section of the bus, which effectively made up into a triple bunk bed, and we all sat down around the lower one while Aisha unpacked a group picnic. I wasn't sure if I should really be eating their food when I wasn't even a member of their tour group but I kept being told that it was 'all inclusive'. If they hadn't all befriended me I'd probably never have known how to get through the border, let alone had a proper meal. We munched away on our 'business lunch' while chatting about our experiences in Urumchi. Uridin wanted to know if I had been to 'Foowkin Beach' while I was in Urumchi. I had never heard of it. It could hardly be a real beach when Urumchi was supposedly the furthest city in the world from any sea. I assumed that the 'beach' must have been by one of the nearby scenic lakes. According to Uridin it was 'very cheapy' and there were 'many sexy girls'. It sounded like a great value holiday resort with plenty of attractive young women. I was amazed that I hadn't heard of it, even if it was still far too cold for gallivanting around on a 'beach'; and I was quite sure it hadn't been mentioned in any of the guidebooks. Apparently Urumchi was famous for it. Whenever Kazakh men visited Urumchi they always went to 'Foowkin Beach'. This time when Uridin said 'Foowkin' he made a lewd gesture … and then it finally clicked.

Apparently, healthy red-blooded Kazakh men never went long without 'foowkin' a 'beach'. Uridin seemed both amazed and alarmed that I had failed to take advantage of such great value entertainment. When he announced to all the ladies that I hadn't 'foowked' a single 'beach' in Urumchi, they were equally taken aback. They were both surprised and disappointed. I felt like I'd let them all down.

More than six hours after arriving at the border post our bus was finally allowed through customs. I really don't know why it took so long. Not a single one of the hundreds of boxes and bags that were stuffed under the coaches appeared to have been opened or checked. Everybody just made an appropriate payment to the customs officials and they let you take whatever you wanted in. Not a single box was unpacked or a single zip unzipped. Anything could have been taken across the border. Even Uridin's box with a picture of a gun on it passed through without comment. Aisha dealt directly with the custom guards 'payments' – it was 'all inclusive'. It was probably this avoidance of import taxes on luxury goods that made the whole trip worthwhile; it was only by avoiding the 'official' payments that the small traders and ordinary people could make a living through their trade along the modern 'Silk Road' trade routes.

Even after the coach had been let through we still had to spend another hour or so loading everything back under the bus. This time around it didn't quite seem to fit in. After a lot of packing and repacking, and swearing – both at and from the driver – we were eventually on our way again. To my surprise, it immediately seemed different. Only a few minutes over the border, the roads, buildings and people all seemed to have changed. Cowboy-type figures were even riding around the fields on horses. Everything seemed more spaced out. So many borders are arbitrary but there was a remarkably clear difference between what was now officially Central Asia and what, just a few miles away – despite being a part of Greater Turkestan – was still very much China.

It was already late at night by the time we finally pulled into the bus station in Almaty. Everybody else seemed to have phoned through on their mobiles to ensure someone was there to help unload all their purchases and drive them home. Uridin's blonde

Russian wife had turned up with his father-in-law to help take home their new kitchen. As soon as I got off the bus I made the mistake of speaking English and was immediately surrounded by predatory taxi drivers. When Uridin saw what was happening he pulled me away and made me sit in their car. I didn't even have a chance to talk to any of the drivers, but apparently they had been asking for silly amounts of money as they knew I was new to town and that the late hour meant no public buses were running.

We all bundled into the car along with the flat-pack kitchen. Rather embarrassingly I was guided into the front passenger seat while Uridin's father-in-law was made to crawl into the boot (once he had finished loading in everything else). Uridin lived towards the top of one of the high-rise flats not far from the bus station. All around it, similar high-rise buildings were being constructed. Even approaching midnight, massive cranes were still piling up the new floors into the floodlit city sky. The recent oil boom in Kazakhstan had inevitably resulted in a property and construction boom in Almaty. Although many construction projects had recently ground to a halt following something of a financial crisis, there still seemed to be plenty of new money pouring into the city, making Almaty probably the most expensive city for thousands of miles. Uridin's high-rise two-bedroom flat was about two years old and much nicer on the inside than the institutional-looking foyer and corridors would suggest. From his eighteenth-floor balcony there was a great view over much of the city, including the bus station that we had just come from. Uridin's young son was delighted with his gift of a machine gun – I assumed it was a toy one, although I wasn't entirely sure – and his slightly older daughter was equally pleased with some bright pink roller blades. A few minutes later she rolled out of the bedroom with them on only to fall flat down onto her arse. For a minute I thought she was going to burst into tears but then she decided not to and more cautiously rose back to her feet.

One of the family's many business lines seemed to be importing the kind of edible seeds that made popular snacks. Their bedroom had boxes of them stacked up high either side of a large wall-mounted plasma TV. The kitchen had already been removed in preparation for the new one so they seemed to be making do with a kind of camping set up. Uridin's wife had plenty of food prepared for us. As the sink was currently missing from the kitchen, we went through to the bathroom – also full of cardboard boxes full of seeds – and washed our hands in a large hot tub-style bath. I pushed the wrong button and squirted water all over the floor and Uridin's leg.

The TV was switched on and seemed to be showing some kind of riot. It was happening just over the border in Kyrgyzstan's capital city Bishkek. I had planned to be there in a few days' time. We sat around the screen munching on huge plates of chicken while the Kyrgyz soldiers randomly machine gunned the demonstrators. I was appalled – this was going to completely ruin my holiday plans. The opposition to President Bakiyev were claiming that his troops had gunned down more than one hundred unarmed civilians (the number of deaths in the initial Bishkek uprising would later be thought to be eighty-eight, but hundreds more were badly injured). Uridin was seriously urging me to reconsider my holiday plans. Apparently there was nothing to see in Kyrgyzstan, anyway, and it was full of 'very cheapy people'. Aisha had also been watching the news from her flat in Almaty. She phoned Uridin and got her son to speak to me in his excellent English. He also strongly suggested that I amended my holiday plans and confirmed that there was nothing worth seeing in Kyrgyzstan apart from a few mountains and lakes. They made me write down their mobile numbers in case I got into any 'trouble'. I was clearly a cause for concern.

Uridin pulled off his shirt to reveal a back full of nasty-looking burns. They were pulsing red, almost circular and evenly spaced. He had been to see an alternative therapist in Urumchi for 'health reasons' and she appeared to have overdone it with a hot-stone treatment. He looked like a torture victim or an over-enthusiastic masochist. I hoped that the 'therapist' had been 'very cheapy'. While Uridin excused himself to visit the box-filled bathroom – he hadn't been able to face the 'not very nice' toilets on the way either – his wife plied me with enormous slices of cream-covered cake while their kids ran around with their new toys. Before Uridin offered to take me to the hostel that I was planning to stay at, she presented me with some bananas as a present. I thanked them for their hospitality and kindness, and was led down to the underground car park by Uridin. On the way we were met by an older man who seemed oddly deferential. Uridin explained that he was always treated with respect as he worked for the police. He flashed me an ID card. He hadn't mentioned this before. Apparently he was some kind of police driver and had been especially trained to manoeuvre out of dangerous situations. He explained that there were some very bad people in Kazakhstan and that sometimes this was necessary. The main streets on the way were wide and well maintained but the side roads were full of potholes and the pavements were cracked. There were plenty of new-looking BMWs and Mercedes around but anywhere outside of the main thoroughfares they would be reduced to crawling just as slowly as the lowliest of Ladas.

As the hotels in Almaty were notoriously expensive, I had planned to stay at the university's ninth dormitory, which was open to travellers. It was difficult to find but fortunately even in the early hours of the morning there were still some staff and students up and about. They showed me to a room full of single beds, and warned me to be careful about locking the door properly and not leaving any valuables in the room. At least I had the room to myself. Uridin seemed less than impressed with my choice of accommodation but it was about as cheap as I was going to get in Almaty and by now I was far too tired to start looking for anywhere else. We said our goodbyes and

I thanked Uridin for all his help – without his and the others' kindness it could have been a very hard and frustrating journey.

Having held everything in since this morning because of appalling roadside toilets, I now really had to go. In hindsight, I really ought to have asked Uridin if I could have used his nice clean Western toilet back at his apartment. The toilets I managed to find did at least have doors but there were no seats, no light bulbs and no windows. There weren't any bins either and piles of used toilet paper had been thrown all over the soaking floor. I had seen some depressing student accommodation in London but this was in a different class altogether. After traipsing up and down all the different floors I eventually found a single toilet that was equally sordid but at least had a working light. I had been tempted to try to wait until the morning when I could check into another place with better facilities, but I knew I wouldn't be able to sleep with the stomach cramps that had now set in. My thigh muscles weren't strong enough to squat over a Western toilet with no seat, so I wiped the edge as clean as I could with my own supply of toilet paper – an absolute essential in this part of the world – and dared to rest my aching thighs down on it. I really didn't want to make any kind of contact with the porcelain but by now I was exhausted. I would have loved to have had a shower straight afterwards but I hadn't been able to locate any during my search for a usable toilet and doubted if they'd be any more hygienic (I found out afterwards that you had to queue up downstairs in order to be handed a key to the mysterious shower room).

Unfortunately, all the travelling, irregular eating and holding it in had not been good for my piles. There was blood everywhere. By now, there was a queue of teenage Kazakh students starting to form outside the single toilet with a light bulb and I was feeling far from relaxed. I finished my business as quickly as I could manage and left my neatly folded used toilet paper in an orderly pile in the corner of the room. I'm not sure why I bothered as everyone else had just thrown their shit covered bog roll all over the place, but I do think it's important to keep up standards. After washing my hands and face as best as I could over what appeared to be a slime-filled trough – using the remains of my mineral water for this as there was no running water – I finally collapsed onto my hard, dusty bed.

* * *

Almaty used to be the capital of Kazakhstan but in 1997 President Nazarbaev moved the capital north to Astana ('Astana' actually means 'capital' in Kazakh). Almaty was earthquake prone and a little too close to China for comfort while Astana was more centrally located and had better transport links to Russia. Despite an enormous amount of investment in infrastructure and architecture, few government employees were overjoyed at the prospect of having to relocate to what was seen as a provincial out-of-the-way city with brutally cold winters. To all intents and purposes, Almaty has remained as the real capital of Kazakhstan and as the place where the real money is to be made. Unfortunately, most of that new money seems to be far from equally distributed. While luxury cars and designer clothes are everywhere to be seen, over one-third of the country is estimated to be living below the poverty line. Even the expensive designer clothes shops appeared to be unevenly distributed along the pot-holed boulevards – while in Europe or America, the high end boutiques would be grouped together in an upmarket shopping area, in Almaty they appeared to be randomly dotted throughout the city. Despite being laid out in an orderly grid, Almaty's development seemed disconcertingly awkward and uneven. It seemed more like a poor city with money than a rich city with poverty. The phrase 'all fur coat and no knickers' came to mind.

Having woken at dawn after only a few hours' sleep, I was keen to find somewhere decent to stay as soon as possible.

My Central Asia Lonely Planet had recommended a place just around the corner from the university, but it was nowhere to be found. Further along was a 'budget' hotel where all the rooms were well over US$100 a night. This wasn't looking good. Most of the other hotels were ridiculously expensive. But there two 'budget' options on the other side of the city. I went back to the university to pick up my backpack and hand over the keys. The staff there didn't seem surprised that I was leaving so early – I can't have been the first foreigner to get out as soon as possible. One of the remaining budget options was supposed to be just across from the train station so I thought it might be an easy one to track down. I managed to find a bus stop where the buses appeared to be heading in the right direction and somehow managed to confirm with a driver that his bus was travelling towards the station. As I sat on the bus, with my backpack between my legs, I attempted to trace out the route along my map. Almaty is all just a big grid, so this wasn't too hard. The final budget hotel was opposite the Zelyony Bazaar, so when I realized we were going right past it I decided to get off there.

This part of Almaty seemed more like the Central Asia I had expected to find. There was rubbish and people everywhere, with stalls of all sorts lining the broken, muddy pavements surrounding the enclosed bazaar. I edged past a tray of fly-ridden goats' heads and into the Turkistan Hotel.

The slightly run down, Soviet-style hotel charged three times more than a similar kind of budget hotel would have charged in China but it still seemed by far the best value option. Accommodation prices in Almaty seemed to be on a par with the more expensive parts of Western Europe but without the same consistency of standards. For what I'd paid for a night at the university in its ninth dormitory I could have stayed at a well-run, clean hostel in virtually any country in the developed world. For now, though, I was just glad to be out of the cold and in a nice warm room with its own functional bathroom. I ordered some coffee from my floor lady – all the old Soviet-style hotels appear to have 'floor ladies' who look after the cleaning and drinks for their designated floor – and had it with the banana that Uridin's wife had given me as a leaving present. I turned on the TV and flicked through to Kazakh MTV. There seemed to be about a fifty-fifty mix between the usual Western pop videos that you get everywhere and the home-produced videos of various Kazakh artists. During my brief time in Kazakhstan I would see these videos and hear these songs almost everywhere I went. While the Western music videos were almost always different every time, there seemed to be only about five or six Kazakh music videos in circulation. I suspected that, as in France or Canada, there was some kind of law that obliged radio and TV stations to ensure that at least 50 per cent of their playlist was made up of Kazakh performers. Left to the free market I doubt any of these acts would have received much recognition at all. Such legislation may have been introduced to encourage the growth of a uniquely Kazakh voice in popular culture but the problem seemed to be that for the main part they were simply attempting to ape what was mainly American youth culture. The stars of one music video in particularly heavy rotation were a girl and boy, both about twelve years old, pretending to be a streetwise urban soul diva and a hard-arsed gangster rapper. As soon as she had finished with wailing out her broken heart and thrusting her booty, he would manfully swagger on in his shell suit and start cussing the bitches. They looked a bit silly. Why weren't they in school?

Another popular act seemed to have taken 1960s Liverpool as a cultural reference point. They all sported Beatle's-style basin haircuts and lounged around stroking acoustic guitars in a vague approximation of the era's psychedelia. They weren't too bad but I really couldn't see them doing much business outside of Kazakhstan. Maybe the next generation of Kazakh musicians, who would have grown up surrounded by Western pop culture, will manage to come up with something that is international and contemporary, and yet uniquely Kazakh? It might take a while.

Having showered, changed and eaten, and feeling a whole lot better, I ventured into the cold Almaty drizzle. I edged my way up through the crowded Zelyony Bazaar towards Panfilov Park. If you've ever seen any tourist promotional photos for Almaty, then they probably had Panfilov Park's Zenkov Cathedral in them. Designed by A.P. Zenkov in 1904, it is one of the few remaining Tsarist-era buildings in Kazakhstan and is considered to be a rival to the more famous St Basil's Cathedral in Moscow. It looks like a big colourful doll's house and, as everything in it is made of wood (including the nails), it was one of the few buildings to survive the 1911 earthquake. Having been used as a museum and a concert hall in the Soviet era, it wasn't returned to the Russian Orthodox Church until 1995. Despite its outwardly bright and cheery exterior, on the inside it is very much a gloom-filled, smoky Orthodox sanctuary. While the brightly coloured wooden domes sprouted out towards whatever light could be grappled from the grey sky, all but a few shards of sunlight were barred from slicing through the incense trails within. Just after a typically grandiose Soviet-style war memorial with the obligatory eternal flame is another Zenkov-designed building, the Museum of Kazakh Musical Instruments. I actually preferred its elegant lines and unpainted wood finish to the more garish and better-known Zenkov Cathedral.

As I carried on up the gentle slope, back towards the university area, I couldn't help feeling that something about Almaty seemed very familiar. There were far fewer Oriental-looking people around than I had expected and far more who looked Eastern European or Russian. In the 1930s, 40s and 50s many Russians, Ukrainians and Germans had been forcefully migrated to the Kazakh steppes. Some had been prisoners sent out to the labour camps while others had arrived to extract Kazakhstan's rich natural resources of coal, iron and oil. In Kazakhstan I no longer stood out as an obvious foreigner. Several times a day people would come and ask me for directions in Russian and then be surprised when I answered apologetically in English. In fact, with my cheap shell suit trousers, baseball cap and bright white trainers I could easily pass for a Russian chav. I fitted right in.

There was something else, though, about the way the people dressed and acted that seemed even more familiar than Eastern Europe. I couldn't quite place what it was about the cheap black leather bomber jackets, side partings and dodgy facial hair on the men, and the shiny calf-length boots and fake fur coats on the women, that seemed so recognizable; and then it hit me – it was like being back in England in the late 1970s or early 1980s. It was like an episode of *Life on Mars*. The only thing missing was black people with Afros. Teenage Kazakh would-be pop stars might have been inspired by the fashions and posturing of American hip-hop artists but there didn't seem to be many black people on the mean streets of Almaty. Surprisingly enough, almost every other ethnic group was, from red heads and blondes to the purely Oriental. Many others, like Uridin, were a complex mixture of ethnicities. Ethnic difference in Central Asia had often been exploited by those in power as a tool for either division or unification. Stalin had deliberately created seemingly arbitrary borders between areas of shared ethnicity or tribal allegiance in order to keep groups of people divided, but, following the collapse of the Soviet Union in 1991, shared ethnicity and culture had been called upon in an attempt to unify the newly independent nations of Central Asia. In reality, there are considerable numbers of all the main Central Asian ethnic groups in all of these countries and Central Asia is largely ethnically heterogeneous. In many respects they're as mongrel as they're Mongol.

While a large proportion of the population of Kazakhstan is made up of a complex mixture of ethnicities and cultures, I couldn't help noticing that most of the customers and staff at the excellent Coffeedelia were very European in appearance. It was a little oasis of posh coffee, cakes and Wi-Fi that wouldn't have seemed out of place in any major Western city. Not surprisingly, it also had the prices to match. I spent more on a cappuccino and a piece of cake than I would have spent on a night's accommodation in most of the Far East, but it was worth it. The excellent coffee and gleaming Western toilets seemed a whole world away from the university's sordid ninth dormitory – although in reality it was just a few blocks up the hill.

Feeling refreshed, I carried on in that direction in search of the Kok-Tobe cable car. You would think it would have been easy to find the cable car station by simply looking down the cables that rose towards Blue Hill (or sometimes 'Green Hill'), a spur of the Tian Shan mountain range that looks down over Almaty. Unfortunately, the line of the cables was obscured by other buildings on the edge of the now-steepening hill, and I could only guess at the general location of the station. When I found a building in the right area with a grand and busy entrance way, I assumed that must be it. I ended up walking through what seemed to be some kind of large government building and getting increasingly lost among the maze of corridors. Nobody seemed to question what I was doing there. At one point I stepped out into what I thought would be another long, anonymous Soviet corridor, only to find myself on a concert hall stage. Fortunately there was nobody in the hall apart from a couple of guys in overalls who took no notice of me. While feeling relieved at the absence of an audience, I couldn't help thinking it would been far funnier if I'd walked straight out on stage into a packed auditorium (on more than one occasion I have overheard references to 'Mr Bean' while I've been attempting to find my way).

After a far more circuitous route than I had anticipated and some elaborate miming of a cable car's ascent that only seemed to increase the confusion, I eventually found the cable car station, only to be rather taken aback at the cost of the ticket. I reluctantly coughed up the required dosh and joined some cheerful Russian tourists in the stationary cabin. It actually seemed quite similar to many of the older-style cable cars in New Zealand – although it was considerably more expensive. We lurched slowly upwards towards the telecommunications tower at the top of Green Hill, from which one could look down over the houses and back yards of the houses on the fringes of the city. Even from high up they looked like shit holes. As the main part of the city faded into the mountains, the 'houses' were reduced to improvised-looking shacks thrown together out of rusty sheets of corrugated iron and whatever junk these new immigrants to the big city could lay their hands on. To the average Kazakh farm labourer Almaty must have seemed unimaginably expensive, but even with something of a financial crisis in full swing it still looked like there would be plenty of work around for unskilled labourers in the booming construction industry. Or maybe there wasn't? Either way, a big city with this much money around was always going to draw in the rural poor.

After lurching to a halt, we spilled out onto the peak and piled into the process of capturing the view on our memory cards. It may have been quite lively in the summer or at the weekends but on a damp, drizzly weekday the park at the summit seemed a little forlorn. To the left were some children's amusement rides that were mainly locked up and to the right was a small zoo that consisted of a few grubby-looking goats, a couple of peacocks and same caged birds. Rather than venturing out to greet the few curious children, they opted to hide out in their shelters. I wandered up and down while munching on an overpriced burger. Not for the only time on this trip I felt like I was visiting a minor holiday resort in an unfashionable part of England during the off season. There were a few Kazakh families and a handful of Russian tourists – probably actually here for 'business' – with their digital SLRs and time to kill, but, as in most of China, I was still the only real foreign tourist. I would assume that there's a few more about in the summer but as this was still officially spring I was surprised that I didn't meet a single other Western tourist during my week in Kazakhstan.

The fun park seemed oddly quiet and subdued apart from what appeared to be a tinny loop of 'I am the Walrus'. I drifted over to the sound of the sixties, to find a set of bronze Beatles statues. As soon as the tannoy on a pole faded into silence, it would repeat once more, 'I am the Walrus' over and over again. These distorted speakers on sticks used to be used for blaring out party propaganda throughout China and the Soviet Union but now they were being used for repeated loops of trippy sixties' psychedelia. Whose idea was this? Why 'I am the Walrus'? You could just about recognize which Beatle was supposed to be which but they all seemed oddly Oriental. They looked more like Mongols with basin cuts than pasty-faced white boys from Liverpool. A group of teenagers ran over to the statues to have their pictures taken with the Kazakh Beatles. One of the boys sat on the knee of what I think was supposed to be Paul McCartney and put his arm around him lovingly while he posed for group snapshots.

It was getting dark by the time that I had traipsed back down to the Turkistan Hotel. As all of Almaty is laid out in a grid and basically slants downwards towards the train station, you would think that it would be easy to get oriented. Unfortunately, the lack of any real landmarks or buildings that stand out over the tree line make it surprisingly difficult to get a handle on where you are. From across the road all the tree-lined parks look the same, so they're no good as landmarks, and a lot of the buildings are grimly nondescript. As the signposts were also all in Cyrillic I found it difficult to match them up to the Anglicized road names on my map (if I was going to spend any time in this part of the world again I would probably try to make the effort to learn the Cyrillic alphabet – it would almost certainly make getting about much easier).

Having eventually made my way back via Panfilov Park and the back end of Zelyony Bazaar, I found myself eating the best donor kebab that I have had anywhere in the world in the green octagonal-shaped café at the edge of the bazaar. Kebabs can vary in quality possibly more than other food in existence but I could have eaten these ones all day. As this café was clearly aimed more at the market stallholders than their designer-label-touting contemporaries, it was also great value. I would become something of a regular over the next few days. After finishing with a mug of Kazakh three-in-one instant coffee and a Bounty chocolate bar, I scuttled on through the drizzle towards the Silk Way City shopping mall in search of an Internet café.

Compared to the bazaar, the shopping mall seemed oddly quiet and sterile. A lot of the shop spaces were still unoccupied. A few soggy souls walked in one end and out the other simply to stay out of the rain for a while. Upstairs there was a handful of teenagers hanging around eating junk food from the few tables and chairs that were scattered along the central aisle. None of the shops seemed busy. Rapidly developing countries always seem to have malls like these, full of expensive imported designer clothes but with few paying customers. In Thailand, people would meet in the malls for the food halls and air conditioning; in Kazakhstan they would come in to get out of the damp and drizzle. I mimed what I wanted to the guy running the mall's Internet café and he handed over a scrap of paper with a logon ID and the number of purchased minutes. There were loads of emails from my wife. She was worried that I hadn't emailed her for nearly a week and wanted to know if the swelling on my throat was still there. She had even phoned my parents in England to see if they had heard anything. I had to explain that the Internet connection in Dunhuang had been down and that the Chinese authorities had effectively banned the Internet in Urumchi. To have been without the Internet in Urumchi when it was easily accessible almost everywhere else in the world seemed bizarrely archaic. Even in Myanmar, where you could supposedly be arrested for bringing in a modem, it was still easy enough to pick up your emails via a proxy server. I called up the *Guardian* website – the service I used for the news wherever I was in the world – and checked out the latest on the situation in Kyrgyzstan. It didn't look good …

The official death toll from the riots in Bishkek had now risen to at least seventy-five with more than three hundred reportedly injured. Dozens of shops had been looted and burned-out cars apparently littered the pavements. The rioters had overrun the palace of President Bakiyev and stolen his lampshades. Another looter had had the barefaced cheek to make off with the President's drainpipes. Even the presidential shrubs had been stolen from Bakiyev's once grand front garden. I was reminded of Uridin's assertion that they were 'very cheapy' people. Maybe they were just poor and pissed off? Price hikes on communal charges for water and electricity appear to have been the last straw in a country of 5 million that was already struggling with mass unemployment and widespread poverty. When Bakiyev had come to power five years earlier in the so-called Tulip Revolution, hopes had been high. When he had turned out to be just another in a long line of dodgy Central Asian dictators, the people had yet again revolted. While sympathizing with the plight of the people I couldn't help feeling that they had been a little bit selfish. Jumping up and down on tanks and breaking the President's windows was all very well, but some people had put a lot of time and effort into planning their holidays only to have their plans disrupted at the last minute. Not wanting to give up on my plans just yet, I emailed my chosen guest house in Bishkek to see if they thought if it would still be a good idea to come and visit.

* * *

The next morning, I hurried through the cold with my still wet hair to the bakery in front of the Turkistan Hotel. I picked out a pastry and emptied a sachet of Kazakh three-in-one coffee into a polystyrene cup and filled it from the communal hot water boiler. A friendly young woman who worked there asked me my name and, as I seemed a bit shy about joining the traders at the high bar-style tables, she cleared a space for me while introducing herself. I actually felt surprisingly at home in Almaty. The people seemed friendly enough and quite a few spoke some English, but they were never pushy or intrusive and were happy to let you have your own space. In fact, all along the Silk Road, the only people who ever set out to exploit you as a tourist seemed to be the taxi drivers. More specifically, it would actually be taxi drivers in places where large numbers of them congregated – such as at bus stations. If you waved down a single taxi away from the others, then the drivers would always seem happy to charge you the same as the locals (in the local currency) but once they all got together they would start asking for ridiculous amounts of money in US dollars. It seemed pretty unlikely that any Western backpacker would ever have shelled out US$100 for a short taxi ride, so where did they get the idea that English speakers were such suckers? Maybe a few American businessmen had paid vastly over the odds a few times – as they knew no better and had generous expense accounts – and then these tales of absurdly lucrative rides had taken off among the Central Asian taxi drivers, only to be exaggerated over time and mutated into some kind of urban myth?

Having returned to my room to brush and plait my still-damp hair, I emerged again to visit Almaty's blue-domed white-marble central mosque. The largest mosque in the country, with room for 3,000 Believers, it was only built in 1999 in response to something of a resurgence of all religions in Kazakhstan after independence was declared in 1991. Although religion was largely suppressed during the Soviet era it was to re-emerge as a core aspect of ethnic identity in the unsettled and confusing years to follow. While Almaty and the territories further north lean more towards Russian Orthodox Christianity – the garish Zenkov Cathedral was reopened as a church in 1995 – the dominant religious group in Kazakhstan is Sunni Muslim. Even though Kazakhstan has a reputation for religious tolerance and any kind of religious extremism is rare, the resurgence of Islam in the south has been a concern for many. If the politicized Islam found in the countries further south were to find a foothold in Kazakhstan, then it seems unlikely that the authorities would remain quite so tolerant.

After another stop at Coffeedelia, I walked up past Respublika Alanghy and the stone-columned Monument to Independence towards the permanent circus. Most big former Soviet cities seem to have both year-round circuses and puppet theatres. There used to be more than seventy permanent circuses in the Soviet Union and over a hundred puppet theatres operating in twenty-five different languages. While the European tradition of circus was often appropriated by the authorities for more pedagogical means, puppetry retained its status as a vital art form.

Although puppets in the Western world largely came to be associated with children's entertainment, in Russia they were thought of as a valid form of contemporary theatre. Well-plotted plays with complex psychologically believable characters grew puppetry into a highly regarded art form. As with cartoons and comics in the West, I suspect they were often used to satirize and make points that might not have been so easily made through other forms of media. Something else you find in many major Soviet cities is state-subsidized theatres for ballet and opera. The kinds of performance that would have been prohibitively expensive in the West were often made available to the general public for the equivalent of a couple of dollars. I suspect that this general policy had more to do with showing off than any real desire by the government to enrich the cultural lives of their citizens. Throughout the Cold War, the Soviet Union was desperate to present itself as superior on every level to the degenerate West. As the prohibitive cost and elitism associated with both ballet and opera meant it was largely associated with the ruling classes, by bringing such 'high art' to the masses they could pretend to be dead sophisticated. As the Americans were watching blockbuster Hollywood movies and listening to rock and roll, the more enlightened Soviet citizens would be enriching their cultural lives at the opera or ballet. Where this fell down was that the youngest and brightest of the population would far rather have been listening to world class rock music and watching decent television or films than being subjected to what their rulers thought would be good for them.

Not all the entertainment, however, involved self-improvement. As well as the permanent circus – where the performers could display the results of their superior Soviet discipline – every major Soviet city also seemed to have its own amusement park. Compared to the rather tired and rusty efforts in China, Almaty's recently constructed Fantasy Land looked state of the art. Unfortunately, along with the circus, it was shut. I walked into a US-style diner and ordered a typically American burger and fries. The flat-screen TV on the wall was permanently tuned into Kazakh MTV. It seemed to be what the young people wanted. Not much further down the newly paved road was a gleaming US-style shopping mall. It was even more expensive and even more devoid of paying customers than the Silk Way City shopping mall. The bored-looking shop girls loitered around the racks of designer label outfits wishing they were somewhere else (like America?).

I somehow managed to get a bus back down to the other side of town and jumped off close to Gorky Park. Yet again, almost every large Soviet city seems to have a Gorky Park. It was pretty much like one of the People's Parks in China but with more kebabs and no temples. There was an unused boating lake, an aqua park (not surprisingly closed at this time of the year) and an assortment of end-of-pier type stalls and amusement rides. Bored-looking attendants thrust their hands into warm fur-lined pockets and shuffled around the few active rides. The guy outside of the ghost train asked me if I liked Almaty. When I shrugged and told him that it was all right he looked confused. 'Why?' he said. 'Why would you like Almaty? America is much better.' When I asked him if he'd been there he admitted that he hadn't but told me that he had a friend who worked there. Everybody you spoke to seemed to have a friend or a relative working in America. It was his dream to, one day, make it to America. I hoped he wouldn't be disappointed.

After yet another visit to my favourite octagonal kebab shop, I headed over to the Internet café at Silk Way City. A quick glance through a few news sites seemed to suggest that the situation in Bishkek had calmed down a bit; there were still packs of youths roaming the streets and making a nuisance of themselves but the army appeared to have given up on shooting them. I had an email waiting for me from my chosen guest house in Bishkek saying that everything was fine in their part of the city and that they would look forward to seeing me the next day. I resolved to give it a go.

* * *

I rushed past the traders setting up their stalls in the early morning cold and into the warmth of the bakery. The friendly girl from the previous morning greeted me by name. I was pleased to see her again but felt a bit embarrassed that I couldn't remember what she was called. It always seemed to be the young who were most friendly, open and curious, and I don't think this is just because they more likely to speak some English than the older generations. After another breakfast of instant three-in-one coffee and pastries, I checked out of the Turkistan Hotel and caught a bus from just outside the market to the same station I had arrived at from China. Having arrived and got off the bus with my backpack I was surrounded by taxi drivers offering to take me all the way to Bishkek. As so many were still going in that direction I assumed that the Kyrgyz border must be still open. For a seat in a shared taxi to the border, they all agreed that the price was US$100. I walked around the corner and straight onto a bus to Bishkek that was just about to leave. The ticket was a fraction under US$7.

During the four-hour journey to the Kyrgyz border we were pulled over several times by police at roadblocks. They were curious about my documents, as I had entered Kazakhstan on an Australian passport but my visa for Kyrgyzstan was in my British one. Having two passports had made things slightly easier when applying for all the visas I would need for this trip while I was staying in Bangkok, but I had later realized that not all countries – such as China or Laos – would allow you to exit on one passport and enter on another. Luckily this hadn't been an issue when entering Kazakhstan but I wasn't 100 per cent sure if this would be the case when entering (or leaving) Kyrgyzstan. The number of police checks clearly indicated that the authorities were still very nervous about the situation in Bishkek but none of the police had discouraged me in any way. It wasn't until we stopped to change money, just before the border post, that one of the younger passengers suggested there might be a problem.

When we eventually pulled up at the border a customs official attempted to explain that only Kyrgyz nationals were being allowed in. The only other non-Kyrgyz passport holder on the bus – a middle-aged Kazakh woman in a headscarf – burst into tears. While my fellow passengers passed through customs, for the second time on this trip I was left standing at the border while my bus carried on without me. Even more frustratingly, Bishkek itself was only a twenty-minute (or so) drive from the border post. I attempted to explain my situation to all the bored young custom officials who were hanging around, just to make sure there was no way I could get in. They all seemed friendly and curious and had a chat among themselves while they passed around both my passports. The one with the best English was pushed forward to speak to me. 'No British, no Australian, no enter,' he patiently explained. 'There is a war on.' When I mumbled that I thought it might be a bit better by now, he shook his head slowly and looked at me with concern. I seemed to be getting that look quite a lot. Fortunately, there was a shared taxi waiting at the border to go back to Almaty. As it only needed one more passenger and the driver couldn't be bothered to try to rip me off, I thought I'd better jump in quick while some transport was still available. After another quick stop to change all my newly acquired Kyrgyz *som* back into Kazakh *tenge*, I was back on the road to Almaty. The journey time by shared taxi was an hour or so less than by bus, but I had still spent most of the day travelling just to end up back at the bus station I had started from.

While flicking through my Central Asia Lonely Planet in the back of the car I had decided on an alternative plan of getting a night bus down to Shymkent, south Kazakhstan's biggest city. From there, it wasn't too far to the Uzbek border and Uzbekistan's capital Tashkent. Unfortunately I didn't have much luck with buying a ticket. I was fairly sure that sleeper buses left from the station every night but when I eventually found someone who spoke some English she just kept telling me to go to the train station. I never really established whether the buses were full or not running for some reason or whether she just didn't want to sell me a ticket. Maybe she just thought that the trains would be better for a foreigner? After wandering around the bus station a few times I eventually found a bus stop where the buses seemed to be going towards the centre of Almaty. I figured that even if I got lost I could always get a taxi and have less chance of being ripped off than if I got one at the bus station.

When a bus turned up I went through my usual routine of pointing at the map. Nobody knew what I was going on about so I got on anyway. I sat next to a young friendly European-looking guy who seemed to agree that I was going somewhere towards the train station, and we starting having the usual conversation about where I came from and what football team I support. This took the usual route of him naming any famous British football players he could think of and me agreeing that, yes, they were famous football players. A darker-skinned guy called Bic, who was sitting behind us, introduced himself in excellent English. It turned out that he spoke several languages and was studying to be a translator. We ended up having a much more in-depth conversation. (I don't think my seat mate minded too much as he had used up all his English phrases and was struggling to come up with the names of any more British footballers.) We spoke about the surprising diversity of ethnicities in Almaty and Central Asia's position as a crossroads between cultures. When I commented, however, that I hadn't seen any black people in Almaty, he didn't seem to know what I meant. He had an excellent vocabulary and almost perfect grammar but didn't seem to know what 'black people' were. I struggled to explain without falling into the kind of racial stereotyping that most middle class English people would feel very uncomfortable with. When it eventually dawned on him what I meant he said 'Ah, you mean niggers!' I explained to him that we don't like to use the word 'niggers' in England, but he didn't seem to understand why. I think 'niggers' was just the word they were taught to describe people of African origin. Apparently, there were some black people in Almaty but you never saw them because they were always in cars.

By the time that I had made it to the train station it was already dark and had sold out of tickets for that night. I bought a second-class sleeper ticket for the following evening and attempted to find the budget hotel just outside the train station that Lonely Planet recommended. I couldn't find it anywhere so started trudging back to the Turkistan Hotel as it appeared to be the only decent budget accommodation in the whole of Almaty. On the way I stopped at a busy Internet café to get out of the drizzle – which was slowly solidifying into sleet – and to break up my tedious trudge across the city. Like most of the cheaper Internet cafés in developing countries it was full of teenagers pretending to blow up their enemies through the same games that teenagers play all over the world. I emailed everyone to let them know that I was still in Almaty because Kyrgyzstan wouldn't let me in (I later realized it was more the case that Kazakhstan wouldn't let me out). Back at the hotel I ended up in a room that was almost the same as I had checked out of in the morning but not quite. The very small differences – such as the brand of the television and some marks on the carpet – led to an unsettling feeling of dislocation.

After what seemed like a very long day of travelling I was (almost) exactly back where I had started. I lay down on my (almost) identical bed and turned on Kazakh MTV. Just as when I had left in the morning, it was still playing the video with the twelve-year-old 'hip-hop artists'. The boy rapper was still pretending to be black.

* * *

I woke to find white everywhere. Overnight the sleet had purified to snow. I really didn't fancy walking around in my lightweight summer clothes getting damp and frozen so I stayed in my room watching Kazakh MTV until it was time to check out. By now, I was quite up on the latest Kazakh hits. After leaving my backpack behind the reception desk I ventured out in search of entertainment. The Almaty City and History of

Repression Museum sounded about as good as it was going to get. Also, it was not too far from Coffeedelia, so that would give me an excuse to go somewhere warm and eat cake.

I eventually tracked down what I thought must be the right building but there were no signs on it. I walked up to the door and a security guard opened it up and invited me in. There was nothing on display around the foyer to indicate that this was any kind of museum. I walked in, anyway, and started wandering around. There were a few pictures on the walls but to be honest I wasn't that impressed. There were no plaques next to them to tell you the artist, title or date and they looked suspiciously like cheap prints from the Kazakh equivalent of Athena. None of this seemed very interesting so I went upstairs to see what was there. It looked like there was some kind of party going on in one of the rooms but a man at the door wouldn't let me in. He held up his finger to his lips in the international sign for silence while we both peered through a gap in the doorway to see what was going on. Somebody was giving some kind of speech in a room full of pictures of bicycles. After a round of applause I was let into the room to have a look around.

The pictures were rubbish – they looked like they'd been drawn by children. Several people were busy snapping away on digital SLRs. One of the photographers had long blonde hair and looked like he might be into heavy metal so I went over to talk to him. It turned out that I was right. Somehow, I had yet again managed to pick out probably the only person in the whole building who spoke good English *and* he was into Sepultura and Pantera. While football is the great shared interest and ice-breaker for most when travelling, for me it's always been rock music. The kind of people who love rock and metal tend to have a lot in common wherever you are in the world. It turned out that Vitaliy's young daughter had won first prize in a competition to draw bicycles that had been run to help promote green awareness and the use of bicycles in Almaty. As in China, a lack of environmental restrictions and the uncritical adulation of cars as a status symbol had led to a growing problem with pollution in the major cities. I couldn't really imagine a similar event being run in China – these values and concerns seemed very much like those of the white middle classes in the developed world. In fact, despite being in Central Asia, and not far at all from the Chinese border, everybody there looked European. Vitaliy's family had been in the freezing north of Kazakhstan for generations but he had moved down to Almaty for his job in IT systems administration. Like many other young professionals he longed to live in Europe or America.

We talked about the rock and metal scene in Kazakhstan and Central Asia, and I seemed to be right in thinking that this part of the world had produced little quality rock music despite having plenty of fans. When established groups *did* play in Almaty they could end up selling out the football stadium rather than the far smaller concert halls they were used to. There seems to be a strong link between the development of economies and the development of all forms of popular culture but particularly that of modern music. It also takes time. A sudden influx of wealth won't necessarily result in any kind of cultural progression and is just as likely to create the kinds of inequalities and insecurities that can result in a desire to inhabit an idealized past. It would be easy to argue that young people in poorer countries don't have the time or money to excel in indulgent pursuits such as performing rock music but I don't think that this is necessarily true. There are plenty of teenagers in developing countries who have the time and money for computer games, and there are also lots of second-rate rock groups. I suspect that the major differences are to be found in the underlying cultural differences that lay the foundations of all development: the same questioning, critical and irreverent mind-set is required for the creation of all real art, such as modern rock music, as is required for the creation of wealth itself.

I asked Vitaliy about Borat. All many people know about Kazakhstan is that it's where Borat comes from. President Nazerbaev had seemed quite upset about this association with the fictional buffoon but Vitaliy just thought it was funny. The internationally successful film *Borat: Cultural Learnings of America for Make Benefit Glorious Nation of Kazakhstan* had been banned in Kazakhstan. All of Vitaliy's friends had seen it on bootlegged DVD and thought it was really funny as well. The only people who seemed offended by it were politicians and foreigners, who thought it was terrible that Borat had made Kazakhstan look bad when they were trying so hard to act like civilized people. Apparently, Sacha Baron Cohen chose Kazakhstan as Borat's country of origin because neither he nor anybody else seemed to know anything about it. Borat could far more convincingly be Romanian, Moldovan or even Turkish. I actually met a tour guide in Cappadocia who was just like him but it was difficult to tell how much he genuinely resembled Borat and how much he had modelled his persona on this international comedy character. The tourists would start off by taking the piss but soon realized he was in on the joke. He was a popular guide – nobody seemed to mind the odd 'offensive' remark as long as he kept them amused.

Having exchanged email addresses with Vitaliy, I carried on towards Respublika Alanghy. In the centre of this ceremonial square is the Monument to Independence on whose stone column is a replica of the Golden Man standing on a winged snow leopard. The Golden Man is a warrior's costume from around the fifth century BC that was found in 1969 in a Saka (Scythia) tomb around 60 kilometres east of Almaty. The elaborate costume, made of more than 4,000 golden pieces, has become a national symbol of Kazakh manhood but it may be neither Kazakh nor even have been made for a man. There is no reason to assume that whoever wore the costume had any real genetic link to modern-day Kazakhs and items left in the grave seem to indicate that the warrior may have been female (around 20 per cent of Scythian graves with armaments were of women).

Overlooking the square is the City Government building – constructed in the neo-classical style that has so widely been adopted as a symbol of Western political power – and the large official Presidential Residence. Nursultan Nazarbaev rose up through the Communist Party to become the first secretary (party leader) in 1989 and to become Kazakhstan's first and only president when independence was forced upon it in 1991. His free market economic policies have made him popular with Western governments, who prefer to turn a blind eye when his political rivals end up in jail or conveniently disappear.

Another large replica of the Golden Man costume took pride of place in the entrance hall of the Central State Museum, just up from the square. Further in, there were statues of fierce nomadic warrior women with their hair divided up into four long braids (in the style of Mohammed), and another section with yurts that was devoted to nomads. While civilization (derived from the Latin '*civilis*', relating to 'city') was spread along the ancient Silk Road cities, other parts of Kazakhstan remained the domain of nomadic horseback traders until well into the twentieth century. For centuries, the nomadic tribes of Central Asia would only settle in order to more effectively exploit other conquered tribes. As these tribes settled down and grew richer and softer they, in turn, would be conquered by other harder and hungrier nomadic tribes. Genghis Khan reportedly warned his sons about getting too used to fine clothes, fast horses and beautiful women. He thought that, if they were to lose their vision, their purpose and hunger, they would end up as no better than slaves. Nomads had always been a threat to those in power who needed their subjects to be tied to the land so they could better exploit them. Their hunger to keep moving may have made their lives harder but they were never enslaved. Some philosophers such as Michel Foucault have argued that the nomads thought and argued in a way that was entirely alien to the Western mind-set but no less valid or meaningful. Others, such as Hegel, have considered nomadic culture simply to be a stepping stone on the way to cultural unity (he was equally dismissive of Confucianism's claim to be a valid alternative to 'Western' thinking and in any way a cohesive philosophy). According to Hegel, all cultures would go through similar stages of development as part of a social evolution towards 'civilization'. For human beings to transcend the whims of nature and to move towards its domination, they would first need to settle and form agricultural communities. Only then could they start to create real wealth and begin to dominate – rather than be dominated by – their environment. More recently, Francis Fukuyama has argued that the end result of this 'social evolution' process would be a globalized culture of 'liberal democracy'. I'm not so sure.

The whole museum seemed to have been set up to impress foreign visitors with the grandeur of Kazakhstan. In the spaces between towering neo-classical columns, elaborate chandeliers hung from great domes. At the bottom of a sweeping staircase was a grand public bathroom that remained surprisingly clean (thankfully, the kind of people who visit museums know better than to stand on the toilet seats). At the back of the foyer was the modern equivalent of a Doric column or a crystal chandelier: a huge plasma television. It showed a constant loop of delighted tourists frolicking in the sun, white water rafting through gorgeous scenery and partying all night long. It looked like a great holiday destination. It was Kazakhstan. I really wasn't sure where all these fun-loving tourists were or even where this version of Kazakhstan was. Despite this seemingly desperate need to show off to foreign visitors, they had neglected to give any explanations in English to the impressively laid out exhibits. The single sign for foreigners said: 'Please don't touch.'

Later that evening I boarded the night train to Shymkent. Everything was dark. As I stumbled through the carriages I held up my ticket to whoever was standing in the corridor. They would squint to make out the Cyrillic writing on the ticket before waving me onwards. I was to share a carriage with a family from somewhere in the north of Kazakhstan. They had already been on the train for nearly two days but seemed well prepared for the journey with their own sets of cutlery and a picnic hamper. They gestured for me to take some green tea and flatbread. The only one who could speak reasonable English was a young, attractive, dark-haired woman who was married to a not-so-attractive middle-aged man with a big belly. They didn't seem like an obvious couple. His gold-toothed, headscarf-wearing mother had their young son on her lap. Apparently, the young woman was a student and her husband, a policeman. I was curious about their back story but had neither the language skills nor the courage to pry any further.

The lights were briefly illuminated as we were slowly yanked out of Almaty but when they yet again dimmed we clambered into our bunks. The dark-haired young woman lay across the carriage from me on the opposite top bunk. We carefully undressed under the sheets as the sound of her blubbery husband and mother-in-law's snoring competed for dominance over the clanking of the train.

Shymkent and Turkistan

Luxury and Authenticity • The Failure of Soviet Consumerism
Reverence and Asceticism

Shymkent was warmer and cheaper than Almaty and seemed a little less European. It used to be a minor Silk Road stop until it was razed by the Mongol hordes but most of it had been rebuilt during Soviet times. Other than the more Islamic-influenced bazaar area it pretty much looks like any other large industrial Soviet city that you've never heard of. I caught a bus from the train station and jumped off at the Fantasy World amusement park when I realized I'd gone too far. I started walking in the direction that I'd come from in search of the Motel Baytarek-Sapar. It was upstairs in a shopping mall and the rooms appeared to have been converted from disused shop spaces. All the rooms had ridiculously high ceilings and large glass windows along one side that had to be obscured by expansive brown curtains. Each room had a skylight but no windows facing outwards. At least the shared bathrooms were OK and it was better value than anything on offer in Almaty.

I hadn't been wandering around Shymkent for long before I realized why I'd lost my place on the map and carried on past the motel on the bus. A whole block of the city was missing. It had been replaced by a giant multiplex cinema complete with bowling alley, food hall and a few shops selling luxury items like DVDs. It didn't seem very busy. Nobody was eating at the food hall as it was so expensive and nobody was going to buy expensive official DVDs when they could easily obtain bootlegged copies on the street for a fraction of the price. At first, the cinema's selection of mainly Hollywood blockbusters looked promising but I then found out they had all been dubbed into Russian. It looked like I'd be sticking to Kazakh MTV for the time being.

Across the street was a more typically Central Asian shopping mall made up of lots of small shops and stalls selling the kind of low quality tat that you could afford but were unlikely ever to desire. Judging by the number of sellers in relation to the number of potential buyers I'm not sure anybody could summon up much enthusiasm over the goods on offer. For a long time Central Asia had been something of a dumping ground for shoddy Russian goods that could not find buyers on the open market. It looked like they were still trying to shift all the tat they had been lumbered with.

I walked down towards the market but it seemed to be closed for the day and the Regional Museum seemed to have shut down all together. For lunch I went into Ladushki. It looked strangely like a primary school canteen. On the walls were brightly coloured paintings and wall hangings in primary colours. The ladies behind the counter looked remarkably like school dinner ladies. After pointing at some chicken, rice and what I assumed to be vegetables, I sat down at a square of Formica-topped tables surrounded by brightly coloured plastic chairs. I wouldn't have thought many tourists ate here, but nobody took much notice of me. They probably just thought I was Russian.

Shymkent had a couple of nice coffee shops and a few decent places to eat but there wasn't much there for a tourist. Later on I would venture into a local café and try *plov* for the first time. This is a mainstay throughout Central Asia that basically consists of a bowl of oily rice with some bits of meat on top. If you were lucky you might also find some grated carrot in it. It was cheap and filling but nothing to get excited about.

Everything seemed to shut early in Shymkent. It didn't seem like much of a party town. When I was finally chucked out of my shopping mall's Internet café at 9pm, there was nowhere to go but my room. I sat in a converted shop and turned on Kazakh MTV. I could almost sing along by now.

* * *

The buffet breakfast included with the room was surprisingly good. Most of the others in the restaurant seemed to be dressed in business suits. As there didn't seem to be any other guests in the motel part that I was staying in, I assumed they had come from the more expensive sister hotel that was also in the shopping mall. After getting some transport trips from the attractive receptionist, I picked up a local bus from outside which dropped me off at a busy market and bus station on the outskirts of Shymkent. From there I managed to buy a ticket to Turkistan – the city, not the historic region of Central Asia – on a bus that would be leaving in half an hour or so. Having failed to find anything of interest or quality in the quite extensive market, I popped into a café where the gold-toothed owner managed to track down a sachet of three-in-one instant coffee for me. When I asked if they had any chocolate she ran out the door. I was starting to worry I might have inadvertently offended her when, a few minutes later, she returned to the café and proudly laid out a selection of chocolate bars in front of me. I wasn't sure if they were all for me or whether I was just supposed to pick out one. Being quite greedy and not wanting to disappoint her after all the effort she had been to, I took the lot. They were rubbish. As in China, the local chocolate and confectionary was ridiculously cheap but incredibly poor quality. Thankfully, also as in China, international brands of chocolate bars such as Mars, Snickers and Bounty were widely available. They were more expensive than in England – which would have made them something of a luxury item for the average Central Asian worker – and the quality of the chocolate wasn't quite as good, but they were still very popular. It was becoming easy to see why Western-branded goods had become such a fetish in this part of the world when for years it only had access to poorly mass-produced Soviet tat.

After about three hours of driving through nothing of any interest at all, I arrived at the Turkistan bus station where I got on a minibus towards the centre. I pointed to a picture of the Yasaui Mausoleum in my Lonely Planet and they nodded. As a white person who couldn't even speak Russian it would have been surprising if I'd been going anywhere else. The mausoleum of the revered Turkic holy man, Kozha Akhmad Yasaui, is Kazakhstan's greatest architectural monument and an important site of pilgrimage. It is said that three visits to Turkistan are the equivalent of one visit to Mecca. The mystical poet and teacher Yasaui (born around 1103) seemed to have had a gift for communicating big ideas to ordinary people. He was enormously popular in his time. Yasaui's original small tomb was already a site of pilgrimage when Timur set about building a far bigger and grander mausoleum in the 1390s. Timur died before he could force his armies of craftsmen and labourers to complete his pet project and 600 years later they still hadn't got around to it. As the side of the Yasaui Mausoleum came into view, I could see they still had the scaffolding erected. This wasn't just there as part of a recent renovation – it had always been like that. They had never even got around to finishing the tiling on that side of the building. I'm not one for the adulation of tyrants but you can't help feeling that without the occasional megalomaniac like Timur, nothing would ever have been done in this part of the world. I'm pretty sure that they'd have finished off his tiling if he'd still been around to crack the whip.

I jumped out of the minibus and set off through some parkland towards the hulking blue-domed monolith before me. On passing the remains of a large defensive wall, the whole complex came into view. As well as the elaborately tiled grandeur of the Yasaui Mausoleum there was also the far more modest replica of the Mausoleum of Rabigha-Sultan Begum (built for Timur's great-granddaughter), a couple of small mosques, the rose garden and a museum that appeared to be closed. There was hardly anybody about but as someone was hanging around the ticket booth I thought I'd better cough up the entrance fee. 'No need,' he said. I'm not sure that he actually worked there but at least I could say that I tried. Before beginning a proper investigation of the complex, I had more pressing needs – I was hungry and there was a promising-looking café facing right on to the Mausoleum.

The great value three-course meal of the day turned out to be not just one of the best meals that I had along the Silk Road but probably one of the best I have ever had anywhere. Every time I began to lower my expectations about the quality of food in any of the countries along the Silk Road I would end up having an unexpectedly fantastic meal for a couple of dollars in some obscure little eatery. I'm not even sure what I ate – I had just pointed to what looked most edible.

Feeling suitably refreshed I resumed my duties as Turkistan's only foreign tourist of the day. I was a little wary of entering into the great mausoleum – not out of any sense of reverence but because there were dozens of pigeons perched on the wooden beams that jutted out from the monolithic walls into the majestic arch of the entrance, and there was bird shit splattered all over the huge cut stones below. A large, shaggy dog had rather unwisely decided to lay down in the shade of the archway. I rushed through to the interior so as to minimize the risk of being shat upon. As in many of these grand buildings, it was surprisingly cool inside. Under the dome in the main chamber lay a vast metal cauldron for holy water that had been given by Timur. Further back laid Yasaui's tomb through a route that resembled an obstacle course. I had assumed that the upper levels were out of bounds only to see a white robed figure up near the rafters. When I asked at the guarded narrow stairway if I could go up (it was actually more a case of pointing at myself and then upwards with a questioning expression), the person politely refused. With my nosiness unrequited I rushed back through the entrance way only to be startled by a yelp from behind. The dozing shaggy dog had been rudely awakened by a pigeon shitting on its head.

Over to the side of the complex was the semi-underground mosque where Yasaui is said to have died in around 1166. He had supposedly retired at the age of sixty-three for the rest of his life to an underground cell in mourning for the Prophet Mohammed who had died at the same age. I can't help feeling that this kind of asceticism is simply a waste – surely such a renowned Sufi teacher and mystical poet could have found a better way to spend his retirement. I'm not suggesting he should have taken up bowls or started an allotment but there must have been better and more useful things for him to do than sitting in a dark hole on his own.

While trying to catch a minibus back to the train station I ran into a couple of small, wiry guys who seemed as out of place in the almost entirely Kazakh city of Turkistan as I did. They both had huge noses and were quite exceptionally ugly. They could have passed for minor characters from the *Lord of the Rings* trilogy. It turned out that they were both from Kurdistan and had somehow wangled a scholarship to study in Turkistan. They seemed a little surprised that I knew that Kurdistan was the one part of Iraq that was open to tourists and that I wanted to visit. They didn't seem to rate it as a holiday destination. They were hurrying to get to the bank before it closed, so they had to rush off; even so, they still found time to get me on a minivan that was running towards the bus station.

It wasn't so easy to remember where to get off. A friendly seventeen-year-old boy who spoke a little English thought he'd better look after me. We got off the bus together, then he led me through a series of back alleys. I was starting to feel a little uncomfortable as I had no idea where I was going and at the very least thought that he might demand some money as a 'guide'. When we eventually found the bus and I offered to buy him a cold drink he rushed off, only pausing to wish me good luck on my travels.

Three hours later, back in Shymkent it seemed almost like another country. It might be pushing it to say that I had travelled back from the past to the present but at the very least it felt as though I had travelled back from the Middle East to Europe. I suspect it will be some time until Turkistan gets a big multiplex cinema like the one in Shymkent. After another decent meal at the Kafe Address I yet again retired to the high ceilinged former shop that was mine for the night. This time I found another music channel to watch. I now had two MTV-style channels to flick between as I sat there on my own with my remaining chocolate. Things were looking up.

Uzbekistan

Tashkent

Life as a Millionaire • Competition and the Black Market • Lost at the Crossroads • A Police State of Boredom • Grandeur from Slavery Lenin Usurped by Globalization • Religious Opposition • Blind Eyes and Massacres • Lost in Culture • U-Girls and Old Bags Soviet Kitsch • Pilgrimage and Animism • Authenticity and the Heritage Industry • Sympathy for the Cute

Unfortunately the bus information I received from the girl at reception wasn't quite as helpful as previously. When I attempted to leave for Uzbekistan I ended up at the wrong bus station and had to take another two *marshrutkas* (minivans) from there to get to the crossroads near the border. A woman with big bleached hair and a bulky fur coat explained to me what was going on and prevented me from accidently paying out ten times the standard fare. She set me up with a seat in a decrepit shared taxi to the actual border and made sure the driver wasn't going to rip me off before she rushed back into the *marshrutka* to continue with her journey. The dusty crossroads was like something out of a grim Western. Despite being miles from any sign of real civilization there were still a couple of old women in headscarves with some dusty-looking junk food spread out over a couple of crude tables. I bought a Snickers bar and asked if they had any toilets (luckily the word in Russian for toilet is similar to the English, so if you pronounce it in enough different ways while attempting to mime your intentions people usually know what you mean). Eventually, after a lot of arm waving and shouted directions from everyone around, I located the makeshift wooden shack. I probably *could* have found it without all the directions – I just needed to follow my nose. When I opened the door I was hit by the stench and then bombarded by flies. Like many of the toilets in Central Asia it was just a pit with a couple of planks over it. If it was this smelly and fly ridden at this time of the year then it must have been unbearable during the scorching summer months.

We made it to the border without the shared taxi disintegrating on the way and I switched back from my Australian to my UK passport without any problems. On my third or fourth passport check on the Uzbekistan side, one of the guards demanded another US$10. When I pretended to be shocked he just laughed, handed back my passport and saluted me.

Before leaving Shymkent I had taken out as much cash as I could from the ATM at the shopping mall as I knew that there was a huge difference between the official rate of exchange that I would get from an ATM in Tashkent and the real black market rate that I could get with cash. Although it was easy enough to look up the current official rate of exchange for the Uzbek *sum,* the only people I could ask about the real rate of exchange were all the people at the border who were trying to get me to exchange money with them. A guy who looked like a tramp shouted out 'change money' and waved a huge brick of crisp new notes at me. It looked like a lot of money for someone who was dressed in little more than rags. Everyone seemed to agree that the rate to the Kazakh *tenge* was 10,000. This sounded about right but I was reluctant to change my money here without really knowing. After the usual ridiculous demands for inflated fares I eventually found a taxi driver who was willing to take me to the beginnings of the Tashkent Metro for what remained of my smaller Kazakh notes. Apparently there was an unofficial money exchange at the metro station where I could get a decent rate for my wad of larger Kazakh bills. After just a few minutes in the car with this driver – he seemed not to belong with the others – he pulled off the main road that led towards Tashkent and started to drive through increasingly narrow back streets that were quite clearly not where I wanted to go. I was starting to feel increasingly uncomfortable with this when he pulled into a drive way that was no longer visible from the road and a heavily muscled man let himself into the back of the taxi. He explained that he was the driver's brother and he had taken me to see him, as his brother knew a little English. He wanted to know how much money I had. I showed him only the smaller bills and explained that I would need to get more money in Tashkent and that his brother had agreed to take me to the metro for what I had left. The big man looked doubtful. Having no idea where I now was, I was hardly in a strong position if they chose to renegotiate. 'OK,' he said, 'my brother is going to sell you. Give him the money.' I handed it over and we were off again.

A few minutes later we arrived at a roundabout and I was told to wait in the car. After a bit of negotiation and a lot of arm waving they came back to the car and both firmly shook my hand before assuring me that my new driver would take me to the metro. They had already paid him so I wasn't to give him any more. I hauled my backpack into yet another shared taxi. My fellow passengers all seemed nice enough but we couldn't have talked much even if they had spoken English as the young, curly haired driver subjected us to some very loud dance music. He drove too fast and recklessly, and the noise was deafening. When I attempted to fasten the seatbelt he pulled it away from me and shook his head. I didn't mind. At least I was safe (in a way) and back on the road.

When we arrived at the metro station on the edge of Tashkent, the driver pointed me in the direction of where I could change money and shook my hand. It took me a while to track down the precise place he meant; it turned out to be a small booth that had been set up to sell mobile phone cards. These small shops were everywhere in Tashkent. As I hadn't seen any ATMs around the metro and I had no Uzbek *sum* at all, I accepted his rate of 10,000. I should have been suspicious that the rate came to an even 10,000 but I was tired and this was the rate that everybody at the border had quoted. I later found out that I should have got around 12,000 but if I had asked for more and he had turned me down then I wouldn't even have had the money for the metro. It was also still significantly more than the official rate that I would have got from a bank or an ATM. What also threw me a bit was the sheer amount of money he was handing over to me. For my small wedge of Kazakh notes I received three great bricks of Uzbekistan's highest currency note (worth about 50 US cents). I felt like a millionaire and in Uzbekistan I technically was. I crammed a bundle into each of the large pockets on my combat trousers and shoved another down towards the bottom of my backpack. When I stood up to leave, the weight of the notes pulled my trousers down so far that I had to tighten my belt.

For one 1,000 *sum* note I received a plastic token that entitled me to ride anywhere on the Tashkent Metro and a tatty 500 *sum* note in change. As well as being ridiculously cheap compared to the London Underground, the Tashkent Metro was also far nicer. Tourists used to avoid using the metro as the police had such a bad reputation for shaking down foreigners to extract bribes, but following something of a crackdown it now seems fine. In contrast to some London tube stations that are drab and grimy, each of Tashkent's twenty-nine stations is an original work of art with a specific theme. The leading artists and architects of Uzbekistan were commissioned to create a spectacular range of stations that range from the majestic to the futuristic. Some stations feature huge arches and chandeliers while others showcase statues, engravings and mosaics. Unfortunately, as it was also designed to double as a nuclear fallout shelter for the residents of Tashkent, and the authorities still veer towards the paranoid, it is illegal to take any pictures.

I got off at the Kosmonavtlar station, which had been done out like a Soviet space ship, and set out towards Ali's B&B.

I couldn't find it. I knew I must be in the right area but there were no signs up anywhere to indicate a guest house. Despite being a little wary of the numerous policemen (*militsia*) and their unenviable reputation, I approached one who seemed happy to point me the right way. I stood outside what appeared to be a building site before being ushered in. Apparently this was Ali's. It was like something out of an Escher painting: windows hung out over nothingness and staircases led to the open sky. I was invited to sit down at a table and after a while one of the builders brought me a pot of tea. I brought out my remaining biscuits from Kazakhstan and we sat there companionably, not saying a word. Ali was coming.

Two hours later I was still sat at the table feeling restless and hungry. I was about to wander off again in search of sustenance when Ali eventually turned up with a group of other middle-aged men. He briefly introduced himself before wandering off again. When he eventually reappeared, I finally got the chance to ask him if they had any rooms. 'No,' he said sadly. They took away my licence. I can no longer take in foreigners.' I didn't want to complain too much as he looked perilously close to bursting into tears but I couldn't help feeling annoyed that nobody had told me this a couple of hours ago. I tried asking him why he could no longer take in tourists but didn't want to push the matter as he was clearly still upset about it.

By now it was already quite dark so Ali suggested that a friend of his would drive me to the Gulnara Guest House, close to Chorsu Bazaar, for 4,000 *sum*. I took up his offer and was soon crammed into a small, flimsy Soviet-style car (my eighth vehicle of the day). Ali had confidently assured me that he knew exactly where the guest house was, but not too surprisingly couldn't find it. After driving around for ages and several stops to interrogate the locals, he eventually pulled up outside an unmarked wooden garage door and knocked loudly. This was it. When I handed over the money to the driver he handed it back to me. Even though he had wasted my time by telling me that he knew where it was when he clearly didn't, I still felt that I ought to pay him. Apparently I had got the wrong end of the stick. He wanted more. As I couldn't be bothered to argue and it wasn't that much, I just gave it to him. At least he'd got me there (eventually).

Gulnara Guest House was a family business, managed by the older son. His mother did the cooking and his younger brothers generally helped out, but I'm not sure what the father did. I was shown to a small room next to the kitchen that faced out onto the shared courtyard and offered a traditional Uzbek meal for a few dollars. As my buffet breakfast at the motel in Shymkent now seemed like a very long time ago, I was more than happy to take them up on their offer. Despite being overburdened with huge wads of Uzbek *sum,* I still agreed to pay for everything in US dollars so as to get a better deal. The manager let me know what the real black market rate was – it seemed to fluctuate quite rapidly – and told me that when he had bought his car in Uzbek *sum* he had had to arrange for two car loads full of cash to be delivered. Nobody seemed to understand the government's reluctance to print notes of a higher denomination and nobody was convinced of the long-term merits of officially over-valuing their currency to such an absurd degree. I was also filled in on the back story to Ali's B&B …

Apparently Ali was a little too fond of the drink and one night he had come into the room of two backpacker girls and made some less-than-appropriate suggestions. The girls had made an official complaint to the authorities and, as it wasn't the first incident of this kind, he had been stripped of his licence to host foreigners. Because there wasn't much other competition in terms of budget accommodation, this had probably worked out very well for Gulnara.

Although there were very few travellers in Central Asia at this – or probably any – time of year, quite a few would seem to end up staying in Tashkent for longer than they had intended in order to sort out all their visas. As Ali's B&B was now closed to foreigners, Gulnara had become the default location for any backpackers. On that first night, however, the only other travellers I met were a Swiss couple who were waiting for their Turkmenistan transit visa. Every morning they would turn up early at the consulate only to be told to try again the next day. Apparently the consulate had moved since the (current) Lonely Planet had been published. This was useful to know, as I would also be heading there myself the next day to try to sort out a visa.

Turkmenistan didn't seem to go out of its way to encourage tourism. Thankfully it had recently increased the three-day transit visa to five days because too many independent travellers were failing to make it across the country in this little time, but staying for longer required travellers to be part of an expensive organized tour. The Swiss couple had driven all the way across Europe and on through Kazakhstan – about the size of Western Europe on its own – to get as far as Tashkent. They planned to circle around back to Europe through Iran and Turkey, but if their Turkmenistan transit visa didn't come through they would be forced to drive back the way they had come.

After eating my fill of Uzbek 'lasagne' and three-layer coffee cake I returned to my narrow room and set my alarm – there were always big queues at the consulate and you had to be there early if you were going to get in.

* * *

I woke with a vicious headache and nausea. After weeks of being too cold and too tired and not eating regularly enough, I finally felt like I was getting ill. The mother of the family found what looked like an old box of painkillers on a kitchen shelf and handed them to me. The writing on the box was in Cyrillic. I took two of them and she said that I'd feel better later on. I doubted it, but if I was to waste any of my days being ill then I would never make it to Istanbul on time.

After breakfast I walked down through the green domes and market traders of Chorsu Bazaar and into the metro. I ascended to sunlight at the Oybek crossroads only to find myself lost – yet again. I knew where I was but not where to go. I guessed the way and got it wrong. Returning to the crossroads I tried again. This time I got it right. A large white wedding cake of a building appeared before me. I trudged up to the grand entrance way only to be pointed further along. Up around the back and around the corner was the real entrance. Bored-looking clusters of would-be visitors stood around in the mud waiting for a sign. I had got there before it opened at 9am but according to the list on the guard house some people had been queuing since 6am (I found out later that a lot of people simply bribed the guards the night before to appear at the top of the next morning's list). I added my name to the bottom then walked over to a small group huddled around a map that was painted onto the bonnet of a sturdy-looking four-wheel drive. They were three Russians and, like the Swiss couple, they had driven right across Kazakhstan and planned to circle around the Caspian Sea. They had come back to the consulate every morning for more than ten days. If they didn't get their visa today they would run out of time and be forced to cut their journey short. Every destination on their route had been carefully painted onto the front of their sponsored expedition vehicle. Until this point they had followed the line of their planned trip without a hitch but now they were stuck and nobody would tell them a thing.

Half an hour later they were called in. A few minutes after that they were back in the muddy, uncovered waiting zone. The consulate was still waiting to hear back from Ashgabat. As the next day was the start of the weekend there was no more time.

They got back into their vehicle, with the now-redundant route map emblazoned across the front, and drove back to where they'd come from.

The consulate closed at 11am but at 10:50am I was still loitering outside along with some others who had turned up before 7am to make sure they were near the top of today's waiting list. They were only just ahead of me and I'd been hanging around for two hours less than them. Fortunately I was now far enough south in Central Asia and far enough into spring to have escaped the brutal chill that still held much of Kazakhstan and China in its grip. To be stuck out here for hours with no shelter in the middle of winter would have been almost unbearably grim. With just a few minutes to go before the consulate shut for the day, the last few stragglers were herded in and told to hurry up with the forms. On entering the grand building with the imposing doorway I found myself in a small, cramped visitor's area facing a bored-looking clerk behind a dusty wall of glass. I couldn't read the form I had been given as it was in Cyrillic, and I couldn't attach my photo to it as the Pritt Stick glue on the table had run out. The clerk behind the counter irritably dug out a form in English and a new glue stick, and told me to hurry. He couldn't speak much English, so one of the Uzbek applicants explained that I needed a five-day transit visa to get across to Iran and that I would have to pay extra for 'express service'. Nobody seemed entirely sure how much this was going to be but I would have to pay it in US dollars and it wouldn't be cheap. As the guards rushed to bundle their remaining 'guests' out of the door, I had my passport returned and was told to come back in a week.

I really didn't have the time or the inclination to hang around in Tashkent, so it looked as if I would have to carry on with my travels then double back to Tashkent to (hopefully) pick up my Turkmenistan transit visa. If I was turned down for no apparent reason – which, apparently, happened quite a lot

– then my plans to travel the whole of the ancient Silk Road would be in ruins. I walked back past the lines of *militsia* towards the crossroads around Oybek Metro and towards a fast food and coffee shop that I had seen on the opposite corner. Everywhere I went in Tashkent seemed to be dotted with young, bored-looking uniformed men with guns. I was far more wary of them than I was of any criminals. Luckily, as Tashkent was Uzbekistan's most cosmopolitan city, I could still pass by quite easily without seeming too obviously like a foreign tourist (at least until I started babbling away in English). A fear of terrorism from militant Islamic groups had led to regular bag and ID checks on the metro but as a pasty-looking white guy I was unlikely to be profiled as a high security risk. Even if I had been planning mischief, then I suspect that most of the *militsia* would have been too comatose with boredom even to have noticed. Sometimes the equally bored street kids around the bazaar would taunt them just for something to do. I suspect that the *militsia* didn't really mind too much as the most excitement they were likely to get all day would be chasing these cheeky teenagers through the stalls and trying to bash them with their truncheons. You couldn't help thinking that all these bored young *militsia* could have been doing something more useful like mending the potholed roads or improving their education but then I don't suppose that it would be a police state.

The fast food and coffee shop I entered could easily have been in Almaty. It was clearly a hangout for the more affluent youngsters. A plasma screen was showing MTV and the toilets were immaculate. Hot dogs, fries and cappuccinos were proudly displayed within the plastic-coated menu. As in Kazakhstan, the youngsters would go for US style and convenience every time over *plov*, kebabs and pit toilets.

I sat there with a latte and my Lonely Planet guidebook, unsure of what to do next. I had originally planned to go from Tashkent to Samarkand and then on to Bukhara before heading over the nearby border to visit the ancient ruins of Merv in Turkmenistan. I had wanted to do the whole Silk Road route by land but now that I was going to have to double back on myself I was seriously considering the option of getting a cheap Uzbekistan Airways flight to Khiva and then travelling back overland to Tashkent via Bukhara and Samarkand. I would still be travelling the whole of the Silk Road by land but with a bit of a detour. While considering my options I decided to walk on to the Fine Arts Museum. When I tried to go in a guard made a cross with his arms across his chest to indicate no entry. I would come across this gesture a lot in Central Asia. As they seemed to be closed for cleaning for the whole day, I carried on to the Alisher Navoi Opera and Ballet Theatre. While much of Tashkent consists of Soviet-style blocks spread out over wide 'centrally planned' boulevards, some of the relatively recent 'showcase' buildings were clearly designed to mimic European grandeur. The Opera House looks like a vanity project from the European Middle Ages but was actually built by Japanese prisoners of war in 1947. I wouldn't normally choose to visit the opera but as the state-subsidized tickets were only around US$2 each I thought I'd give it a go.

Having purchased my tickets for the early evening performance of *The Fisher King*, I carried on towards the far more contemporary but equally flashy Senate building. President Islam Karimov's offices were apparently somewhere in the south of the building, set back from Mustaqillik Maydoni (Independence Square), the site of epic, Soviet-style national parades (there used to be a big statue of Lenin in the middle of the square but this was replaced in 1992 by a giant globe). Karimov had been the head of the Communist Party and became President of Uzbekistan upon independence in 1991. Ever since then Karimov has won every 'democratic' election with a considerable majority. As you might have guessed, any real form of opposition is rather frowned upon.

Both Birlik (Unity) and the Islamic Renaissance Party (IRP), along with any other parties with a religious platform, have been banned from taking part. Any use of religion to win political support is dealt with in a particularly brutal manner. Although around 85 per cent of Uzbekistan's population consider themselves to be Muslims, the vast majority are quite moderate. However, a series of bombings in Tashkent in 1999 that were blamed on the fundamentalist 'Wahabis', and the fear of a rise in the kind of politicized Islam found further south in Iran, had led to an unprecedented rise in police harassment, imprisonment and torture.

As Uzbekistan had allowed the USA and NATO to set up bases in the south of the country for use in the war against Afghanistan, and seemed so enthusiastic about halting the spread of politicized Islam, the US government had chosen to turn a blind eye to such blatant human rights abuses and continued to prop up the Karimov government with huge amounts of US taxpayers' aid money. This all came to something of a head with the Andijon Massacre. When local businessmen from the eastern city of Andijon were arrested and charged with being members of a local Islamic movement, their allies stormed the prison, leading to a massive but largely peaceful demonstration in Andijon's main square. The National Security Service troops then started to fire indiscriminately into the crowd. Estimates of how many were killed seem to vary enormously; the government put the official figure at 187 while others reckoned it was more than 5,000. A defector from Uzbekistan's secret service alleged that around 1,500 had been killed. After this massacre of unarmed protesters it became increasingly difficult for the Western powers to continue in their support of the Karimov regime. As the West was forced into distancing itself from the totalitarian state, Uzbekistan instead turned towards Russia and China, who supported the regime's response in Andijon.

I carried on past the strangely cold and remote Senate building to the mawkish Crying Mother Monument. Karimov seems to have built similar monuments to this, along with the obligatory eternal flame, in most of the major Uzbek cities. They commemorate the 400,000 Uzbek soldiers who died during the Second World War. While killing time before my night at the opera I also visited the vaguely impressive but unremarkable history museum and art gallery. I couldn't help feeling that their main reason for existing was simply that they were something any major capital city needed to possess in order to be taken seriously. The nearby Mir shopping centre and food court was equally anonymous – despite being in the middle of Asia, you could have been almost anywhere in post-Soviet Eastern Europe.

I decided that rather than having to keep doubling back to Tashkent on long overland journeys just to pick up my Turkmenistan visa, I would head off to the Uzbekistan Airways office and try to get a cheap ticket to Khiva. Apparently, it was a huge great building that I couldn't possibly miss. I did. I traipsed backwards and forwards for ages and everybody seemed to think that it was somewhere slightly different. As I was running out of time, I eventually had to give up and rush back over town for a bit of 'culture'.

With my combat trousers and denim jacket I thought I might seem a little underdressed for the opera but it didn't seem to matter. As in many large Soviet cities, because it was cheaper to visit the opera or the ballet than go to the cinema it seemed like far less of an event than it would in England. Having said that, they had still gone out of their way to try to make the opera house itself as lavish, ornate and imposing as possible. I knew nothing about *The Fisher King* other than the name itself, so I bought a programme with an English explanation – but it didn't help much. For the first few minutes of the performance I was vaguely amused by the elaborate sets and costumes, although the music did nothing for me and the dancing was surprisingly ropey. While I know as little about dance as I do about opera, they performers were clearly out of step and line with each other. The whole thing seemed more like an extravagant school play with a couple of hired-in opera singers than anything you would expect to see on a West End stage. Fortunately, the whole performance lasted less than an hour.

Although it was still early evening and had only just begun to get dark, the ornately tiled and chandeliered metro station seemed surprisingly quiet and forlorn. Flat-screen televisions suspended from elaborately carved columns looped continuous advertisements that attempted to reproduce a Shania Twain video in which she herself is parodying a Robert Palmer video. While glamorous young Eurasian models touted the latest in the 'U-Girl' clothing range – lower quality copies of the same kind of thing that you would see anywhere in America or Europe – two large old Uzbek cleaning ladies in overalls and headscarves laboriously pushed huge grey brooms up and down the station like worn-out beasts of burden slowly tilling wasted land. These poor old Uzbek women would never make it as 'U-Girls'.

The only passengers were me and an old man with two fir trees. He hauled them into the carriage and then propped them up on the escalators as we rose up into the now nearly abandoned Chorsu Bazaar. I hurried through the dark and nearly empty market alleys and the piles of decomposing fruit and vegetables to make it back onto the illuminated main street where some uniformed men were blowing four- or five-feet-long bugles outside the entrance to a hotel. It might have been a celebration or it might have not.

* * *

After a surprisingly decent breakfast at the Gulnara Guest House, I found that the main shared bathroom was occupied, so I used the smaller one, which housed the boiler, just next to it. (I had tended to avoid this room because the boiler made it too hot and the shower wasn't as effective.) I had already showered and washed my hair before breakfast to give it a chance to dry before setting off for the day but after using the toilet I still wanted to wash my bottom to soothe my throbbing haemorrhoids (my headache and nausea from the morning before had miraculously disappeared by the middle of the morning but my bottom was holding up less well to the strains of constant travel). I didn't want to get completely wet again under this bathroom's huge non-detachable showerhead but this bathroom did have a bidet.

I've never entirely got the hang of using bidets but being an adventurous type I thought I'd give it a go. This was a big mistake. I cautiously turned on the tap, and a stream of water instantly squirted out over the front of my trousers. It looked like I'd wet myself. Refusing to give up on my mission, I twisted the taps until a steady stream of moderately warm water was flowing upwards and outwards into the bowl of the troublesome bidet. Just as I eased my arse into the flow of tepid water, the temperature shot up to near boiling. I struggled not to yelp out in pain as my piles received third degree burns and I grabbed out for the taps in a panic. I turned the wrong way and a steaming jet of water squirted out over me and the floor of the bathroom. Both the front and the back of my trousers now featured large embarrassing wet patches. To make matters worse, my bottom hurt. Having dried myself off as best I could, I emerged from the bathroom only to be greeted by the Swiss couple. I held my towel over my wet crotch while they told me about how they still hadn't been granted their Turkmenistan visa and would now have to wait until after the weekend. As I couldn't really walk back to my room normally without them noticing the large wet patch spread across the back of my trousers,

I attempted to gradually edge my way towards my room, crab-style, while still chatting to them. I think I got away with it.

As the guest house was fully booked for this evening and I hadn't been able to get a flight to Khiva, I decided to get the metro over to the main train station and try to get a ticket for tonight's sleeper to Bukhara. After a couple of days there I could then work my way back to Tashkent via Samarkand. Having been directed around the station a few times I joined what seemed to be the right queue, only to get stuck behind some middle-aged women with carrier bags full of cash. It looked like they'd just robbed a bank but they were probably only buying tickets for their immediate family. After checking the availability, they handed over brick after brick of crisp new 1,000 *sum* notes. Luckily the cashier had a counting machine that she just fed the wads of cash through. If she'd had to count them herself we'd have been there all day. It looked like I was going to be there all day anyway as everybody just kept pushing in front of me but a man at the front had noticed what was happening and brought me to the cashier's attention. Having handed over my own epic pile of cash, I was now booked into a second-class sleeper for tonight and was free to roam the streets of Tashkent.

I got off the metro near Navoi Park and walked over to the monument to Alisher Navoi (considered by many to be the founder of Turkic literature). The park is known for having some of the ugliest and most garish Soviet-era buildings of all time. They all looked like they belonged on a very cheaply made film set. There were even Venetian-style bridges that rose up on one side of a road only to come back down again on the same side. Functionality and style came a very distant second to pointless decoration. For the first and only time on this trip I was approached by a beggar who was obviously targeting foreign tourists. He spoke surprisingly good English and was probably one of the ugliest children I have ever seen. I wasn't even sure if he *was* a child, as despite only being the size of a ten-year-old he was bald and his unusually dark skin was exceptionally leathery.

I suspected that he had been selected by someone in control of the park to work as a professional beggar. Unfortunately, he was so hideous and yet so strangely confident that most people would just have wanted to get away from him. He may have been clever and wise beyond his years but he simply wasn't 'cute' enough to pull in the big bucks; his only hope of success would be to guilt trip the visitors into paying him to go away.

After walking on past the usual man-made boating lake and amusements, I carried on towards Khast Imom, the official religious centre of Uzbekistan. The Moyie Mubarek Library Museum holds what is supposed to be Tashkent's most important site: the seventh-century Osman Koran that was first brought to Tashkent by Timur and is thought to be the oldest in the world. I find it difficult to get excited about the idea of looking at an old book. It's not like they're even going to let me pick it up and flick through it. Such 'tourist attractions' seem to appeal to the kind of primitive animistic beliefs that lie buried all around us but are rarely acknowledged. So many still seem willing to surrender their rationality when presented with a suitably revered fetish that has been deemed to be of value by those in authority. It's not just objects – whether a splinter of the cross or the crown jewels – that become infused with a value that is no way intrinsic to themselves, but also places. Many tourists or pilgrims will go to great lengths and expense to visit a place where something significant may or may not have happened when there is nothing much to see apart from the gift shop. Even when there is something to be touched, or held or captured through photography, it is often only a copy of what was once there. Little remains of most 'ancient' oriental temples as they were mainly constructed from wood that has to be replaced every few decades. Even monolithic stone structures such as Stonehenge have been 'restored' to a degree that few in the heritage industry seem comfortable with admitting to. None of this really matters, as I couldn't find it anyway. I walked all around the Khast Imom area trying to find my way into something interesting but eventually grew tired of walking around in circles. I surrendered to confusion and left for the circus.

Although I missed the puppet theatre in Tashkent it seemed to have everything else that you would expect to find in a major Soviet city: the flashy opera house; the parks with man-made boating lakes; the grand bazaar full of old tat; the rickety amusement parks; the closed up water-park; and the circus. The circus in Tashkent was staging some kind of dolphin spectacular. If someone tried to run a show like that in England they would probably be inundated with placard-wearing protesters objecting to the 'exploitation' of animals that are deemed to be 'cute' (as with human beings, people tend to care less about the ugly ones). In a country where forced child labour is still widespread, however, few people are likely to make that much of a fuss about the mistreatment of any animals (even really 'cute' and 'clever' ones).

After walking back towards the guest house, via the Kulkedash Medressa (an Islamic school), the Juma (Friday) Mosque, and the Chorsu Bazaar, I picked up my backpack and set off for the main train station. When I eventually located my shared sleeping carriage, I was welcomed in by an Uzbek family with a picnic, and a younger guy from Andijon who worked in IT. They offered me some tea, which I was pleased to accept, and the contents of a bag of horse meat, which I wasn't so sure about. The young IT guy thought I must be a vegetarian and, as the meat looked like it had been hanging around for a while, I decided not to disagree with him.

The train seemed surprisingly comfortable and my fare for a bed for a night on it – despite the huge wedge of notes I had handed over to the cashier – was actually less than I had been paying for a night at the guest house. We settled down into the rhythm of the train and rolled on through the night towards the ancient Silk Road city of Bukhara.

Bukhara

Cultural Tourism for the Old at Heart • Layers of Belief
Health and Safety • Being Exotic • Crime and Punishment
Masters of Puppets • The World through a Lens

Bukhara was conquered by Genghis Khan in 1220 and then again in 1370 by Timur. As the Silk Road went into decline over the following centuries, Bukhara was ruled by a series of increasingly disreputable Emirs before eventually being absorbed by the USSR in 1924.

I arrived at Kagan in the early morning, was shown on to a *marshrutka* by the Andijon IT guy, then set off for the Lyabi-Hauz (Tajik for 'around the pool') in the centre of Bukhara. Most of the guest houses in Bukhara seemed to inhabit the narrow alleyways branching off from the restaurants surrounding this scenic central pool. While trying and failing to find a bed and breakfast that had been recommended to me, I was approached by the owners of another guest house and decided to stay there instead as it seemed like such good value. I showered, had a cooked breakfast in the pleasant courtyard and was ready to hit the tourist trail.

For the first time in quite a while, I would be far from the only tourist wandering around. There were literally coachloads of them but they were mainly over fifty and from either Germany or France. I had seen these expensive 'cultural' Silk Road tours advertised in magazines but had never met anybody who had been on one. For some reason this part of the world is only known as a tourist destination to the French and Germans. Nobody I knew in England even seemed very sure about where Uzbekistan actually was. This seems rather odd as Bukhara, Samarkand and Khiva are all great places to visit. If the Uzbekistan government were to stop making it such a hassle to get a visa and were to hire a decent PR firm to promote its many attractions, then tourism could really take off. Perhaps fortunately, for the moment, I would often find myself the only tourist at one of Bukhara's many mosques, *medressas* or monuments. This could all change in a moment, however, as a coachfull of camera-wielding geriatrics pulled up outside only to be herded through by a flag-waving guide. Within minutes the whole place would be flooded by wobbly bellied pensioners only to fall into an eerie silence a few minutes later as their guide rushed them on to their next photographic opportunity. It looked like fun.

I liked the Kalon Minaret. It was probably the tallest building in Central Asia when it was built in 1127. Genghis Khan liked it as well. In fact he was so impressed that he decided not to knock it down. He must have been having a good day. Another favourite was Central Asia's oldest surviving mosque, the Maghoki-Attar (the pit of the herbalists). It's now a carpet museum. If you pay to go in they'll show you a partially excavated section in the corner where you can see through the various historical layers to its previous incarnations as both a Buddhist and a Zoroastrian temple (up until the sixteenth century, Bukhara's sizeable population of Jews was also allowed to use the mosque in the evenings as a synagogue).

I thought about visiting the Borzi Kord public bath house for a good steaming and a massage but was scared off by a very large and hairy man who was flashing around his dangly bits in the reception area. Instead I opted for a nice cup of tea at Silk Road Spices. The business was clearly aimed at the coachloads of 'cultural' tourists and was quite expensive for Uzbekistan – but worth it. For a set price I could sample as many types of exotic teas and coffees as I liked within the beautifully restored teahouse. I also managed to eat most of the four plates of local sweets that were included in the price.

Bukhara's oldest building, the Ark, is a huge fortified city within the city that dates back to the fifth century. From

Bukhara's main square, the Registan, the huge fortress-like structure, still looks to be in pretty good condition but you don't have to walk very far down to the side to see how badly it was damaged by the Red Army's bombings in the 1920s. There's a number of small museums in the sections that remain standing in the royal quarters but there wasn't much worth seeing once you had paid to go inside.

On my way back down the stone steps, a local with a stall full of tourist tat beckoned me over. He said he could get me into the part of the Ark that tourists weren't allowed in if I gave him some money to pay off a policeman. This sounded a bit dodgy but apparently there were great views and it was really worth it. After a bit of hesitation I agreed and he left me with his stall while he wandered off to find his accomplice. I followed the policeman over to a large gateway where he unpadlocked a heavy chain and hurriedly ushered me through. The gates slammed behind me and I was left standing on my own in the ruins of the Ark. As I stumbled my way through sliding dirt, debris and rocks, I couldn't help feeling that the stallholder and policeman were being rather irresponsible – this clearly wasn't a safe place to let tourists wander around on their own. If they'd let in the old bids from the coaches it would have been a blood bath. I'm not sure if there is such a thing as 'health and safety' in Uzbekistan, but if there were those in charge would be going mental (that might have been why there was a great big gate in the way with a heavy chain around it). Nearly falling into another hole, I skidded down to the edge of the Ark's monolithic walls. The stallholder had been right – the view was worth it. I could see right down over the top of all the old *medressas,* mosques and minarets of the beautiful Silk Road city.

After managing to clamber back without any injuries I walked over to chat to the stallholder. He clearly wasn't used to seeing independent travellers and was surprised to find I was on my own. I normally shy away from tourist stalls but as he was so genuine and friendly, and his stories were so entertaining, I bought a couple of Zoroastrian-style necklaces from him (up until the Arab conquest in the eighth century, when many of their fire-temples were destroyed or converted into mosques, Zoroastrianism was the dominant religion in Bukhara).

As well as the French and German pensioners, there were also plenty of Uzbekistan tourists. In the main square outside the Ark, I was approached by plenty of Uzbek youngsters who wanted to have their photo taken with me. A group of beautiful young girls from Tashkent took turns at putting their arms around me while their friend took pictures on their camera phones. Unlike the more traditionally dressed local women they wore tight fitting fashionable clothes, left their beautiful waist-length hair to fall freely, and were confident and vivacious – they were definitely 'U-Girls'. When I asked them why they wanted to have their picture taken with me they said it was because they liked me. This didn't seem to make much sense. I think I was just a bit of a novelty but that was OK. I could hardly traipse around Asia taking pictures of colourful locals and then complain when I turned out to be the 'exotic' one.

A friendly but more traditionally dressed young woman would wave to me whenever I passed by her restaurant at the back of the Lyabi-Hauz. It was behind an old *medressa* that had now been converted to put on dinner and traditional dance shows for the coachloads of Euro biddies, and featured three eight-foot tall traditional pots for some reason. I wasn't sure if they were just there for decoration or actually had some kind of purpose. The small outside restaurant's menu was limited but excellent – I was wary of eating there when I was the only customer but ended up with the best shashlik kebabs that I have ever tasted. Despite now turning dark, Bukhara still seemed like a very safe place to wander around through the mazes of alleys and now near empty bazaars. I ended up around the other side of the Ark and decided to try to at least find the entrance to the Zindon jail that I had somehow missed out earlier in the day. I wandered around the back of the Ark into an unlit area where two silhouetted figures began to approach me. The two *militsia* (policemen) came over to say that I shouldn't be down here and started to demand payment. They then remembered their manners and took turns at shaking my hand. I thanked them for their help and starting walking back towards the road. When they asked again for money I agreed that Bukhara was very nice and that the people were very friendly. This seemed to confuse them so they ran off into what appeared to be a bar to get a friend who spoke better English. As I was almost back on the lit road, their friend caught up with me to say that I didn't understand and that they were the police. When I agreed and thanked him he looked a bit discouraged. I almost felt sorry for them. The *militsia* went back to the bar and I went back to my B&B.

* * *

The next morning I went to jail (the Zindon jail that I had been looking for in the dark). You could visit the dungeons and the torture chamber. At the gate, a gold-toothed woman in a headscarf asked where I was from and then told me that 'the bug pit is for English'. The bug pit was the dungeon that had been used to hold Colonel Stoddart and Captain Conolly when they had come to visit Emir Nasrullah Khan about a problem with Afghanistan (does this sound familiar?). He was so upset they hadn't brought him a present that he had their heads cut off. Stoddart and Conolly's friends and families were so annoyed about this that they saved up to send out their own emissary, a clergyman called Joseph Wolff. The Khan probably would have beheaded him as well but thought that he looked so funny dressed up in all his clerical regalia that he let him off.

I wasn't sure where to go next so I wandered off past the Soviet water tower in front of the Ark towards Samani Park and the obligatory Crying Mother Monument. I then decided to be clever and take a shortcut back. I got very lost. I suspect that very few tourists in Bukhara ever go out of the main tourist zone but I have a tendency to find myself in places where I don't belong. Surprisingly there were plenty of mosques, *medressas* and monuments outside of the centre that don't seem to be mentioned in any guidebooks but would be considered to be worthwhile tourist attractions in Tashkent or Kazakhstan. Unfortunately, I had no idea what they were or where I was. I thought that one grand *medressa* I had came across might be one that was marked on my map. When I attempted to open the door and look through I heard several girls scream and then run away. A minute later they returned to the door and timidly poked their heads around. Their curiosity had clearly come out on top of any fear they may have held about a strange man on their doorstep. They handed around my map and then pointed to somewhere far off the page. I thanked them for their help and randomly wandered off in the hope of finding some kind of landmark. After far too long I eventually came across the large tennis complex on the edge of my map – Uzbekistan has excellent tennis facilities as President Karimov is a big fan – and from there I could find my way back into the tourist zone.

Having failed to be blown away at the opera I thought I might be better suited to the puppet show. The previous evening's performance had been cancelled but tonight I was in luck. The venue was a permanent puppet theatre at the far end of the pool with school hall-type foldable chairs lined up in front of the 'stage'. None of the coach parties had booked up for tonight but they were going to run it anyway for just me and two guys and a girl from Germany. They had all come to Uzbekistan to visit a friend of theirs who had been working in Tashkent but for some reason she had had her visa revoked just as they were leaving to visit her. They were now holidaying in Uzbekistan while their friend had been sent back to Germany. For a puppet show there was surprisingly little use of the puppets. Most of the show consisted of five attractive young women standing in front of the Punch and Judy-type stage and telling stories. Every now and again one of them would say: 'I know a song about that. Shall we sing it?' They would then go off into their next number. It was a bit like being in a TV show for under-fives. Then one guy in the troupe did a 'wrestling' act where, by bending over in a special costume with his hands on the floor, he impersonated two midgets embraced in a struggle. I was slightly disappointed that the puppets didn't get much of a look in but it was more on my level than the national opera company.

Afterwards we chatted with the performers and then left to look at a couple of photography galleries. The Germans were leaving Bukhara tomorrow and one of them was interested in purchasing some arty-looking prints of the city. The photography in both of the galleries was of a consistently high standard but in many ways quite derivative – even for somebody who is far from an expert it was easy to pick out the influence of iconic American photographers such as Diane Arbus. The visual art on display was far more evolved than other Uzbek expressions of popular culture but the Western influence was still very strong.

Feeling inspired by the art and the early evening light, I left to take more of my own photographs of beautiful Bukhara before the sun finally set. Once the only light remaining came from the crescent moon above I returned to Lyabi-Hauz for a meal around the glistening, mulberry tree-lined pool. It was a wonderfully dream-like and romantic location but it seemed a little sad to be sitting there on my own. As I tore off the meat from the skewers of my shashlyk kebabs I thought of my wife and wished that for this moment, at least, she was here by my side.

Samarkand

Ancient Crossroads • Blood in the Sand • Heads Held High
Restoration • Propagation of the Wicked • Memento Mori
Trapped Spirits • Winning Hearts and Minds • Knowledge and Power
Murder in Samarkand • Interests as Perceived

Samarkand is set on the crossroads of China, India and Persia, and is one of Central Asia's oldest cities dating back to around the fifth century BC. After being conquered by Alexander the Great in 329 BC and destroyed by Genghis Khan in 1220, it then went on to become the majestic capital for Timur after he settled there in 1370. Having grown to become the second largest city in the world it would later go into decline again but was somewhat revived when the Russians linked it up to their Trans-Caspian railway network. It even became the capital of the Uzbek SSR in 1924 but was soon replaced by Tashkent.

After another fried breakfast in the courtyard of my Bukharan B&B, I caught a battered Trabant-like taxi to the bus station on the outskirts of the town, where I was quickly rushed on to the bus to Samarkand. I was the only person sitting on it. When I asked when it was leaving they said when it's full. This bus standing next to it was almost full. When I asked where that one was going they reluctantly admitted that that one was going to Samarkand as well. It was the rival bus company. I made them get my backpack out from underneath and switched buses. Five minutes later we were on our way.

I ended up on the back seat with some friendly but rather grubby-looking old men. They had very few teeth left between them and amused themselves by passing around a plastic bottle full of green slime that they would take turns gobbing into. They offered me some chewing tobacco, which I declined as politely as possible, and then they started going through my carry-on bag to see if they could find anything interesting. I showed them my passports and let them listen to my Discman. One of them wanted to keep my CDs as a 'present' but I took them back and gave him some biscuits instead. I doubt if he was much of a metal fan anyway.

After two or three hours of driving through nothing very much at all, we stopped at an Uzbek version of a service station. It was almost as grim as the roadside stops in China. I went in and out of the toilets as quickly as possible but decided not to risk the food in the café. Instead I bought a hygienically wrapped Snickers bar from a stall at the side and loitered in the car park. It didn't take long before some of my fellow passengers came over to practise their English on me. I ended up chatting to one of the younger ones with a moustache who had recently gotten married. She spoke good English as she was studying to be a translator. I had to keep reminding myself not to stare at her upper lip while she was talking. After we had all piled back on the bus, she came up to the back seat and handed me a glittery woman's watch. She had wanted to give me a present but didn't have anything that was suitable for a man so had decided to give me the watch as a present for my wife. I was very touched but also quite embarrassed. It seemed like too big a present for somebody you had only just met. I would have been pleased with a cup of tea or a biscuit.

On arriving at the Samarkand bus station, I caught a *marshrutka* into the centre of the city. I had no idea where I was going but when I caught site of what appeared to be the three grand edifices of the Registan, I decided to jump off. Luckily I had chosen to get off in a sensible place as after checking my map properly I realized I was just a few minutes' walk from the Antica B&B. After wandering through some narrow alleyways just off from a park and the Guri Amir Mausoleum, I was let through a large wooden gate and into the family's courtyard. I opted for a small room that looked like it used to be some kind of outhouse or shed, as it was the cheapest option. While my passport details were being written down I was given a large pot of tea and plenty of biscuits. I also signed up for a traditional Uzbek meal that took place in a traditional Samarkand house that had recently been restored by the family.

Once I had checked in and dumped my bags, I set off towards Samarkand's most famous site, the Registan. This group of three huge *medressas* surrounding a large tiled courtyard was constructed by Timur and his successors from around 1400 (with the help of a lot of skilled craftsmen and even larger numbers of less willing slaves). These are the oldest such buildings in Samarkand, as Genghis Khan had made a point of knocking down everything else when he had visited about 150 years earlier. 'Registan' is Persian for 'the place of sand' – it was strewn across the ground to soak up the blood from the executions that were regularly held there up until the beginning of the twentieth century. Timur would stick his victims' heads on vertical spikes around the Registan while gathering his followers close to him to hear his mighty proclamations. The hordes of visitors today are more likely to be gathering around a tour guide with a brightly coloured flag – as opposed to a human head – on the end of a stick held up high. By the time that I had arrived, however, the tour groups were being carted back to their hotels for an organized evening of feasting and dance. The only treasures that these hordes departed with were decorative plates and t-shirts from the multiple gift shops that inhabited the former cells of religious scholars.

From a distance the Registan looked hugely impressive but closer up you could see the real damage. Along with many other buildings in Samarkand, the Registan was heavily restored during the Soviet era. Some of the liberties taken during the restoration process have been heavily criticized but at least they kept them from falling down all together. Scaffolding was still in use to support the back walls and large areas that faced away from the front were missing most of their tile work. Hopefully there will be money to restore them all properly once Karimov finally wakes up to how much could be made through tourism.

On entering the complex I was approached by a security guard who suggested I climb to the top of one of the minarets for a fantastic view of the Registan and Samarkand during the fast-approaching sunset. The minaret was out of bounds to tourists but this could all be arranged for a fee. As he was asking for a ridiculous amount of money I politely refused. He said to come and see him if I changed my mind. I carried on through the various sections of the imposing *medressas* while the stallholders who had yet to pack up for the day did their best to flog me tacky souvenirs. I somehow managed to resist. Despite the monumental grandeur of the complex I couldn't help feeling that these buildings were all starting to look very similar. There was only so much elaborate tile work that I could admire in a day.

Having completed the obligatory circuit of the buildings I was yet again approached by the security guard who was so keen to send me to the top of a minaret. Now that I was ready to leave, the price being quoted for his services began to drop dramatically. As he saw that my interest had been reawakened, he hiked the price back up again and told me that if I climbed the tower then I would have a child within a year. Genghis Khan is thought to have fathered hundreds of children and to have millions of descendants (almost everybody from Central Asia is thought to be related to Genghis Khan to some degree) but I was reluctant to surrender any of my freedom for a child, and cared little for the propagation of my genes. As I turned to walk away, his price fell back down again so I finally gave in and we shook on it. As with the ruined part of the Ark in

Bukhara, I'm not sure that the Uzbekistan Health and Safety Organisation would have approved (if such an organization actually existed). I had assumed that he would guide me along the ruined stairway to the top but, after unlocking the heavy wooden door and ushering me through, he then locked it behind me. I was to shout out when I had finished. I cautiously edged my way up the crumbling stairways, ducking under fractured wooden beams and trying not to slip on the dirt and gravel. This really wouldn't be a very clever place to slip and break your leg. After sliding up past some wiring at the top, I could poke my head up through the top of the minaret and look down on the majestically domed and minareted skyline of Samarkand as the sun began to set. I was tempted to gob on some tourists below but managed to resist – it would have spoiled the moment.

Back at the Antica guest house I met Stefan and Ruth from Belgium who had also signed up for the meal at the historic house. They were only on a three-week holiday and having flown into Tashkent they had been planning to fly home from Bishkek in Kyrgyzstan. They had received an email from a friend saying that he thought the border was now open again but they weren't sure. A couple of German psychologists were also coming along. They were supposed to be flying back home in a couple of days but all the flights had been cancelled owing to the volcanic eruptions in Iceland. She desperately wanted to get back in time for her sister's wedding. Once everybody was assembled in the Antica courtyard we were led off through some potholed back alleys as the light began to dim and the temperature dropped dramatically. After taking off our shoes we were led into an atmospheric old house that had been in the family for years. With their income from tourism they could now begin the slow and laborious task of restoring it to its former glory. Between courses of pleasant but unsubstantial Uzbek dishes, we were given a lecture about the history of the house. It was a nice enough evening but I still felt a little hungry when were marched back through the poorly illuminated back streets, too busy concentrating on looking on where we were treading to take in the surroundings. Back in my small, shed-like room, I filled up on biscuits before dragging two heavy blankets over my narrow, sloping bed in an attempt to stay warm.

* * *

In the dining room of the guest house, where a buffet breakfast was served, everyone's eyes were drawn to the CNN news channel on the large plasma screen. It looked like the German psychologists wouldn't make it back for the wedding – most of the flights across northern Europe had been cancelled. Stefan and Ruth still weren't sure if they would be let into Kyrgyzstan but had decided to head for the border near Osh and hope for the best.

I headed off past the Registan towards Shah-I-Zinda, the avenue of mausoleums. The name means 'Tomb of the Living King' and refers to an inner shrine that is possibly the grave of one of Mohammed's cousins. It began to take on its current form when Timur started to bury his family there in the fourteenth century but was heavily restored in 2005 as part of Karimov's plan to 'beautify' Uzbekistan's architectural monuments. At the top of a steep avenue of tiled shrines, cut into the hillside, lies a large cemetery for the less wealthy or revered. For those who could never afford a mausoleum of their own, there were still huge granite gravestones featuring photographs of those buried below. Many of the headstones would show individual pictures of a married couple but the ages wouldn't match. A young husband may have been pictured next to an old wife. She may have died thirty or forty years later. On some of the tombstones their pictures looked too young for the age that they died at. Maybe they didn't have any good pictures of when they were older or maybe nobody wanted them to be remembered like that? Other smaller graves just had pictures of children on them, all dressed up in their Sunday best with their hair neatly combed. If the parents had known that their children were dying, would they have taken them along to a professional photographer to make sure they had a decent reminder for all eternity? All of the photographs seemed strangely formal, as if they were dressed up for a baptism, or a wedding or a funeral. None of them looked like they were having much fun. What if you died suddenly without a single decent image? I nearly always look gormless in snapshots. I would be rolling in my grave if somebody stuck one of those on my headstone. I would probably be forced to come back as a ghost and vandalize my tombstone before I could rot in peace.

After walking back through the Siob bazaar and past the colonial-style State Art Museum, I found Stefan and Ruth in an Internet café across from the Registan. They had grown tired of looking at mosques, *medressas* and mausoleums – however impressive they may at first seem – and were now slowly and laboriously attempting to upload their pictures onto their travel blog and get some more information on the situation in Kyrgyzstan. The torturously slow broadband speeds in Uzbekistan meant they had been in there for quite a while. After joining them for coffee and some excellent cake in a nearby café, I continued to explore the city. Rather than being a city with a well-preserved ancient centre, like Bukhara, Samarkand is closer to a modern Soviet city such as Tashkent but with pockets of ancient structures dotted all around. I traipsed on through the more Soviet part of the city around Navoi Park – yes, there is yet another Navoi Park in Samarkand as well as yet another Crying Mother Monument – but there really wasn't much to see in this part of the town and what there was to see seemed to be in the process of being rebuilt. After some shashlyk kebabs at a *chaikhana* (cheap local eateries serving mainly dumplings, soup, *plov*, kebabs and beer) I was starting to run out of things to do. What I had thought was an art gallery had turned out to be more of a tourist shop, and a lot of the highly stylized architecture was starting to look remarkably similar. I cautiously wandered into the forecourt of the Aini Museum, unsure of where I was or where I was going, and was enthusiastically greeted by the curator. I got the feeling that nobody had bothered to visit him for a while.

The poet and writer Saddridin Aini (1878–1954) is generally considered to be the founder of Tajik and Uzbek literature and is revered in Uzbekistan in the same way as contemporaries such as Tolstoy are revered in Russia. The curator took me around the house pointing out such items of 'interest' as Aini's writing desk and bed. I'm really not sure how looking at an old desk is supposed to increase my appreciation of a cultural icon (if anybody is interested I got my one from Argos when it was on special offer but it's a bit wobbly). Maybe, deep down, many people still believe that an individual's spirit can somehow connect to them via inanimate objects? While he carried on in Russian, I nodded my head, pretending to understand and occasionally repeating a phrase that I could comprehend. At the end of the tour, he gave me a brochure in English and then charged me for the leaflet and the tour. He seemed to be able to communicate this part of the tour well enough in English but I didn't really mind.

While enjoying yet another pot of tea and reading through my Aini brochure in the courtyard of the Antica guest house, I met Jimmy and Kiaro. They were both Fulbright Scholars who had studied Russian at their US universities and were now doing 'research' at the Almaty University in Kazakhstan. It didn't sound as if anybody took much notice of the 'research' they were doing but it gave them a chance to practise their Russian and avoid getting a proper job for another couple of years. The Fulbright Scholars are given grants to study or do research abroad in the hope of creating good relations between the US and other countries. In other words, like the Peace Corps, they primarily exist for reasons of 'soft power' (the US Peace Corps left Uzbekistan for security reasons in 2005 following the Andijon Massacre). As Central Asia has a lot of oil, and isn't the Middle East, the US has been particularly keen to win its heart and mind, but this hasn't always been easy. All the murders and torturing in Uzbekistan have caused a bit of a strain on their relationship of late. China has also recently set up its own scholarship schemes and version of the Peace Corps, but I couldn't see many Central Asians falling in love with the culture and values of China. All the best-educated and most ambitious youngsters seem to aspire to be – if not American exactly – at least more or less Western. China may be a growing superpower but it will be a long time before it can ever seriously compete with the music, art, literature, television, film and sophisticated level of bullshit of the West. Half of the youngsters I met along the Silk Road had fallen for the idea of living in America or Western Europe but I didn't meet anyone who dreamed of starting a new life in either China or Russia.

Jimmy and Kiaro were going to the restored house meal tonight and were waiting for an American military guy to meet them who Kiaro had previously met on a plane in Kazakhstan, before bumping into him again in Samarkand. I was persuaded to join them along with a French woman whose Polish husband was ill in bed. When their guest walked into the courtyard, it was very clear that he belonged to the military. People like that just seem to ooze some kind of indefinable military presence. He, himself, admitted that lots of people seem to assume that he is in the military and can consequently be a little wary of him. I never seem to have that problem – people are far more likely to assume that I am some kind of student, musician or artist and are more likely to look out for me than feel threatened by me. I always seem to be the one in a crowd who people will pick out to ask directions from (I may not be a lot of use as I very rarely know where I am or exactly where I'm going but at least I'm approachable).

When the group for tonight's meal was assembled we were once again herded off. Soldier boy was also a kind of student, as he was on some kind of military programme to become an 'expert' on Central Asia. Apparently, the US military needed people to learn more about the region as they could no longer ignore its growing importance and it was increasingly apparent that the average US soldier couldn't even point out Central Asia on a map. He was to be trained as some kind of specialist on the area and was allowed to go off on trips such as this one to Samarkand, provided he wrote it all up properly when he returned to his base at Astana in Kazakhstan (it seems even more unlikely that anybody ever actually read these 'reports' than that anybody ever read the Fulbright Scholars 'research'). He had attended and spoken at various conferences and meetings where a range of aspects of US relations in the region had been discussed. Unfortunately, he seemed to know very little and what reading he had done seemed to consist of the officially sanctioned book list that had been passed down to him by his military superiors. When the discussion turned to *Murder in Samarkand* by the former British ambassador to Uzbekistan, Craig Murray, it seemed very odd that he hadn't even heard of a bestseller that had brought up so many awkward questions about US foreign policy; when Murray had made a nuisance of himself by complaining rather too loudly about the Uzbekistan government boiling members of the public to death, it made things very awkward for the US forces, who were so keen to maintain good relations with the Karimov regime (as well as Uzbekistan's substantial natural resources there was also the matter of the US army base near the Afghan border to consider). After pressure from the US government, Murray was eventually forced out of his position by the British authorities. Kiaro had admired the moral position that the ambassador had taken in regards to the torture but thought that it was a shame that he was such 'a sleaze' (he had left his wife for a glamorous young Uzbek woman who was probably young enough to be his daughter).

When the conversation broadened out into the area of whether the US government should really have been bank-rolling dodgy Third World dictators, soldier boy insisted that the US government's only responsibility was to best represent the interests of the USA. Despite the fact that the perceived interests of the USA by those in power seem to be the same as the interests of those who are actually in power, there can be a big difference between the short-term interests of a vested interest and the long-term interests of the world as a whole; short-term goals of the US such as arming and training the Mujahideen in Afghanistan haven't always turned out to be such good ideas in the long term. Soldier boy couldn't seem to grasp that, while putting aside any moral concerns about disreputable regimes might have military or financial benefits in the short term, it might not necessarily be in the long-term interests of world security, as a whole, to simply turn a blind eye to torture, massacres and kleptocracy (everybody else at the table seemed to take a more straightforward moral stance in regards to US foreign policy).

As Central Asia looks set to become increasingly significant as a focus for the 'clash of civilizations' that is likely to be unleashed over hearts, minds and money in the coming decades, it seems somewhat alarming that those who are currently being groomed as 'expert' advisers for the region seem to understand so little (I am sure that both Jimmy or Kiaro would have been far better candidates for such a position but then they would never have joined the military in the first place).

Despite – or perhaps because of – the heated debate, we enjoyed the meal, the vodka and the discussion (although we were made to shut up for a while to listen to a history of the old house). As we all stumbled back to the guest house through the dimly lit back streets, I arranged to share a taxi to the train station the next morning with the French woman and her poorly husband who had failed to make it out for the night (all the seats had sold out but the owners of Antica seemed to think that for a little extra payment we could still get on the train to Tashkent).

Tashkent (again)

Breakfast Apocalypse • Gypsy Dancer • Prodigal Sons • The Threat of the Other • Merging and Melting • The Only Way • In Search of the Mighty Dollar • Marx Usurped by the Scourge of God Restless and Wild • There Can Be No Alternative

During the buffet breakfast most of the guest house's residents' attention was again taken up by the large television in the corner. A lot of people's travel plans had now been disturbed by the volcanic eruption in Iceland, the uprising in Kyrgyzstan and a disastrous earthquake in China. It was like viewing the apocalypse over coffee and croissants. I met an old French guy with a grey beard and a worn-out expression who was cycling all the way from France to China. He was now in his tenth year. I have met plenty of crazy cyclists before but this seemed a little excessive. After a bit of clarification it eventually turned out that he had actually been doing the trip in stages over the last decade or so; each year he would take all his annual leave in one go and then fly to the furthest point he had made it to on his last vacation and carry on through the next section of his trip. He hadn't been able to get a visa for the Turkmenistan section, so he was going to have to try to go back and complete that leg of his journey at a later date. It really didn't look as if all the strain and exertion was doing him a lot of good. I hoped that he'd make it.

The French woman's husband didn't look too good either. His face was as grey as it was lined. He should have stayed in bed but they were running out of time and needed to move on from Samarkand. The brother of a woman from the guest house picked us up at the end of our alley in a battered old Soviet-style taxi to take us to the train station. If we couldn't get on the fast morning train that was coming up from

Bukhara, then he would take us to the bus station instead. As we expected, all the normal train tickets had gone but they still had a few 'luxury' train tickets left. We couldn't seem to work out why these tickets were any different from the normal tickets except that they were four times more expensive and still available. Our driver suggested that for a fee he could sort out a far more affordable option directly with the ticket inspector. This seemed a bit dodgy. Surely they either had seats or they didn't? I didn't want to end up standing for the whole journey and we were also somewhat concerned about getting dragged into the whole rigmarole of petty corruption and bribery. We needn't have worried too much. By paying the guards directly they actually let us stay in their own unused sleeping cabin. The friendly guard pushed his bedding aside so that we could all sit down along the foldout bed that faced out towards a line of ticket inspectors' hats. I thought the inspectors deserved any little extra money they could get by going out of their way to accommodate the occasional tourist – we weren't depriving anybody else of a seat and in the name of laissez-faire economics we were each working the system to our mutual advantage (at least that's how I justified it).

We parted ways at the Tashkent Central Station and I caught the metro back up to the Gulnara guest house. On arrival I was somewhat taken back to find a long line of tables taking up the courtyard and overflowing with affluent-looking French tourists. Apparently, the guest house would take in tour groups for big set lunches. Later on they would have a coachload of geriatric Germans arriving for a large set meal and an after-dinner dance show. Luckily I had reserved a room for my first night back in Tashkent but they couldn't guarantee me anything for the following night as all the rooms had been booked out by a group of French architectural students (they had got stuck in Tashkent after the Icelandic volcanic eruptions had caused their flight to be cancelled).

The mother of the guest house was worried that my family might have been harmed by the volcano in Europe. I explained that Iceland wasn't that close to England and that my Mum had actually been worried about me because of the earthquake in China. She probably should have been more worried about the fact that I had resolved to try again to get into Kyrgyzstan after (hopefully) picking up my Turkmenistan transit visa. Apart from the fact that the Kyrgyz visa had cost so much and hadn't been used, I also had another reason to try to fit this one more country into my trip: I had worked out that if I made it to Kyrgyzstan then I would have visited a hundred countries in total by the time that I returned to England. Although on one level I knew that this kind of country counting was kind of silly, I still felt the need to reach such a milestone. I knew that I would never leave my mark on the world in the same way that Genghis Khan or Timur had, but through experiencing a lot of the world, I hoped it would somehow leave its mark on me. If I missed out on the chance to visit Kyrgyzstan this time then I would probably never get to go there at all and would risk not reaching a hundred countries before I died. One problem with my plan was that I only had a single entry visa for Uzbekistan and that even if I managed to get across the border into Osh then I wouldn't be able to get back into Uzbekistan to continue my journey. The manager at the guest house seemed to think that it was possible to extend your visa at the passport office at the airport so I took a bus over there and attempted to track down the necessary officials. As you may have guessed this was far from easy. After much pointless waiting around and being passed from one office to another I was eventually referred on to some uniformed customs guards who seemed a little confused by my request. They all stood around passing my passport to each other and then asked me if I was a journalist. When I said that I wasn't they looked a bit sceptical but still seemed friendly enough. I'm sure that as individuals they would have been more than happy to help me but in the end they had to admit that there was nothing they could do. The only way around it would be to apply for another new visa for Uzbekistan but I simply didn't have the time to waste (or want to pay out all that money yet again). It looked like I would be denied my century.

I walked up to the nearest Internet café to check on the news again and to reassure my friends and family that I had yet to be annihilated by any kind of natural (or unnatural) disaster. I ignored my wife's enquiry as to the lump on my throat as I didn't want to worry her (I also hadn't told her that the one other person I had met with a similar lump had been subjected to years of chemotherapy). On returning to the guest house, I met Neil from Israel, Angelo from Italy and a slightly frumpy-looking German girl of Turkish descent called Jeanine. She was some kind of German academic with a special interest in Uzbekistan – she was even familiar with the works of the poet and writer Aini. As the coachload of German tourists began to fill up two central lines of tables running through the courtyard, we sat cross-legged at the far end on one of the raised wooden seating platforms that were draped in traditional-style carpets (this may have looked far cooler and much more fun than sitting upright along a school dinner-style row of tables but it would soon become very uncomfortable – I would constantly have to keep shifting my weight around to get to anywhere approaching less than numb). Towards the end of the meal a free-spirited dancer with a headfull of braids falling down to her waist, launched into her 'cultural' performance. Overweight Germans with expensive video cameras kept standing up and getting in the way while trying to capture the eye rolling, wrist wriggling and hair spinning in full HD. The dancer's outfit and dancing seemed closer to that of Eastern European gypsies than anything you would normally associate with Central Asia. Rather surprisingly, Jeannine joined in with the traditional but still quite sexy dancing, towards the end of the show, and turned out to be rather adept at the wrist wriggling and hip thrusting.

While taking in the entertainment, and chatting around our knee-height table, it became clear that we had all met several of the same people while travelling around the region. Neil seemed to assume that I would know David from America. There may only have been a small amount of backpackers in Central Asia but I couldn't be expected to have met all of them. We stayed up talking until quite late but I eventually retired to my small upstairs room with the intention of getting up early the next morning. I lay there in the narrow bed thinking how strange it was that I would be expected to have met every other traveller along the Silk Road.

* * *

The next morning I met David from America outside the Turkmen Embassy. He had been coming here early every morning for days in the hope of picking up his transit visa. He had been through exactly the same process in Almaty to get his Uzbek visa and was getting rather tired of the whole rigmarole. As he'd been stuck in expensive Almaty for over a week, the only place that he'd been able to afford to stay in were the university dormitories that I'd left after one night. Agreeing that the accommodation was as grim as I'd remembered, he insisted that his shoestring budget had left him no other choice. As his extended stay in Almaty had eaten up his limited budget rather more quickly than he had anticipated he was now staying at a very cheap but depressing guest house in Tashkent that also seemed to double as a brothel. It didn't sound as if he was having much fun.

There were so many people loitering outside the embassy that despite getting there before they even opened the gates I was concerned that I wouldn't get in before they closed it up for the morning. David had been getting there every morning for 6am but hadn't always managed to get in before they turned the remainders away at eleven. With ten minutes to go, David was let in but I was still standing there. A local guy just ahead of me in the queue said that if I trusted him he would take in my passport with him to check if my visa was ready. I handed it over as he was let in with the last of the day. David returned to the gates looking downtrodden. There was still no news – he would have to come back tomorrow. A couple of minutes later the guy who had taken my passport rushed back to the gate and persuaded the security guard to let me through. After handing over the exact amount in unfolded US dollars they finally told me to come back at three in the afternoon to pick up my visa. I may have failed in my mission to make it to Kyrgyzstan but at least I would be allowed to enter Turkmenistan.

With time to kill I caught the metro up towards Water World, the Central Asian Plov Centre and Tashkent Land: Uzbekistan's answer to Disneyland. Water World still hadn't opened for the summer, I couldn't find the Central Asian Plov Centre and, once I got to the old-fashioned looking Tashkent Land, I couldn't summon up the enthusiasm to buy a ticket and then go around the rides on my own. Even by my standards that seemed a little too desperate.

After returning to the embassy to pick up my Turkmen transit visa, I set about trying to find the Uzbek airline office but also with no luck. Everybody seemed to think it was somewhere else. As I was already too late to go overland on the night train via Bukhara and the flights to Khiva for tomorrow didn't leave until the late afternoon, I decided to give up and return to the guest house. They had kept my backpack in the downstairs storage room and had promised to let me sleep in the dining room if I had to stay another night.

Just after I got back, Moses and Nicholas from Singapore staggered in under the weight of two massive backpacks. They had also had trouble with finding the guest house and were disappointed to find that all the rooms were still booked out to the French architectural students who were still waiting for the flights to Europe to resume. Relief spread across their faces as the family also offered to let them sleep in the dining room (as they were only charging us US$2 less each to all sleep on the floor than they would have charged us for individual rooms, our hosts were actually doing quite well out of the Icelandic volcano). As they had been travelling along the Silk Road in the opposite direction to me, we had plenty to talk about. I led them out to where there were a couple of Internet cafés and we ordered some plastic-covered microwaveable burgers in a small café. Moses was half-Indian and half-Chinese, and his parents were born-again Christians – all his brothers and sisters had been named after biblical characters. Nicholas was unusually tall for someone of Chinese descent and had found himself being stared at a lot. This had been particularly uncomfortable when he had been forced to use one of the communal squat toilets with no doors – apparently the locals had found the site of a tourist taking a shit quite fascinating. They were on their way to China via Kazakhstan. Nicholas could speak some passable Chinese as his mother often spoke it at home, but Moses' family only ever spoke in English. Despite both only being a few generations removed from their Chinese ancestors this would be their first visit for both of them. China was just as much of a foreign country to them as it was to me.

After leaving them at an Internet café and returning to the guest house, I found out that the black market rate for the Uzbek *sum* against the US dollar had dropped dramatically. Apparently the government had just decided to introduce some kind of in-between official exchange rate for businesses that meant that there was no longer such a huge divide between the official and real rates of exchange. It seemed that they would do something like this every now and again whenever the imaginary official rate became too difficult to sustain. As I had been about to exchange some more of my dollars for *sum*, this would actually make things quite a bit more expensive for me. Angelo seemed to think that one of the black market money exchangers could still give him a pretty good rate for his dollars but the manager of the guest house thought that it would take a while before it crept back to the usual rate (these random fluctuations in the value of the Uzbek currency might allow easy fast pickings for those in the know but couldn't be in the long-term interests of the Uzbek economy).

Once Moses and Nicholas had returned, we sat cross-legged around the low table with Angelo and Neil while feasting on Uzbek 'lasagne' and drinking green tea. Moses and Nicholas had recently finished their compulsory service in the Singapore army and Neil had had to spend about three years in the Israeli army. It seemed difficult to imagine why Singapore needed its own army when it was so well integrated with the surrounding economies that any serious attack upon its independence could only result in financial disaster all around. They, however, seemed to think that compulsory military service was an unfortunate necessity and that without its own well-trained army, Singapore could be seriously under threat from its neighbours. I suspected that compulsory military service had as much to do with the control of its own citizenry as to do with any real or imagined threat from 'foreigners'. As Singapore lacks any real ethnic or cultural identity of its own and is more likely to simply absorb outside influences than be absorbed by them, it would seem that the only real concern of Singapore's elites would be the threat to their own standing within the existing system (a perceived threat by 'outsiders' – whether real or imagined – will always help in propping up the status quo).

The threat to Israel by 'outsiders' is, however, far from imagined. A lot of their neighbours would be happy to see Israel wiped off the face of the planet. The Jews have always defined themselves as a racially and culturally unique group of people whose strong sense of identity has only been strengthened over millennia of persecution. In reality, however, they are maybe not as culturally homogenous or ethnically distinct as is often imagined. As Jewish traders played an important role in the Silk Road trade, they dispersed their ideas, culture and DNA – as well as their goods – along the Silk Road cities of China, Central Asia and the Middle East. The Bukharan Jews have been in Central Asia for over 2,500 years and formed a sizable community within the ancient Silk Road city of Bukhara itself. Despite the odds they always managed to hold onto their Jewish identity. Other sizable Jewish populations further along the Silk Road in Chinese cities such as Kaifeng fared less well in preserving their culture or ethnicity. Over time they intermarried with the ethnic Chinese and became increasingly Chinese in both appearance and culture.

When I questioned the whole concept of race, Neil seemed to balk at the suggestion that those who define themselves as Jewish might not be as ethnically distinct as they imagined. On pointing out that some Jews had fair hair and light-coloured skin whereas some others were extremely dark, he conceded that Jewishness was primarily cultural. This culture, however, is founded upon the idea that the Jews are 'the chosen people' and are somehow intrinsically better than everybody else – it's not hard to see how such beliefs might antagonize their neighbours and lead to persecution. While other 'Peoples of the Book' such as Christians and Muslims might believe they are the only ones who are truly right, being evangelical in nature they have an obligation to show others 'the true path' regardless of race or ethnicity. Jews, however, believe they belong to 'the chosen people' simply by being born into it (some claim it is possible to 'convert' to being a Jew but such 'converts' are rarely accepted as 'real Jews'). Recent studies have shown that the genetic make-up of Jews and Arabs is almost identical, while at the same time people of Chinese or African appearance have used DNA testing to prove they are of Jewish descent. In a world that is becoming increasingly globalized it is becoming increasingly apparent that we are all fundamentally more global than was once commonly believed.

* * *

The next morning I made the mistake of changing US dollars at the guest house for the current black market rate. I had needed a couple of bricks of Uzbek *sum* if I was to buy a cheap flight to Khiva. Later on in the day I would bump into Angelo – he had managed to track down the money-changer at the market who had delivered on his promise of a far better deal. This was a bit annoying. I was also concerned that I was going through my stash of US dollars a little faster than anticipated. I needed to keep enough in cash for Turkmenistan and Iran as the ATMs or banks would rarely accept foreign credit or debit cards.

After several frustrating hours trying to track down the recently moved Uzbek Airline office, I eventually queued up at the well-disguised counter only to be told that that they had no more tickets to Khiva for several days. I then bought another ticket for the sleeper train to Bukhara, and descended to the metro in search of the mighty dollar. The ATMs at the Hotel Intercontinental didn't seem to be working for me but I was directed to the exchange counter by a very helpful hotel manager. After feeling somewhat disconcerted at how easy it had been to use my British debit card to take out US$500 at a decent rate and without any commission, I bumped into Moses. Even though there was just a handful of backpackers in Central Asia at the time, they all seemed to meet up with each other at the same guest houses, the same embassies and now at probably the only place where you could easily get your hands on those so-essential greenbacks. Moses had been about to pick up his visa at the Kazakhstan embassy but the woman at the desk had refused to take his US dollars as they had been folded. He hoped that the hotel would have some perfect, unfolded dollar bills left so that he could continue on his journey.

As I still had several hours left before I had to pick up my backpack from the guest house and catch the evening's train, I walked on down towards the Amir Timur Maydoni, from where many of Tashkent's main streets radiate. There used to be a bust of Marx in the centre of the park, but this had now been replaced by a statue of a tubby Timur (Tamerlane) on a prancing horse. Upon independence, Karimov set about resurrecting Timur as a national hero for Uzbekistan. It seems more than a little odd that Karimov should have selected a mass-murdering tyrant as a hero for Uzbekistan when it was the Uzbek people themselves who eventually crushed the remains of the Timurid Empire. Timur is reckoned to have killed more people than Hitler and Stalin combined; when he wasn't stacking up towers of skulls he was cementing together even more gruesome towers made of still-writhing prisoners. Karimov seemed to have adopted Timur as a potent symbol of power and independence that could be appropriated for his own means. While Soviet era academics were prevented from celebrating any of Timur's artistic, architectural or organizational triumphs, the academics of today are heavily discouraged from drawing attention to any of Timur's many faults.

I walked over to the Amir Timur Museum where several groups of school children were excitedly waiting to pay their respects to their esteemed ancestor. The museum was hurriedly constructed in 1996 as a tribute to the newly adopted national hero. In style it was closer to a Las Vegas casino than to the more staid national museums of the West. Huge garish pictures surrounded the walls and a film set-style staircase twisted around the oval sanctuary towards the chandeliered dome that rose majestically above. They could easily have made some cash by hiring it out for weddings – instead, many newlyweds made do with celebrating their union in front of Timur's statue. 'The Scourge of God' drew freely from both Islam and the laws of Genghis Khan to justify his actions but chose to disregard any aspects that were inconvenient. Timur was actually of Turkic descent but formed marriage alliances with Genghis Khan's descendants to gain status and credibility. He also unashamedly used Islam as a tool for gaining popular support whenever it was to his political or military advantage (in a way that would now be heavily cracked down upon under Karimov's regime). Timur thought of himself as a great 'player' and likened his political prowess to that of a chess master. He may have 'settled' to a certain extent among his magnificent architectural achievements at Samarkand but in order to stay in power he had to keep moving on and conquering new lands. Like Genghis Khan, he retained his nomadic spirit and was scared of becoming too soft, too settled or too comfortable. Also, like Genghis and many leaders of today, he was a master manipulator of both image and fear – he could only sustain his position of power by perpetuating a fear not so much of himself as of any alternative. Maybe that is what Karimov really sees in him?

Khiva

Torn Apart • Slaves to the Grind • Desertification
Black Death Renaissance • Shackled and For Sale
Standing to Attention • Love for the Other

Yet again I rolled into Bukhara on the night train. This time I knew where to get the *marshrutka* into town and where to go once I got there. I knew that I would feel really rough if I had just gone straight from the train station to the long-distance bus station so instead I returned to the guest house where I had stayed before and asked if I could just rent a room for a couple of hours and get some breakfast. I offered US$6 instead of the US$10 I had paid previously and they seemed happy to accept. After a chance to change my clothes, use a decent bathroom and sit down for a proper breakfast, I felt surprisingly refreshed and ready to continue with my journey. I paid another couple of dollars to a friend of the guest house's manager to take me to the bus station from where I negotiated a place in a battered shared taxi that was heading to Khiva. We were soon heading out of the sprawling suburbs of Bukhara and on into an increasingly hot and harsh landscape.

As we clattered through the Kyzylkum Desert, the driver reached across and offered me some pills. When I asked him what they were, he shrugged. Sometimes the drivers would take nicotine pills rather than smoking, but the chewing tobacco had already been passed around. When it was time to spit out the dregs, they would push open their doors and gob out huge streams of brown spittle into the passing desert. If the timings were wrong and the wind in the wrong direction, the back seat passengers would be splattered with the chewed-out remains. I was wary of accepting an unknown quantity of what I assumed to be amphetamines. The Uzbek guys on the back seat laughed at my hesitation and reached forward to grab a handful.

I had gotten used to being in vehicles that were pulled over by the *militsia*. After checking our documents and a brief exchange with the driver, we would be on our way. This time was different. As a foreigner, I had expected to be the one who was subjected to the third degree from the armed police, but they didn't even ask me see my passport. They asked me what country I was from but just to pass the time. As we dragged ourselves out of the sweltering taxi, the relief at escaping the cramped metal box soon evaporated with direct exposure to the brutal midday sun. We shuffled around in the desolation and waited. More *militsia* emerged to needle the passengers and poke around the car. They grew bored and wandered off. We waited some more. The driver returned to the taxi with yet another armed interrogator and they drove off into the desert. Nobody asked what was going on. When the taxi returned and parked further up on the other side of the road, we all hauled up our bags again and trudged over. The tatty old taxi had straddled a previously unseen inspection pit from where the search began in earnest. Once the contents of the car had been emptied – including the seats padding and covers – they used whatever they could find to tear it apart. Our driver lowered himself into the pit and joined in. As screws and bolts and other bits of metal were hastily removed, they were left abandoned in the roadside dust. I thought about jumping down and joining in – at least the car above would provide some protection from the unforgiving sun – but instead sank into the same infectious lethargy that had consumed my fellow passengers.

After far too long, a transit van pulled up next to the inspection pit. I had assumed the occupants would be more *militsia* but they just looked like normal Uzbek guys in jeans and t-shirts. They stood for a while, observing the deconstruction, before also jumping into the pit and collaborating in the carnage. I asked another of the passengers what they were looking for – I think he understood but just shrugged. We crouched alongside our dismantled ride and passed around the remains of our warm drinking water. Eventually, the *militsia* – and anybody else who had joined in – lost interest and wandered away, leaving us to try to put it all back together again as best as we could. As we were about to leave, I noticed that some of the nuts and bolts from below had been left behind. I passed them over to the taxi driver who stared at them for a few seconds before shrugging and throwing them onto the floor of the passenger seat. It didn't seem to matter. We headed back to the wilderness.

We eventually rattled into Urgench, the capital of Khorezm, where the other passengers were dropped off. Around twenty minutes or so later we were slowly rumbling through ancient gateways onto the cobbled streets of Ichon-Qala, the walled centre of historic Khiva. I found another great value room at Meros Guest House and set out to explore the city as the light began to fade.

Following a Soviet conservation programme in the 1970s and 1980s, Khiva has a reputation for being something of an overly sanitized 'museum-city'. While it's true that the attraction rich centre of Ichon-Qala revolves around the needs of the coachloads of French and German tourists, by the early evening it can often seem almost deserted by the tourists who have been bussed of to their nights of 'cultural' entertainment. You also don't have to wander very far out of the centre to see that it's not quite as sanitized as you might first believe. Away from the tourist zones there is still a great deal of poverty and up until well into the twentieth century, Khiva was still a centre for the trade in Persian and Kurdish slaves. Widespread slavery only came to an end in the 1920s under the Bolsheviks but bonded and forced child labour is still quite common within Uzbekistan, especially within the cotton industry.

Standing proud around the corner from the Meros Guest House was a magical mixture of mosques, minarets and *medressas* that just about managed to seem more like an ancient city than an old-world theme park. As dusk embraced the city and the stallholders put their offerings to rest for the night, I wandered through the stone-laid streets taking in sight after sight. Soon after entering a dilapidated alley you would emerge in front of yet another mosque or *medressa* where small grubby children would enthusiastically greet you with a friendly 'hello'. This would soon be followed by a plea for 'bon-bon'. They wanted pens and had learnt to expect them from tourists. I tried to explain that I had no extra pens to give away. They seemed doubtful but unconcerned – there would be other tourists with other pens but not tonight. Even Katya the camel seemed resigned to the fact that no more tourists would be clambering up on her back for today. After an unremarkable meal in an attractive and centrally located *chaikhana* – that was strangely devoid of the clearly desired tourists – I returned to the guest house.

Sitting on the sofa outside my room were three young Dutch guys. They were brothers with a shared desire to be somewhere different. Tomorrow they would leave for Nukus to visit the acclaimed art museum. From there they were heading for the port of Moynaq. It used to be a fishing town but the coast of the Aral Sea now lies more than 150 kilometres away. Tourists go to take pictures of beached ships rusting in the newly formed Aral Desert. The Aral Sea used to be the fourth largest lake in the world and about half the size of England until Soviet planners starting tapping the rivers that fed it in order to irrigate the cotton fields. Despite Uzbekistan's mainly poor-quality desert soil, the Soviet Union decided that intensive cotton production would lead to a great leap forward economically for the Soviet textile industry. As cotton production rose, the Aral Sea shrank dramatically. The level of the sea dropped by about 16 metres, it dried up into two smaller parts, and as well as most of the fish dying so did much of the other surrounding wildlife. As the once-sizable fishing industry collapsed and the environmental devastation led to a whole host of health problems, most of the former population deserted the surrounding towns.

Along with the competition over oil and natural gas there is likely to be increasing tension along the Silk Road over access to the remaining water supplies as both global warming and population continue to rise. With the health and livelihoods of so many in the region destroyed there is a widespread concern that current levels of dissatisfaction will inevitably bolster the support of the politicized Islamic groups that the current regime feel so threatened by; this will, in all likelihood, only result in further repression, human rights abuses and the kind of political instability that only perpetuates poverty.

As if things couldn't get any worse for the former fishing communities of the Aral Sea, there is also the matter of 'Voz', the Soviet Union's main testing site for biological weapons. Vozrozhdeniye (Renaissance) Island used to be isolated in the middle of the Aral Sea but the sea has now shrunk so much that it will soon be connected to the mainland. Biological and chemical weapons were buried in huge pits on the island in stainless steel canisters and there is now a real fear that spores from these buried plagues could leak out and be spread into the wider environment through what remains of the local wildlife. In some of the pits, anthrax sludge is already beginning to leach up through the sand and a number of plagues are believed to have originated in the area and then been spread along the Silk Road. It may well be that the Silk Road itself will undergo something of a renaissance itself – only this time instead of carrying silk, art and precious jewels, it will instead be carrying smallpox, anthrax and the bubonic plague.

* * *

The atmosphere within the walled fortress of Ichon-Qala was completely different the next morning. The stone clad streets were bustling with coachloads of Uzbek school children and French or German coffin dodgers. The stall in front of Katya the camel was doing a roaring trade in silly hats and the cheap but poor-quality ice-creams were proving to be (if not exactly popular) at least good sellers.

Khiva has existed since way before the eighth century as a minor fort and Silk Road trading town, but it wasn't until well after Timur laid waste to Konye-Urgench ('old' Urgench – just over the border in Turkmenistan) in 1388 that Khiva rose to prominence. When the Uzbek Shaybanids succeeded what was left of the Timurid Empire, they founded a new state in Khorezm and in 1592 chose Khiva as their capital. For more than three centuries, much of Khiva's wealth derived from the busy slave market. Most of the slaves were brought by Turkmen tribesman from the surrounding deserts and steppes but when Russia began to expand its empire into Central Asia many of its citizens also found themselves shackled and for sale in the market. It wasn't until 1873 that the Russians finally forced the Khanate into becoming a mere vassal of the Tsar and not until 1920 that the Bolsheviks finally dispensed with the Khan all together.

I bought an entrance ticket for Kuhna Ark: the fortress and residence of the former Khans. A series of small museums featured displays in the rooms that not so long ago made up the arsenal, barracks and harem of the former rulers. The Zindon (Khan's jail) shows pictures of those who displeased the Khan being thrown from the tops of the minarets or being tied up in sacks with furious wild cats. I edged past hordes of Uzbek school children stomping up the Ark's tower at the edge of the West Gate. From there you could look down on to the nearby Kalta Minor Minaret. This squat but ornate tower was begun in 1851 by Mohammed Amin Khan who dreamed of it becoming the tallest minaret in the world. Unfortunately the Khan dropped dead in 1855 so his massive erection remained short and stumpy but perfectly formed. The tallest minaret in Khiva is a part of the Islom-Hoja Medressa that was constructed as recently as 1910. I gave a dumpy woman in a headscarf some money to go up it and began my ascent around the spiralling stone stairs. This was made rather awkward by the sheer number of canoodling young couples in the way. As you approached they would meekly pull away from each other and make out as if they just happened to be pausing for breath before squeezing into the wall to let you through. I can't remember ever seeing young Uzbek couples kissing or even holding hands in the streets but it seemed to be perfectly acceptable to indulge in a quick game of tonsil tennis as camera-wielding tourists barged past in a dimly lit minaret. Maybe this was the 'in place' for young Khivans to take their dates? Maybe it was lucky?

From the top you could see down on to the whole of the fortified inner city and out towards the huge rusting Ferris wheel in a park beyond the grand North Gate. It may have seemed like a busy tourist site by Silk Road standards but if Khiva were almost anywhere else in the world then it would be as overflowing with tourists as St Mark's Square in Venice or the Acropolis in Rome. As it was, by the late afternoon most of the school buses and tourist coaches had departed for the day leaving behind just a few locals, stallholders and independently minded travellers to wander the winding alleyways in search of green tea, *plov* and kebabs.

Back at the Meros Guest House I bumped into Jimmy and Kiaro, who I had met in Samarkand the week before. When the conversation turned to relationships, they both half-mockingly professed a desire to meet that special other person. I couldn't help wondering why they weren't together; they were both young, attractive, from the same kind of background and shared the same interests. I was going to ask them why they couldn't just pork each other but I thought that this might raise some awkward questions (I am rarely this restrained when it comes to my deep-rooted nosiness but for once I managed to resist the temptation to pry). Jimmy asked me if I was planning to write a book. As I hadn't mentioned anything about this I was a little surprised by the question. When I replied that I was, he wanted to know if he would be in it. I told him that he might be so had to promise to make him look good (it was probably Kiaro's fault that they weren't playing Mr Wobbly hides his helmet).

* * *

I still had another day to wait before I could enter Turkmenistan as I had had to give exact dates for my five-day transit visa and I had wanted to allow enough time to have visited Osh in Kyrgyzstan – assuming I had managed to sort out my visa difficulties. I decided to explore a bit further afield and set off out of the walled old city and into the sprawling outer city of Dishon-Qala. Beyond the heavily restored tourist zone, Khiva looked pretty much like any other Soviet Central Asian city. In contrast to the atmospheric winding lanes within Ichon-Qala, the streets were too wide for the amount of traffic and the buildings were spaced too far from each other to give any sense of community. The dusty park attracted some crowds but the dilapidated old Ferris wheel seemed to have ground to a halt some time ago.

Not far from the fortified walled city were the remains of another large stone wall. It used to go on for 6 kilometres and completely surround the whole of the city but only a rubbish-strewn section of the crumbling ramparts remained. It wasn't the kind of place any other tourists went to. Other than the typically ornate Isfandiyar Palace, there was little to see. I couldn't even find any decent normal shops. I would assume that most of the locals did their real shopping in the much larger Urgench as the shops within the inner city seemed almost entirely aimed at tourists. When I had asked for a deodorant at the Deichon Bazaar near the East Gate, the seller had tried to charge me US$10 for it so I decided to try instead at the types of shops the locals would visit. When I did eventually track down the closest thing they seemed to have to a supermarket (actually more like a Soviet-stocked corner shop), I was surprised at how expensive just normal everyday products were. Despite most of the goods' poor quality and generally low level of wages, many everyday items turned out to be far more expensive than in the West. Luckily the food, transport and particularly the accommodation were still great value.

My feet were now quite sore from all the traipsing up and down I'd been doing over the past couple of days, so I hobbled back to Meros Guest House for a rest. On a table in the dining room sat a proudly displayed hardback book by Christopher Aslan Alexander called *A Carpet Ride to Khiva.* I picked it up and started to flick through. The book revolved around the British author's seven-year stay in Khiva and the work he did in setting up a traditional carpet-making business in a disused *medressa.* As well as helping to employ and pass on skills to many people who otherwise had been denied the opportunity, he also helped to set up the guest house I was staying in while he lived there as their long-time lodger. Only on being denied entry back into Uzbekistan did he return to England and write the book (I ordered it off Amazon when I, myself, returned to England).

After reading the first couple of chapters, the family chatted to me about Alexander's stay in the house and suggested I visit the carpet factory featured in the book. I normally avoid those kinds of places like the plague as I worry that I'll get hassled into buying the kinds of things that, even if I wanted, I would not want to carry. Fortunately, when I explained at the factory about the book they were more than happy to show me around. It was probably quite clear from my appearance that I was unlikely to be ordering a full-sized traditionally hand-made carpet at thousands of dollars, but they seemed to be happy to take the long-haul road of simply letting people know that they exist.

I took another walk along the top of the city walls to once more catch the sunset over the mystical skyline of Khiva, then returned to the Bir Gumbaz restaurant with its perfect view of the Kalta Minor Minaret. After paying for my green tea and a large bowl of *plov,* I still had some Uzbek *sum* that I wanted to use up before I left for Turkmenistan the next morning. I didn't quite have enough to pay for a Bounty chocolate bar but the lady who ran the restaurant let me take it anyway. They were nice like that.

Turkmenistan

Dashogus and Konye-Urgench

Divide and Rule • Dancing for Dictators • The Decline and Fall of Civilization • The Never-Ending March of Time • Deformed in the Desert • Prayers of the Barren • Like Father, Like Son Fighting for Freedom • Drunk and Disorderly

I paid in US dollars to be driven the hour or so from Khiva to the Turkmenistan border post. This was by far the easiest and most practical option. Not many foreigners crossed at this point and the customs guards seemed confused as to what I was doing there. When one of them asked me why I would want to visit Turkmenistan, I mumbled something about how I thought it would be interesting. 'Why?' he said, as his expression changed from curiosity to pity. After negotiating through the various obstacles on both sides of the border I eventually emerged the other side of some large metal gates into Turkmenistan. There was a single small wooden money exchange booth that was closed up and a few would-be taxis. I joined a nearly full shared taxi heading just down the road to Dashogus and paid my share with a couple of US dollars.

Dashogus (pronounced 'dash house') is different from the rest of Turkmenistan. Being just over the border from Uzbekistan, many of the population are actually of Uzbek rather than Turkmen descent. This part of Central Asia used to be a part of Khorezm, but when Stalin divided up the Soviet Union he deliberately tore apart regions with arbitrary borders in order to keep them divided and therefore easier to control.

In less than twenty minutes we were cruising along the main strip of Dashogus past widely spaced anonymous concrete buildings. This was apparently the town centre but there was hardly anyone on the streets and there appeared to be virtually no shops. The driver dropped me off outside Hotel Dashogus, the only real budget hotel, and I hauled my backpack up to reception. It didn't look too promising. The whole reception area resembled a building site and after being passed around a few times I eventually had it confirmed that the whole hotel was closed for renovation. Unfortunately, as well as being the only real budget choice, Hotel Dashogus was by far the biggest in the whole area. Consequently most of the other more expensive hotels in the town were now full up. I was told that the Hotel Uzboy was full and when I eventually tracked down the Hotel Diyarbekir I was rather abruptly informed that they had no room and half-heartedly pointed in the direction of some other hotel. Not surprisingly, with no map or proper directions, I couldn't find it. Feeling a little frustrated I returned to the Hotel Diyarbekir to see if I could persuade someone to write down some directions to this other hotel for me. As I walked back through the foyer the surly middle-aged receptionist barked 'passport' at me. Having already handed over my passport at least ten times in the last hour or so, I handed it over yet again without a thought. 'Forty dollars,' she demanded. It began to dawn on me that she had actually deemed to let me stay in her hotel after all and wasn't just randomly demanding to inspect my passport in order to satisfy her own nosiness or deeply ingrained sense of petty bureaucracy. I hadn't really wanted to spend that much but I thought it was best to take a room while I still had a chance. I handed over the cash and was led into a suite with a separate balcony, bedroom and dining room complete with chandelier. This seemed a bit posh for me – I was more used to dossing in hostels.

Alone in the room, I began to notice that it wasn't quite as upmarket as I'd first thought. There were stains on the carpet, the paint was starting to peel off and there were cracks across the ceiling. The hotel had supposedly been built just a few years ago but it was already going to seed. The inevitable decline of once flashy but shoddily made and poorly maintained buildings would become something of a recurrent theme within Turkmenistan; every new attempt at grandiosity seemed doomed to rapid disrepair. I turned on the old-fashioned portable TV to see if there was anything worth watching. There really wasn't. All of the channels seemed to be showing rows of Turkmen citizens marching up and down in rather ridiculous-looking national costumes. Despite having died a few years earlier, former President Saparmurat ('Turkmenbashi') Niyazov still managed to have his picture raised on giant placards over the goose-stepping masses (it may actually have been the current President Berdymukhamedov as he looks remarkably similar to Turkmenbashi and is rumoured to be his illegitimate son). Although most of the people outside were dressed in the usual Soviet garb of cheap grey suits, jeans or tracksuits, all of the citizens shown on television seemed to be subjugating themselves to their glorious leader while decked out in fancy dress. It looked like a Nazi rally for Morris dancers.

There didn't seem to be anywhere open to change money so I set off in search of something resembling a bank. Instead I found a bar at the side of the road that also offered food and a reasonable rate for my dollars. They only seemed to have one kind of dish on the menu so I ordered that. They brought me two dishes that were both chicken and didn't seem to mind when I sent one back. It seemed like it was a bit of a novelty to them to have anybody turn up at all. Everyone around the bar seemed friendly and keen to help. I got the feeling I could easily have found somewhere cheaper – or even free – to stay for the night, if I had just turned up at this bar to start with. They even bundled me off in a ridiculously cheap taxi where I caught another absurdly cheap, shared taxi that was heading towards Konye-Urgench (as the state-subsidized petrol is only a few pence a litre, one of the main sources of revenue for the residents of Dashogus is smuggling fuel across the Uzbek border).

The other guys in the shared taxi couldn't speak much English but they were curious and friendly. I showed them pictures from my trip on the screen of my compact digital camera as we rattled through the barren landscape. After about ninety minutes or so the driver dropped the other guys off around the nondescript centre of modern-day Konye-Urgench and then took me to the Nejameddin Kubra Mausoleum. There wasn't much to see here either apart from a few small mausoleums and a museum. Ten minutes was enough to have seen everything and I was a bit disappointed that that was all there was to it. I hadn't realized but the sights of the ancient city were actually in two locations and this was just the smaller one. Fortunately the driver then dropped me off at the larger complex of southern monuments before leaving me to make my own way back to Dashogus.

The grand but desolate southern monuments protruded from the lifeless soil as the few remaining flowerings of what was once an oasis of civilization. Genghis Khan laid siege to the city in 1221 in revenge for the murder of his envoys in Otrar by Mohammed II. The citizens put up a good fight but were eventually drowned by the Mongol hordes when they managed to divert the waters of the Amu-Darya across the city. The city was eventually re-established under Mongol rule as part of the Golden Horde but was flattened again by Timur in 1388 as he considered the revitalized city of Urgench to be a threat to Samarkand. The city again lived through a minor renaissance in the sixteenth century but was eventually abandoned for good when the Amu-Darya changed its course. Konye-Urgench has now been recognized by UNESCO as a World Heritage Site, but it is unlikely ever to rival nearby Khiva as an international tourist attraction (even if the Turkmen government were to deem to honour its potential visitors with tourist visas).

Not far from the small wooden ticket booth, and a rather smelly public pit toilet, towered the Turabeg Khanym complex.

Many have assumed that this building was a mausoleum but as it appears to have had some kind of heating system this seems unlikely. The component parts of a geometric mosaic across the underside of its dome make up a giant calendar – it apparently signifies humanity's insignificance in the march of time. Further on was the slightly wonky Gutlug Timur Minaret, the only surviving part of Urgench's main mosque and one of the tallest minarets in Central Asia. It looked like it might not be for much longer. As I walked over to get a closer look I turned around to respond to a cheery 'good morning' (it was the middle of the afternoon but as I had only just been reminded of our insignificance in time it seemed petty to quibble). Unfortunately I was neither cool nor collected enough not to flinch at the site of my greeter's head. He looked like a fully sized dwarf in a shell suit. Northern Turkmenistan is noted for its exceptionally high rates of birth defects – the closer you get to the blighted area around the remains of the Aral Sea, the more deformities you are likely to encounter (this is often blamed on the pesticides, and other chemicals used in the intense cultivation of cotton, that were blown across the surrounding villages and towns as the fields dried to desert). I tried to seem open and friendly but I think he could tell that I had been somewhat alarmed by his unfortunate appearance. I moved swiftly on towards some more isolated mausoleums that may once have been Zoroastrian temples (hardly anybody seems to agree on anything about Konye-Urgench) and up a dusty mound to the Kyrk Molla burial site. Apparently, this is where the citizens of Konye-Urgench held their last stand against the marauding Mongols. Old rags and bits of cloth had been tied onto head-high sticks that were planted into the desolate soil – this was something of a fertility ritual for local women who also come to roll down the mounds in the hope of being impregnated. Why anybody would associate such desolate remains of civilization, and multiple mounds of once-slaughtered corpses, with getting up the duff seems difficult to imagine – you could hardly imagine a more barren, more ruined and less fertile location.

Apart from the single wooden ticket shack and the shared pit toilet there were few of the facilities that you would expect at a World Heritage Site. There were hardly even any tourists – there was only me and a couple of Turkmen families in headscarves and shell suits. I really wasn't sure how I was going to get back to Dashogus for the night so I started walking down the road from the entrance way in the hope of getting a lift to the bus station (although as I didn't have a map I had no idea where it was). Just down from the main gates was a small general store with a few tables and chairs. As I suspected that it might be a while until I found anywhere else, I popped in for my usual Central Asian snack of a Snickers bar and a cup of three-in-one instant coffee. The woman who worked there spoke a little English and seemed keen to talk. She was only thirty but her cheap floral dress and general style would generally have been seen on a much older woman in Europe. While the clothes and styles of Kazakhstan were reminiscent of the fashions of 1970s Britain, many of the styles to be found on young women in this part of Turkmenistan were closer to that of the 1950s. In this part of Central Asia most people still married young and wore the same styles as their parents and their parents before them. Despite being only a few miles from the Uzbek border, the U-Girls from cosmopolitan Tashkent seemed to belong to another time and place all together.

I showed the woman some pictures on my camera from my trip but when I pointed out my wife she was clearly bothered by something. She seemed to be quite shocked at her cut-off denim shorts. To expose the top of your thighs in public was clearly inappropriate behaviour for a young lady in northern Turkmenistan. Just to make sure I had got the point, she lifted up her granny dress over her knickers and pointed to the top of her thigh. I apologized for my wife's scandalous exposure of her upper leg and was thankfully forgiven. (A few months later I happened across a picture of this woman on the Internet when I was searching through some information on Turkmenistan. I know this sounds unreasonable but I felt annoyed that she had clearly been fraternizing with some other foreigners. I wouldn't be at all surprised if she had showed those tourists her knickers as well. Hussy.)

I carried on walking down the road but it was starting to get dark and there were hardly any cars around. I had been hoping to come across a taxi but as this seemed unlikely I decided to start sticking my arm out at any car that came along the road. The second or third one to come along stopped and for a small fee took me to the bus station where I easily found another shared taxi heading back to Dashogus where they dropped me off right outside the hotel.

The woman at reception barked 'passport' at me again. This didn't really seem necessary as I had already shown her my passport when I checked in but I had resigned myself to the endless checking of passports and other official documents (as well as the multiple passport checks I had encountered when crossing the border, I had also had to show my passport and sign some official-looking documents at both of the Konye-Urgench archaeological sites). Once it had been deemed appropriate to allow me access to my room, I dumped my bag in my 'luxury' suite and headed off to a nearby Internet café where I again had to hand over my passport for the duration of my stay. I had been under the impression that the Internet facilities in Turkmenistan would be poor to non-existent so was surprised to find that this new-looking Internet café had far faster broadband than anywhere I had tried in Uzbekistan. I wondered how much of my Internet activity was really going to be logged against my passport details. It seemed difficult to believe that any government would really care about anything I said or did, but at the same time I knew that the monitoring of Internet activity and even the bugging of some hotel rooms was still a reality in paranoid former Soviet states. I checked a few sites to see what was being censored but found that only the usual Facebook, YouTube and a few travel sites were being blocked. It seemed a little strange when about twenty minutes later a young guy with perfect English – unusual enough in itself – came in and introduced himself as an IT specialist. He pointed at my combat trousers and wanted to know if I was in the military. I turned around to show him my long plaited hair as I thought this would make it clear I wasn't a member of anybody's army. His response was a blank stare, so I politely explained I was here on holiday. Despite appearing a little incredulous he politely managed not to blurt out 'why?' When he said that he also worked as a translator for the US Peace Corps, it was my turn to seem surprised. I had been led to believe by the American soldier I had met in Samarkand that the US had basically given up on all 'soft diplomacy' with Turkmenistan. (I looked this up later on and found out that even after the Peace Corps had withdrawn from Uzbekistan, in response to the Andijon Massacre, it had still continued to maintain a presence throughout Turkmenistan.) Maybe Turkmenistan had just infected me with its paranoia?

For a town of its size, Dashogus didn't seem to have many places to eat in. I decided to check out the Kafe Manet but it appeared to have been taken over by a wedding party. I was about to walk out of the foyer in search of somewhere else when I was spotted by a group of young drunken guys in neatly ironed shirts and chinos. Misha introduced himself and explained that his family had booked out the whole restaurant for his nineteen-year-old brother's wedding. They insisted that I joined them for shots of vodka and plenty of food. It would have seemed churlish to refuse. I was dragged over to a table near the dad and granny dancing and plied with plates of whatever dishes remained. As soon as I took a sip of vodka they would fill up my glass to the top again. Not having drunk for a while I was soon feeling the effects of the undiluted spirit. I couldn't fault their warmth and generosity but as they all became increasingly drunk I began to become more uncomfortable. I had clearly been adopted as some kind of exotic foreigner who was somehow bringing honour to Misha and his friends simply by virtue of being from abroad. I didn't want to seem impolite but the huge amounts of vodka that I was being pressured into gulping back were starting to make my head spin.

As their older relatives were clearly beginning to leave and the restaurant was already cleaning up, I thanked them all for their hospitality and tried to say goodbye. Misha wasn't having it. He insisted that I stay at his house tonight and be his guest. This was going to get awkward. As well as having already paid out US$40 to the hotel, I also knew enough to be a little wary of excessive vodka drinking in former Soviet countries. The atmosphere could very quickly change. Added to which, I had no intention of waking up in the middle of nowhere in some stranger's house when they were all badly hung over.

I thanked them again and tried to leave but Misha grabbed my arm and begged me to say at his house. The more desperate he became for me to stay with him, the more I wanted to escape. I tried explaining that I needed to get up early tomorrow to catch the bus to Ashgabat but this didn't seem to help. I explained that all my things were still at the hotel and I needed to go back there. By now we were out on the street and taking turns at taking pictures of each other. They all wanted to have their picture taken next to me. Eventually they relented and I staggered back to my tatty hotel suite. I turned on the TV while I used the bathroom. On every available channel the masses were still dancing for dictators. I crawled into my double bed and surrendered to my vodka-driven dreams.

Ashgabat

Desolation Angels • Different Worlds • Ozymandias Reborn When Babies Rule the World • Islam's Resurgence • The Adulation of Tyrants • Spiritual Guidance • Tearing Down the House • Ivory Towers Turkmenbashi's Land of Fairy Tales • There be Monsters • Jesus Christ Pose • Well-Ordered Emptiness • Masters and Slaves • Lost and Found Ethnic Diversity • State of Control

After breakfast on my own in the hotel dining room, I caught another cheap taxi to Bai Bazaar in the hope of getting a bus to Ashgabat. The crowded bazaar was clearly where all the normal people went shopping rather than in the deserted downtown area that I had been staying in. Before I could actually make it from the taxi to the bus, however, I was mobbed by the long-distance taxi drivers. They started off demanding US$200 but the price rapidly came down as I got closer and closer to the soon-to-be-departing bus. By the time I had clambered my way through the crowds to climb on board, their price had dropped down to US$30. The bus driver laughed at their persistence and then asked for the equivalent of US$4 in Turkmen *manat*. This felt like a good deal for a 600-kilometre ride from one end of the country to the other across the entire length of the Karakum Desert.

The bus seemed to be mainly full of old men with tatty tweed jackets, patchy grey stubble and missing teeth (although as this was northern Turkmenistan they may only have been about thirty-five). Mineral bottles full of green sludge rolled up and down under the seats as we trundled out of the city and into yet more desolation. The friendly old guy sitting next to me picked up one of the sludge bottles as it rattled past and gobbed his chewed-out tobacco into it before letting it roll on under the other passengers. I turned down his kind offer of some rancid-looking chewing tobacco and offered him some biscuits that I had bought in the bazaar. This seemed to please him.

After three hours or so of trundling through the desert, with nothing much to see apart from the occasional two-humped Bactrian camel, we eventually pulled up next to some ruined concrete buildings in the middle of nowhere. We all wandered off to our little patches of scrub and small, gritty sand dunes to empty our bladders while we had the chance. The old guy who had been sitting next to me seemed keen to lead me into the ruined shell of these abandoned outposts. Through the doorway of one half-destroyed building was a small makeshift café. Other passengers ushered me to join them on an ornate Turkmen carpet laid down among the rubble, while two old women in floral aprons brought us out mugs of Nescafé 3-in-1. They appeared to have boiled up the water on a fire in another room through a hole in the wall. I wondered how our baristas had arrived at these ruins in the middle of the Karakum Desert; we had seen no signs of habitation since leaving behind the outskirts of Dashogus and there seemed to be little opportunity for making any money in this inhospitable terrain, outside of boiling up water for instant coffee.

On returning to civilization – or at least the outskirts of Turkmenistan's capital, Ashgabat – the bus driver called his teenage son on his mobile phone, as he could speak good English. They went out of their way to find a taxi that would take me, for an agreed price, to the Amanov Homestay. As this wasn't really an official hotel and only travellers on transit visas – as opposed to full guides requiring tourist visas – can actually stay there, it was kind of difficult to find. When we eventually got there, the driver demanded far more money. I gave him what we had agreed on and he solemnly nodded. I was allocated a narrow, bumpy bed in a dorm I would share with two guys from Berlin who had driven up from Iran. Having their own four-wheel drive had meant they could visit the Kow Ata Underground Lake (where you could swim in the sulphurous pools 65 metres underground) and would also be able to visit the Darvaza Gas Craters on the way to Konye-Urgench. These fire craters in the middle of the Karakum Desert have often been likened to the gates of hell. I recognized another four-wheel drive parked outside. It belonged to the Swiss couple I had previously met in Tashkent.

I wanted to find somewhere nearby to eat as it was already dark and I hadn't had anything other than biscuits since my hotel breakfast. The homestay was only a couple of blocks back from an immaculately maintained strip of park and shiny new tower blocks that ran through the centre of the city. Most of the run-down suburbs of the city, with dirt roads and crumbling walls like those around the Amanov Homestay, were steadily being bulldozed to make way for broad, open, Soviet-style boulevards, dotted with shiny white towers that seemed closer in style to Vegas casinos than to apartment blocks. The only nearby eatery was a posh café with outside seating that overlooked the fastidiously manicured lawns and ornate fountains of the park. The affluent and urbane clientele seemed to belong in a different world from the workers left scratching for a living in the dusty wastelands of more rural Turkmenistan. After settling up the bill for a very average and overpriced meal (by Central Asian standards) I was drawn up along the Vegas-style strip towards the ever-changing illuminations of the Arch of Neutrality. As the bright neon lights glowed from a lurid green to an ostentatious purple, I began to make out a shining golden figure perched above what seemed to resemble a giant toy spaceship from the 1950s. The surrounding spotlights picked out the 12-metre-high polished gold statue of President Niyazov (Turkmenbashi) standing proud upon just one of his many notoriously costly vanity projects. As the money had begun to pour in from Turkmenistan's huge reserves of natural gas, rather than investing in education, infrastructure or healthcare, Turkmenbashi had blown much of it on some of the most ill-conceived projects ever imagined by any of the world's dodgiest dictators. As well as a series of absurdly expensive monuments, museums and ministry buildings, he also blew millions on a 'House of Creativity' for journalists that was shaped like a giant book; an artificial river to run through Ashgabat; a giant man-made lake in the middle of one of the hottest deserts in the world (with water diverted from the rapidly diminishing Aral Sea); and in 2004 he exceeded even himself by ordering the construction of an ice palace just outside of Ashgabat that would be 'big and grand enough for one thousand people'.

As it was getting dark and I was keen to avoid being caught outside by the *militsia* after the evening curfew, I made my way back from the base of the Arch of Neutrality through the narrow strip of perfectly maintained park. I walked towards a young soldier, parading backwards and forwards, stiff legged, between the illuminated fountains and the neatly clipped shrubbery. Half-way through his solo procession, he started goose-stepping like a demented Nazi storm trooper. I was sure that he was about to stick his finger over his lip and execute an extravagant leg-swinging turnaround in the style of Basil Fawlty, when he noticed me watching and abruptly came to a halt. As I walked past, he said something. I didn't understand, so he pointed at my watch. When I showed him the time, his face dropped even further – it was clearly going to be some time before he finished his shift of pointlessly waiting. Even the funny walk couldn't cheer him up.

* * *

The next morning both the Swiss couple (whom I had only just met again) and the two guys from Berlin, took turns reversing their four-wheel drives out of the homestay's courtyard on to the pot-holed side road. The Swiss were heading for the Iranian border – the woman already decked out in the required headscarf

– and the Germans were planning to stop off at the renowned Tolkuchka Bazaar before stopping again at the Darvaza Gas Craters on the way to Konye-Urgench. After all the hustle and bustle of their preparations it seemed strangely quiet to be left in the courtyard on my own, sat at a picnic table with my Nescafé 3-in-1 and a slightly stale bread roll from the nearby corner shop. The owners then decided to let out their coop of pigeons so I retreated under the dormitory's awning to make sure they didn't crap on me.

After finishing my breakfast I walked back towards the Arch of Neutrality and the grandiose Independence Square. In order to make the neo-colonial-style government buildings as impressive as possible, huge television screens had been mounted up above the square. Their high-tech flashiness was rather let down by the fact that the only thing that seemed to be shown on them was the amateurish-looking national news channel. From what I could make out it seemed to be following the standard Soviet line of letting all the people know how lucky they were to be living in such a wonderful country under such a great leader. Nobody seemed to take a lot of notice. It must have stopped seeming funny a long time ago. The Arch of Neutrality looked just as odd, but far less colourful in the cold light of day. If you were to stare upwards to the great man for long enough then you could just about make out the golden statue slowly twirling around so that it always faced towards the sun.

I caught an escalator up one of the feet, in order to catch the lift to the top of the tower. I had expected it to be a real tourist centre – if only for day trippers to Ashgabat – and was surprised to find that the only people inside were a couple of men in grey suits at one of the tables, and an old woman with a mop. Inside it looked more like a run-down council building than anything you would expect to find inside a giant toy space ship. From the upper windows you could gaze down on to the parade grounds of Independence Square and the golden-domed

Palace of Turkmenbashi (this area was currently all boarded up and undergoing some extensive-looking rebuilding – I suspect that it had already started to fall down). To the left of the Ministry of Fairness (no, this isn't a joke), the Ruhhyet Palace and the Parliament buildings (all built by the French corporation Boygues Construction) was the equally bizarre Earthquake Memorial. On top of the museum built to commemorate the disastrous earthquake of 1948, in which it is estimated that over 176,000 people were killed (more than 10 per cent of the Turkmen SSR at the time), was a large bronze statue of a globe with an angry-looking bull on top of it. On closer inspection you could see that there was a baby sitting on top of the bull. The baby is supposed to be Turkmenbashi.

I walked around the Earthquake Museum but all the doors were locked. I shouldn't have been surprised. Slightly further down, beyond a small female-only army of state gardeners, was the Soviet war memorial with the obligatory eternal flame. Further on from this centre of state-sponsored ostentation stood the Azadi Mosque. Similar in size, scale and style to the Blue Mosque in Istanbul, it was inaugurated as recently as 1998. During Soviet times all religious observance had been heavily discouraged and it wasn't until after independence was forced upon it in 1991 that Turkmenistan's Islamic roots were officially permitted to resurface. Islam's resurgence, however, was heavily restricted. As long as Islam was associated with subservience and conformity, then Turkmenbashi would happily encompass it within the rigid state structures. He embraced traditional cultural values in an attempt to both gain popular support and to perpetuate the belief in the virtue of submission to a strong tribal leader. He even claimed that his own pseudo-spiritual writings in the *Rukhnama* (*Book of the Soul*) appeared by a miracle of Allah and would therefore be great for the Turkmen nation. This not-so-small green book became required reading for all Turkmen citizens, and all students were required to pass a formal exam on the *Rukhnama* before they could graduate. They even had to take a test on it before they could pass their driving test (the actual driving part probably wasn't such a priority). When the dumpy dictator spent more than US$100 million of the state's money on an enormous mosque in his home village of Kipchak, he made sure that his spiritual writings were engraved across the walls, side by side with extracts from the Koran. He even went on to claim that he was, in fact, the 'thirteenth prophet'. When Turkmenistan's Grand Mufti objected to having to read from the *Rukhnama* during services, he was jailed for twenty-two years under charges of treason.

The epically proportioned Azadi Mosque was pretty much empty. It could hold up to 5,000 Believers but there were only three other people in it and they were just the cleaners. I left my grubby trainers outside and wandered around in my socks as the three old ladies dragged their vacuum cleaners up and down expensive-looking Turkmen carpets. I tried to ask one of the cleaners if it was OK to take some pictures by pointing at my camera and then around the mosque. She just shrugged in a 'yeah, whatever' kind of way. On the way out I was warmly greeted by a devout-looking young man who shook my hand enthusiastically. He seemed delighted that a foreigner had bothered to visit his mosque. After a series of unfortunate deaths during its construction, it had never really caught on as a place of worship. Turkmenbashi seemed to go off the idea of Islam a bit when some religious groups refused to acknowledge him as their one and only true leader. As in Uzbekistan, the young, poor and frustrated who were drawn towards radical Islam as the only conceivable path towards political change were jailed, tortured and disappeared. Before dying of a massive heart attack in 2006, the tubby tyrant decided that enough was enough and banned the building of any more mosques.

The international posh coffee culture had even made it as far as Turkmenistan. Despite the pitifully low average wage in a country with such great wealth in natural resources, there were clearly still some people around in Ashgabat who had managed to get their hands on some of the wealth that Turkmenbashi had neglected to siphon off into his Swiss bank accounts. When the nouveau riche weren't blowing it on Vegas-style apartment blocks or imported Mercedes, they could hang out at the 'Coffee House'. You could tell it was aiming at an affluent clientele as there was a large plasma screen on the wall that was permanently tuned in to MTV. After indulging in a cappuccino and checking out the latest in a long line of bling-flashing Soviet R&B stars, I decided to check out what appeared to be Ashgabat's only bookshop. Other than a few ancient-looking picture books on the glories of Turkmenistan, and a couple of outdated thrillers, there appeared to be nothing to buy that wasn't written by, or in praise of, Turkmenbashi. Not surprisingly, the *Rukhnama* took pride of place among the Miras Bookshop displays. Turkmenbashi seemed to have overcome all Turkmen rivals to his literary dominance by having them jailed, and he certainly wouldn't have approved of any un-Turkmen literature polluting the thoughts of his citizens.

Feeling in need of some entertainment I decided to try to find my way to Turkmenbashi's Land of Fairy Tales. In order to build the US$50 million amusement park, Niyazov had ordered the bulldozing of the homes of hundreds of ordinary Ashgabat residents who were never properly compensated. Still, for that kind of money it looked set to seriously rival Disneyland itself. Unfortunately, I hadn't journeyed far down the road to this world of fun and fantasy before I found myself completely lost. I had confidently followed the road to the Promised Land, only to find that it led to ruins. All over Ashgabat, the run-down rambling houses of the poor were being torn down and replaced by yet more strangely isolated tower blocks. In this city of constant destruction and construction, no map would stay up to date for long. I walked back and up around the building site in search of a road or a landmark that would help me to get my bearings. I found myself at a crossroads and yet again checked my guidebook. Either side of me, bored, young military policemen loitered inconsolably. Everywhere you went in Ashgabat they would be standing around, guns in their holsters, heads in the clouds.

I decided not to ask directions from these bored young men with guns and, instead, traipsed down a long, straight boulevard, with sparsely spaced out tower blocks on either side. I assumed that these shiny white skyscrapers were blocks of flats built to house Ashgabat's displaced residents – except that nobody seemed to be living in them. There was the occasional gardener and plenty of cars were passing by, but there was little evidence of life or occupation within the gleaming, ivory towers. If the bubonic plague were to desolate Las Vegas, it would look like this. Outside of the showcase museums and public buildings in the centre of the city there seemed little in the way of entertainment for ordinary people. There were a few decent restaurants and I had noticed a couple of nightclubs but the strict curfew meant that anyone found walking around after ten at night would risk arrest from the hordes of bored young soldiers. There used to be cinemas but Niyazov forced them to close as he considered movies to be un-Turkmen. He had them changed into puppet theatres as he considered puppetry to be more in keeping with the Turkmen culture. He also banned opera, ballet and most theatre but was quite keen on traditional song and dance, providing it was used to praise the many virtues of their glorious leader. Still, at least he had built a big theme park to keep everyone amused. At US$50 million it was bound to be brilliant.

I didn't seem to be getting any closer to this Turkmen wonderland. I'd found a few people who seemed to understand a bit of English but they weren't much help. They were all very nice but seemed a little concerned that I was looking for a fairyland. My attempts at miming a roller coaster only added to the confusion. As I had already been walking for about forty minutes and all I could see ahead were yet more miles of the sparsely spaced Vegas tower blocks, I decided to head back. After another mile or so, I had the idea of getting up around the back of the tower blocks on the other side, to get a better view over the city. I couldn't be sure but I thought I had spotted the top of a giant plastic mountain. Between the Promised Land and me lay yet another building site. I couldn't be bothered to walk all the way back again along the official footpath, so decided just to walk straight through the construction zone. Strangely enough, loads of other people seemed to be doing the same thing. Everybody seemed to avoid walking along the wide, clean, official footpaths that seemed to lead you nowhere and left you feeling far more exposed than if you were stood out in the middle of a desert (until fairly recently this is exactly what much of it was). They seemed far happier to be squelching through muddy tracks and dodging industrial machinery. At least there was some human life to be found among the noise, dirt and chaos. I emerged onto some scrappy grassland and stepped through a broken fence towards a narrow, blue rail track. I could see the mountain now and it was definitely plastic. I had made it to the land of fairy tales.

As the grass was so overgrown, I headed off along the rail tracks, towards a huge brown lizard. There was a door in the side but it seemed to be locked and there were no signs or pictures to indicate what lay within the belly of the beast. I still wasn't sure if the amusement park was actually open. A few people were wandering around but the pedalos on the lake were still bound together and the train had yet to join me on the tracks. As I ducked around the lizard's head, I caught sight of a small blue rollercoaster. It was running and there were people on it. Their screams drew me closer.

I had been hoping for a kind of Central Asian Disneyland but it looked more like the kind of run-down amusement park that might still open up for a few months in the summer at one of the smaller British seaside towns. The rides were small, tired looking and mostly closed. There were a few stalls selling soft drinks and snacks, some operational dodgems and the small blue rollercoaster. I needed some vouchers before I could go on any rides and was directed to a woman in a headscarf at a drinks stall. She looked too young to be wearing a headscarf. Contrary to Turkmenbashi's preference for traditional Turkmen costumes, most of the young people at the land of fairy tales were just wearing jeans and t-shirts. She was probably a poor person. After buying some vouchers for about 80 cents each – the other rides only cost one voucher but the roller coaster cost two as it was the biggest and the best – I got into the front car and sat there on my own, feeling a bit silly. After a while, two middle-aged Turkmen women got in behind me. A few minutes later, the operator realized that this was about as busy as it was going to get and sent us trundling on our way. Every time we sped up or spun around a corner, the two women screamed. I clutched my bag between my legs and held on tight. A minute later it was all over. I needed more. The dodgems didn't tempt me – they were full of young kids and even I would have felt a bit silly as the only adult in among them. Instead, I went on the spinning teacup ride. I was their only customer. It wasn't that great. There seemed to be some kind of log flume that came out of the big plastic mountain. I followed a Turkmen family who had also spotted it. As we wound up the steps through the moulded plastic boulders, I became infected with their enthusiasm. Maybe this was where all the US$50 million went. I felt far more disappointed for them than for myself when we came up against yet another locked gate. Who knows how far they had come and how long they had saved for their big day out? Their faces dropped and we all trudged back down the plastic hill in search of more fun.

There was an opening – a way into the plastic mountain! Who knew what lay within? It turned out to be monsters. It looked like a kind of ghost train ride but without the train. The three young women at the desk seemed a bit surprised to see me. I'm not sure how much they understood me, but I pointed at the door and waved some vouchers at them. One of them took a voucher and led me into the darkness. As we walked into each room, she would stand to the side and press a button on the wall. A low, dramatic voice would then start to say something in Turkmen, while I stood admiringly in front of some papier mâché mythical creatures. She made me wait until the entire recording had finished before letting me go through to the next room where the whole process was repeated.

This room seemed to have some big cauldrons in it and what may have been wizards. I couldn't understand a word of the accompanying sound recording, but felt obliged to stand there looking respectful. In the room after, the woman offered to take my picture in front of some trolls (or, at least, the Turkmen equivalent to a troll). As monsters go, they seemed quite nice. We emerged from the darkness towards Soviet-style strip lighting, and I thanked my guide for my visit to the underworld and went in search of the toilets. They were huge and had clearly been designed to deal with crowds of hundreds. At first glance, they looked surprisingly posh, but on closer inspection it became clear that most of the toilets were now locked up or broken. I eventually found one that seemed usable but then I couldn't find the flush. There was a button on the side of the cubicle so I tried pushing that. Water squirted up through a hose and over my leg. As the back of the toilet seemed to have caved into the back of the wall, I reached through the hole and tried pulling something. This seemed to work and the toilet flushed. My next challenge would be washing my hands. Dozens of sinks were lined up in rows through the centre of the bathroom but none of them actually produced any water. Eventually I found a single working tap but as the sink below had been shattered, the water sprayed back over the front of my trousers. I pulled down my t-shirt as low as it would go and hoped that the gloom within the plastic mountain would help to hide the wet patches around my crotch. The grand opening to Turkmenbashi's Land of Fairy Tales had only been five years ago.

I still had some ride vouchers to use so emerged from the mountain to see if any of the other rides had opened up. A crowd of teenagers were queuing up for what looked like a revolving disk with benches facing inwards from the outer edge. I joined the queue and handed over the last of my vouchers. The kids at the front were urging their mates to join them but several refused. I should have wondered why. We walked up the steps and through a gate at the side on to the circular platform. We slowly spread out over the lightly padded benches and faced each other in anticipation. Two of the girls jammed their legs through the side of the entrance gate as if attempting to lock themselves in place. The disk started spinning and tilting and bumping up and down. I awkwardly grabbed the metal bar behind so as not to be thrown off the bench and down on to the kids across from me. As we spun into an almost vertical tilt we suddenly stopped. On the other side of the circle they lay on their backs looking up while on my side we held on to the metal bar at the back with all our strength. I couldn't believe there were no safety barriers or seatbelts. If we were to fall or slip we would crash down on those below, leaving cuts, bruises and broken bones in our wake. This would never be allowed in a civilized country! In most countries they would be terrified of being sued for millions if anybody was injured but I couldn't see that happening in Turkmenistan (not many dictators get taken to court in their own countries for negligence).

Just as I was losing my grip, we dropped down and started to spin around again. I followed the local's example and locked my arms around the bar above the bench – my arms might get dislocated but at least I'd have less chance of falling. I could see now why those two girls had locked their arms and legs around the bars at the entrance. I was starting to relax a bit when the real bumping kicked in. It was like being given the bumps by a hyperactive Turkmen troll. As I started to slide off the bench, the pummelling intensified. The edge of the bench pounded into the small of my back again and again. I willed for it to stop but the battering was relentless. Even the teenagers seemed shocked by the intensity of the assault. I couldn't be sure but I think the operator might even have let out an evil cackle before finally letting up on the bumping for more spinning and tilting. Just as we had almost slowed to a halt and some were heading towards the exit gate, he turned it up again and sent them sprawling across the floor. He eventually let us out and we hobbled back down the steps, nursing bruises and strains. Some of the survivors got back into the queue to have another go.

I staggered towards the exit, which actually turned out to be the grand entrance. It was a great hall with statues of Turkmen folk heroes and murals depicting their fairy tales. It pretty much looked like a low-budget Disneyland attraction that had been adapted to seem more 'Turkmen' – except that it hadn't been done on a low budget at all. In a country where most ordinary people are still dirt poor, it had cost a fortune.

I didn't know where I was and I wanted to go back to the Homestay. If I could only make my way to the centre of the city then I knew that I could find my way back. I scanned the skyline in the hope that somehow I would be shown the way and was rewarded by a shining light on the horizon. It was the last of the sunlight glistening off the 12-metre gold statue of Turkmenbashi stood arms wide open atop the mighty Arch of Neutrality. I was no longer lost. I limped towards my saviour.

* * *

The next morning I set off to visit the Turkmenbashi Cableway (yet another one of Niyazov's vanity projects – this one came in at US$20 million). I walked over to the nearby crossroads and stuck my arm out. Eventually I got a lift in a shared taxi with a driver who agreed a fare in *manat* and didn't simply demand an extortionate fee in US dollars as soon as he realized I was a foreigner. I was feeling quite pleased with both my language and negotiating skills until he took me to the cement works. I felt that my roadside mime of a cable car going through the mountains had been more than clear enough. Why would he have thought that I wanted to go to some factory in a muddy industrial estate? My attempts to point out the distant mountains were somewhat hampered by the ominously dark clouds that obscured the Kopet Dag. We drove off again but just seemed to be circling around. I was beginning to think that there probably wasn't much point in going up the cableway, anyway, with weather like this, when what appeared to be a giant ornate plunger came into view. I realized that this must be the Monument to the Independence of Turkmenistan, so asked the driver to drop me off there.

Underneath the monument was the Museum of Turkmen Values and not far across the road was the grand and rather lonely looking National Museum. These buildings appeared simply to have been abandoned at the end of the eerily spaced out and empty Berzengi suburb. Only old school Soviet city planning and pretension could ever have led to such well-ordered emptiness. I couldn't be bothered to enter either of the museums as I didn't want to pay out another US$10 to each of them just to look at some more old jewellery and pots. It didn't look as if anybody else was bothering to visit them either. Instead, I circled the Monument to Independence on my own, taking pictures of the surrounding statues of Turkmen warriors, the elaborate displays of fountains and the tackily ornate tower of the monument itself. It would have made a fine job of unblocking a pretentious giant's toilet.

I carried on through the empty park in the direction of the city centre and towards the Mayan-style pyramid that is the Altyn Asyr Shopping Centre. The building itself is supposedly the biggest fountain in the world. Unfortunately, up close it looks like just another Soviet-style grey concrete lump with some water dribbling down its sides. Inside was even more disappointing. Most of the shop spaces were empty. It seemed more like a run-down Eastern European council building than the upmarket international shopping centre it aspired to be. I got the lift to top of the pyramid and walked out into a surprisingly pleasant-looking restaurant with good views over the surrounding park and the city. After a quick look at the menu to make sure the prices weren't too extortionate, I sat down next to the large plate glass windows overlooking Ashgabat and ordered some ice-cream with waffles and a coffee. The service, the location and the ornate presentation of my dessert were all immaculate. On one day in Turkmenistan I would be drinking instant coffee from an old chipped mug among the rubble in some burnt-out ruins in the middle of the desert, and on the next slurping my morning coffee at an upmarket restaurant at the top of a concrete pyramid. Such huge contrasts in lifestyle seemed ever-present in Turkmenistan. While wealthy urbanites cruised along immaculate boulevards in their top of the range Mercedes, only a few metres back from these showcase streets, a class of workers only one generation removed from being desert nomads could be found driving over-laden donkeys and carts over pot-holed dirt tracks. I circled around the top of the pyramid staring out over the sparsely spaced out marble towers, the newly built ring roads and the well-ordered parks. On the horizon, beyond the last vestiges of sprinkler-saturated greenery, I could make out something else: it was the desert, waiting to return.

I carried on walking back towards the city. From my elevated position at the top of the pyramid I had made sure of my direction but if I followed the roads I was meant to I would soon find myself lost. Instead, I opted to follow my own sense of direction. Whenever a pathway ended in a building site I would simply carry on through the construction. Whenever a government ministry got in my way I would simply cut across its grounds. At first I had expected to be hassled by the multiple *militsia* but they seemed to take little notice – it would have taken far more than a little trespassing to have raised them from their lethargy.

On returning once more to the centre, I carried on to the Russian Bazaar. This large, crowded market was clearly where most people still chose to do their shopping rather than in the sterile and half-empty shopping malls that could only be reached by car. While the women in the more upmarket malls and restaurants around Ashgabat seemed generally European in both their facial features and style of dress, the women around the markets were far more likely to be found with the traditional Turkmen outfits and the two long plaits that were so favoured by Turkmenbashi (he was less approving of the Soviet-style gold dentistry that is also popular). When independence from the Soviet Union was forced upon it in 1991, many Russians left the country as it was made increasingly hard for them to find work without speaking Turkmen. You wouldn't necessarily have known this from Ashgabat, however, as most of the people with money seemed very Russian in style. The range of physical types to be found in Ashgabat was also far wider and more international than you might expect within such a closed country. As well as dark-skinned Turkmen tribesmen and affluent-looking blonde Russians there were also a surprising number of green- or blue-eyed red heads in traditional costumes. Many Turkmen, such as the inhabitants of nearby Nokhur, believe themselves to be descendants of Alexander the Great. They have their own variety of the Turkmen language and prefer to marry among themselves in order to preserve both their looks and the culture. Although lighter skin and hair colour is usually associated with higher levels of wealth and education, the red-headed Nokhur tribes people were something of an exception – for years, Nokhur was something of a byword among Soviet Turkmen for everything rural and backwards. As with Karimov in Uzbekistan, Niyazov attempted to build upon the ethnic identity of his people as a way of constructing a strong sense of national identity that was independent from its Soviet past (with him, of course, as 'Turkmenbashi' – 'leader of the Turkmen'). In reality, however, the Turkmen are a mixture of everything from Oghuz and Seljuk Turks to Persians, Arabs, Mongols and Europeans. The real identity of the Turkmen came from their pride in the nomadic lifestyle but their freedoms were heavily restricted with the advent of the Soviet era. It may be easier to control a state where the people are united but it's far harder to control a state when the people won't stay still.

After eating a chocolate hedgehog I returned to the Amonov Homestay where I met Nicco and Sarah. They were cycling from Europe to China and had just crossed over from Iran. As it would be impossible to cycle all the way across the Karakum Desert on a five-day transit visa, they had spent most of the day trying to sort out some transportation that would allow them to take their bikes on board. When they hadn't been doing that, they seemed to have been taking pictures of each other wearing large furry Turkmen-style hats. As I had had some decent *plov* earlier in the day at 'The World Trade Centre' (another small half-empty shopping mall just in front of the Arch of Neutrality) we decided to head over there for a cheap evening meal. Unfortunately almost everything in the city centre, including the single Internet café, was closed by 9pm. So, instead, we settled on a pleasant coffee shop in the mall that sorted us out with some decent kebabs.

Nicco and Sarah had enjoyed Iran but had had some problems. On one occasion they had been flustered by a 'plain clothes policeman' who had panicked them into showing him the contents of their money belt. Only after returning to their hotel did they notice that US$300 was missing. Apparently this kind of scam was quite common. They had also flown back to Europe from Tehran for a week after Nicco's granddad had died. They had hoped to be on the road for a long time but it was already becoming clear that their savings might not last as long as they had intended. I wondered how many of the people I had met along the Silk Road that they, in turn, would run into. There were only so many places to go and so many others to meet.

Iran

Mashhad

Veiled Intentions • Fall Among Thieves • Modern-Day Pilgrims
Eat the Rich • In League with Satan • Islam/Submission
Alien Animation • Opium Dreams • Global Infection

The owner of the Aminov Homestay in Ashgabat waved down a taxi for me and made it clear to the driver that I would only pay him US$5. We were soon driving along a surprisingly green but misty corridor through the Kopet Dag mountain range. When we pulled up at the customs point for departing Turkmenistan and I handed over the promised US$5, he looked a little disappointed. I thought he was going to ask for more but then realized it was the quality of the note itself rather than the amount that he was disappointed with. When I offered to exchange the slightly crumpled note I had handed him for a far crisper new one, he was delighted.

It was quick and easy enough to pass through the isolated customs post, and on the other side there was a nearly full minibus waiting to ferry passengers across the no-man's-land to the Iranian customs. I was asked for another US$10 to join an already packed vehicle that I thought was only going a couple of kilometres down the road, and hesitated at paying when it had only cost US$5 to be brought here all the way from Ashgabat. I was pretty sure that nobody else on board was paying anything like that much and I was probably right. Unfortunately, my hesitation meant that I missed that bus and had to wait around in the damp mountain cold for another one, which I still ended up paying the same for. Being stuck in the middle of nowhere with no other competition there was nothing else I could do. In the end, the no-man's land between the two countries turned out to be closer to 20 kilometres of swerving mountain road than the straightforward 2 kilometres that I had imagined.

Everyone at the Iranian customs post seemed exceptionally friendly and welcoming. I couldn't imagine that many Iranians were likely to receive such a welcome to the UK. On officially entering Iran I was immediately approached by a number of very enthusiastic taxi drivers. They were very keen to inform me that there were no longer any buses going from the border to Mashhad and the set price for a taxi was US$45. When I looked a little doubtful they pointed out a whiteboard in the taxi office with 'Mashhad – $45' scrawled across it in marker pen, as if this was proof of an incontrovertible fact of life. As I really wasn't keen to cough up this much money for a ride I wandered off in the hope that either one of the taxi drivers would break ranks and come down in price or another option would present itself. After a while, I was approached by a young guy who offered to take me as far as Quchan on the back of his motorbike for US$10. From there I would be able to catch a bus to Mashhad. Within seconds of accepting his offer I received another one. The same guy said that his friend would now take me all the way to Mashhad in his taxi for US$20. It soon became clear that this driver had been intending to go to Mashhad anyway as we first had to go back to his house to pick up his friend and his wife. They piled in their suitcases and we were off on our way through some surprisingly attractive mountain scenery.

Mashhad, the capital of the Khorasan region, is Iran's second biggest city and has a population of nearly 3 million. It is hardly known at all in the West but it is actually a major tourist destination – around 20 million Muslim pilgrims visit Mashhad every year to pay their respects to the martyred eighth Imam, Imam Reza. As it's not really on the main international tourist circuit, only a few Westerners ever seem to visit it and most of them seem to stay at Vali's Non-Smoking Homestay. As we pulled out of the manic traffic – the driving in Iran is notoriously bad and most of the cars seem to have dents in them – I handed over my map to the driver so that he could see where to drop me off. He then handed it around to the others to have a look at and they seemed to come to some agreement before taking me to an office car park. We all got out of the car and the security guards took it in turns to shake my hand. I wasn't sure what I was doing here and neither were the security guards but they seemed more than happy to welcome me in. Having eventually managed to explain that this wasn't where I wanted to go, the driver phoned up Vali on his mobile phone for directions and we were soon back to weaving in and out of traffic jams among some of the worst drivers in the world. They seemed to take a macho pride – yes, it did only seem to be men behind the wheel – in trying not to swerve out of each other's way until the very last moment. This clearly didn't always work out as in the five or ten minutes it took to drive across town to Vali's house, I saw two crashes take place (none of the passengers in any of the cars were allowed to wear seatbelts as this may have implied a lack of faith in the drivers' abilities and hurt their feelings).

On finally pulling into the right side street, the wild-haired and wiry Vali emerged from his family home and welcomed me in. Before being allowed to approach the delicate subject of money I was invited to sit down on the carpet-strewn floor to drink tea (as well as sharing his small house with whatever backpackers happened to turn up, there were also a lot of carpets around, as Vali's other source of income came from selling them). Vali poured the tea first, then told me there were no beds left in the shared dormitory downstairs but that I shouldn't worry as I could stay in his son Reza's bed instead for the same price. He also suggested that I ate with them that evening. It all seemed very reasonable but I was a bit uncomfortable about taking over his son's bedroom. Vali assured me this wasn't a problem as it was his income from tourism that was paying for Reza's computer equipment and IT course. I dumped my backpack in the kind of messy, teenage boy's bedroom – strewn with CDs, techno junk and used tissues – that you could find anywhere in the world, and headed out on to the carpet-covered balcony to meet some of the other guests.

Propped up on cushions across the balcony was the ultra scruffy Mathias from Germany, blonde-haired *uber* traveller Rolf from Denmark, and three young Japanese guys who had all started out by travelling on their own but had later teamed up. The youngest one – he was only nineteen – was lying across the floor in a Parker coat that was zipped up to the top. He looked like an oriental Kenny from South Park (after he had been killed). All you could see through the fur-lined hood was his fringe and a hair lip.

Rolf claimed to have been travelling for seven years. He hadn't really as he kept going back to his parent's house – he just hadn't had a proper job for that long. There was a map of the world in his bedroom that he was slowly and steadily marking up as red as he attempted to visit every country on it. When I asked him how he was managing to finance all his travels he said that it was a secret but later admitted to being a 'human guinea pig'. Whenever he ran out of money he would return to his parents' house and sign up for whatever medical trials were on offer. Sometimes he would have to stay in the hospitals so that he could more easily be monitored. Once he came to the end of whatever clinical trials he had signed up for, and had saved up some more money, he would resume his world travels.

Mathias was also a big traveller. He was enjoying a year's sabbatical from his job as a high school teacher to train in new areas and travel, and felt liberated from no longer having to cut his hair or even change his clothes very much. He looked as if he was wearing old dishrags. Later on he would look somewhat put out when he stated that it was only necessary to shower once a week and nobody reacted. When Mathias rushed to add that he was only joking, Rolf simply shrugged and claimed that he looked the type.

Before the communal dinner on the floor of the patio, we were joined by the Swiss couple that I had met in both Tashkent and Ashgabat, and three other young women who were leaving for Tehran later that evening in order to fly back to Europe the next day. Even within the closed walls of Vali's house, all the women still felt obliged to keep their hair covered with granny-style headscarves. Vali's wife was covered from head to foot in a standard issue black burka while his daughter remained equally, but more colourfully hidden, under a patterned green effort. When Vali's teenage son, Reza, turned up, he happily wandered around in just a pair of boxer shorts. This didn't seem very fair. Vali told me that, when he had suggested to his wife that there was no need to wear the full-length burka, she had felt very uncomfortable with the idea; it was just what she was used to and she would have felt that people were staring at her if she were to go out in anything less. Even the Western women at the dinner table – well, floor, actually – seemed less approachable in their headscarves. You couldn't see their faces properly when they were turned away from you and could only read their expressions fully when they were facing you directly – to approach them directly or to expect their undivided attention seemed almost invasive. I also couldn't help feeling that by covering themselves up in this way under the auspices of respect for local culture, they were in some way collaborating with, and perpetuating, the systematic denial of many women's individuality (I know this is easy to say as a man, when you could wear pretty much what you want, but I did previously travel around most of the Middle East in only t-shirts and shorts – if anyone is unduly offended by the sight of my naked, hairy calves they really do need to sort out their priorities). The young European women had even immersed themselves in local culture to the extent of buying a Persian carpet, which they were arranging for Vali to post home for them. This seemed to prompt a rather too-well-prepared talk from Vali on the wonders of Persian carpets and how much cheaper it is to buy them here in Mashhad, and managed to stall all the surrounding conversations for a few moments, but we soon moved on to the subject of theft. I mentioned the story about the fake policeman from the couple I met in Ashgabat, and Vali warned us to be careful of similar scams. As the evening moved on and my back became increasingly uncomfortable from sitting on the floor for too long, we passed around a sour yoghurt drink from a glass tumbler and swapped tales of robbery (at one point it looked as if Mathias was going to win with a rather unfortunate mugging in Sierra Leone but Rolf stormed in to take the crown with a disastrous armed robbery in Chad). Eventually I retired to my single room – or at least to the now-exiled Reza's room – and cleared a path through the assorted rubbish across the floor to my bed for the night (they had put some sheets over the top for me to sleep on but had left Reza's old one ones underneath so that they wouldn't have to change them).

* * *

After breakfast I had arranged with Mathias to visit Mashhad's biggest attraction, the collection of sacred precincts known as Haram-e Razavi that surround Imam Reza's Holy Shrine. Vali, however, was concerned that I only had T-shirts to wear so lent me a long sleeved black shirt to wear over the top. Apparently my combat trousers were fine and plain t-shirts would normally be OK but all of my ones seem to have pictures on them. Mathias even managed to dig out a slightly less grubby long sleeved top from somewhere at the bottom of his backpack. Looking slightly – but not much – more presentable, we set off through Mashhad's grimy urban sprawl on a pilgrimage of our own. Mashhad was already a site of pilgrimage before Genghis Khan and his Mongol hordes ransacked Khorasan in the 1220s. He may actually have helped Mashhad's rise to prominence as the ancient Silk Road city was left relatively unscathed and therefore drew in large numbers of refugees from other less fortunate cities in the surrounding area. It later became a Timurid city after Timur's brutal sacking of Khorasan in 1389. It was Timur's son, Shah Rokh, and his wife, Gohar Shad (after whom the main mosque is named), who enlarged the shrine into a major pilgrimage site. The complex was further developed by devotees in the twentieth century and is still being expanded today. The story goes that Imam Reza was murdered by the Caliph, Ma'mun, when the religious leader's popularity began to be seen as a threat to his authority. He was supposedly poisoned by grapes in 818, but even today thousands of devout Muslims still make their way to Mashhad to weep at his shrine.

The concept of pilgrimage seems to be universal among all religions and is even widespread among secular groups. It seems to connect to some deep-rooted kind of animism, in the sense that the spirit and soul of beings can somehow be found in inanimate objects and revered locations. This phenomenon is not only found among the avowedly spiritual but also among groups of tourists who feel that they can somehow connect to something beyond their ordinary existence by virtue of visiting the sites of seemingly significant events. Modern-day pilgrims are just as likely to visit memorials to war heroes or pop stars as they are to visit the remains of the religious elites. The real significance of pilgrimage, however, may not be found in the final destination, but in the journey itself. Those who endure the hardship, expense and difficulties of a challenging journey are often awarded status, among their fellow believers, as those who have had the courage to reach out towards something more. It is often said that one of the aims of pilgrimage is to transcend the ego but this seems unconvincing when so many cultures award prestige or even honorific title to those who make such a quest – the striving, patience and willingness to open up to the new forms of experience may all contribute to something akin to spiritual growth, but in no way contribute to a transcending of the self. We carried on by foot, through the grey of modern Mashhad towards the glistening domes and minarets of the shrine, where we joined queues of Pilgrims from all over the Islamic world – they took turns standing together while their fellow devotees captured their likeness on their mobile phones (you wouldn't want to go all this way and spend all that money without having something as proof of your faith, wealth and experience).

When it was our turn to enter the Haram-e Razavi, we were asked to step aside and a phone call was made. A few minutes later a smartly dressed young man turned up and introduced himself. He was a scholar of Islam and here to be our free guide (and keep an eye on us). After dropping off our bags and cameras in exchange for a token, we were marched off to watch a DVD (you couldn't take any pictures using a dedicated camera but rather inconsistently it was fine to take them from a mobile phone). Also joining us were a coachload of pilgrims from somewhere in the Gulf, all decked out in matching red tour shirts. Our guide raised his eyes upwards in a dismissive gesture. Apparently these people were too religious. They didn't look too religious to me – they looked more like a tour group of enthusiasts on an 'all ages' special interest tour. As we were herded towards our seating for the video show, the atmosphere was closer to that among an audience at a pop concert than to what you would normally find within a mosque. It looked like they were having a good time and enjoying their pilgrimage. They probably only got to go on a pilgrimage once a year and had probably worked hard for it, so I was pleased that they seemed to be having fun. When they had finished photographing all the fancy buildings on their mobile phones, and stocked up on presents for their relatives from the gift shop, they would probably all head off together for a nice session at one of Mashhad's more upmarket teahouses.

Having sat through a history of the shrine, which pretty much went in one ear and out the other, we looked around at some old pots and manuscripts in the museum. Neither of us could summon up the enthusiasm to check out either the stamp or coin collections. A lot of the buildings in the part of the complex that we were allowed into were still being built. I couldn't help thinking it might have been a better use of money and time to concentrate on looking after the already large complex of far superior older buildings. The newest additions, like many newer Islamic buildings, looked alarmingly like add-ons from a stage set; flimsy decorated boards were simply stuck on over hastily wired metal frames to add yet more instant glamour to the ever expanding complex of holy constructions. They wouldn't let us into the good bit where Imam Reza's tomb is, in the inner sanctuary of the Holy Shrine building. They asked us if we were Muslims and we were politely turned away after confessing to our infidel status. (We later found out that the three Japanese guys simply walked straight into the inner sanctuary – nobody bothered to question them as Mashhad apparently has quite a large number of oriental-looking residents.)

Having entered into every part of the complex that we could access, we walked back across the city in the general direction of Vali's. For a city this size there was actually very little to see and surprisingly few places to eat. Nobody seemed to go out much. We eventually found a small burger and kebab bar that looked no better or worse than the few others we had come across, and settled for plastic-covered microwavable burgers and a small bottle of a local variant of cola. The foods available seemed limited and of poor quality but the people we met were friendly and keen to know what we thought about Iran. They seemed to think that everyone in the West thought Iran was full of terrorists and were keen to dispel this notion; people would repeatedly stop us in the streets to welcome us and then tell us how crazy all their politicians are.

Most ordinary people like to moan about their leaders but the contempt of most ordinary Iranians for their politicians was on a different level all together. For many years Iran was held up as an example of a country that was a democracy but was far from liberal – in reality, the veneer of democracy established by Iran's elites is increasingly losing any credibility among the people of Iran and the world as a whole, and most of the ordinary people that you meet on the streets are far more liberal and open to international influence than many would imagine.

We returned to Vali's, to find Reza blasting out some very Germanic-sounding heavy metal from his bedroom. Despite the unreliability of the Internet around Mashhad – every now and again there would be a bit of a crackdown and it would all be cut off – Reza could still quite easily download hard rock and metal tracks from all over the world. I knew that metal had quite a significant underground following within Iran and asked Reza if he got to go to many gigs around Mashhad. He shook his head sadly – all live music throughout the region had been banned by the Imam of Mashhad in 2007; the religious leader believed that all live music and dance is *haram* (not allowed according to Islam) and that any venues where such activities occurred were places of Satan. This hadn't gone down too well with the large number of young people (about two-thirds of Iran's 70 million population are under thirty years of age), but many felt intimidated by the cleric's domination of the state (in 2008 around 230 heavy metal fans were arrested as 'Satan worshippers' at an underground concert in Tehran, and in 2009 another 104 rock fans were arrested at a gig in Shiraz for being 'unIslamic'). Reza and his friend weren't afraid to criticize the regime but Vali, his father, grew uncomfortable at their contempt for those in power. Vali thought it was better not to get involved in politics. He probably knew of many who had suffered for their political convictions and was afraid that Reza and his friends might find themselves in trouble. Many of the young people in Iran are, however, far less wary of having their voices heard. Despite attempts by the state, the Internet has proved to be largely unpoliceable, and has given many of Iran's disgruntled population a space in which to question the establishment (Farsi is one of the most commonly used languages in blogs). Iran may still be in the grip of the cancerous religious elite but it seems difficult to believe that things won't change – there are simply too many intelligent and determined young people out there for something not to give. As time marches on, ever more will stand up for their rights and refuse to submit to the authority of the religious establishment. I only hope that Vali's warnings of caution don't prove to be too prescient.

The communal meal across the balcony was set for earlier that evening as the three European girls had to rush to get their night bus to Tehran from where they would fly home. Vali had persuaded me to stay an extra day so that I could join him on his 'eco tourism' tour of Kang, the nearby stepped village. Nobody was entirely sure what 'eco tourism' really was – other than a marketing term – but Vali seemed to have picked up on the phrase as a credible and fashionable way to describe doing things on the cheap. That was fine by me. I wasn't entirely clear how I was supposed to be saving the planet by going on a day trip but at least it wouldn't cost me much. Rolf had done the trip with Vali before and actually preferred Kang to the better-known stepped village of Masuleh, near the Caspian Sea. As the family seemed to know Rolf quite well, he was suckered into laying out the floor with plates and cutlery and passing around the various dishes. The last time he had visited he had even been commandeered into helping to dig Vali's grave. I'm not entirely sure why Vali was getting tourists to dig his grave, as opposed to members of his immediate family, or why he felt the need to organize this in advance. Maybe he just liked to be prepared?

Rolf had previously stayed here while preparing for a trip to Afghanistan a few years earlier, which he was writing a book about (I'm not sure if this was ever published in any form, as he intended to use a pen name to preserve his anonymity; this seemed hopelessly optimistic). He affected a philosophical fatalism about whether the book would be published or not, and claimed that it was just something to do while submitting to life as a human guinea pig. It seemed difficult to believe that anybody could put that much time and effort into creating something and yet not be too concerned about whether or not it actually saw the light of the day. If he genuinely wasn't that bothered then I doubt if it could really be any good – any form of real art, whether it is travel literature or heavy metal, can only transcend the prosaic if born from a real fire for creation and a genuine striving for more. Nobody is ever likely to leave a mark on the world – let alone change it for good – if they simply submit to the will of the gods.

* * *

Before I could leave for Kang with Vali, I had a confession to make. I had blocked the downstairs squat toilet. Vali didn't seem too bothered about this and said that he kept meaning to put a bin in there for toilet paper. His skill with the plunger seemed to suggest that this was something of a regular occurrence. He asked if I could give him the money for the trip before we left so that he could pay our bus fares from it. I was pleased to do so as I rather liked Vali's unusually direct approach to money – I far preferred his direct, but entirely reasonable, requests for payment than the often-stressful palaver surrounding payment in some Islamic countries (especially when they try out the guilt-edged 'whatever you like' approach). He handed over a sturdy walking stick and we set off to catch a series of public buses to the scenic stepped village.

After changing at a bus station on the far outskirts of Mashhad, we piled on to a smaller and rustier bus which wound its way through the surrounding villages. As we swerved around blind corners, picking up farmers on the way, I told Vali about the only Kang I knew – the space monster from *The Simpsons*. He had never even heard of *The Simpsons* but was sure that Reza would have done. We got off near the village and began to walk up a hill on the other side. As it grew steeper we used the long wooden walking sticks to propel ourselves up along the country tracks, through orchards and past beehives to a rocky hillside peak. From there we had picture postcard views across to the stacked mud brick houses piled up upon the facing hillside. Vali pointed out the public bathhouse, next to the stream at the bottom of the valley. As few of the houses had their own bathrooms, each of the families would pay an annual fee to be granted once weekly access to the communal bathing facilities (whether they needed it or not). We skidded and stumbled down through the fields to the crumbling bridge that spanned the stream, and then made our way up through narrow stone pathways, winding in and out of crumbling mud brick houses with protruding Ottoman-style wooden balconies that looked as if they might splinter into pieces given a strong enough wind. Everybody who lived there seemed to know Vali. One family invited us into their courtyard to see their animals and some dumpy, apron-clad women let us watch as they prepared their weekly bread in a large communal outside oven; the women contentedly grumbled and chatted among themselves as they piled in more firewood under the stone oven walls and slid in mounds of just pummelled dough.

Vali led me through more of the maze and down a side alley to a friend's house where we took off our shoes before being welcomed in. We sat down on the floor with the young children and their granny while the mother of the house brought us tea and biscuits. Her dyed blonde hair fell out of the headscarf and across her face as she leant forward to pour me more tea and pass me more snacks. Vali wanted to know why I wasn't taking their pictures. I always feel a bit uncomfortable about taking pictures of people I don't really know, simply on the basis of them being a bit foreign looking, but they seemed to expect it. They all mugged for the camera like the professionals they were and then checked out their pictures on the camera's screen to make sure that I had adequately captured their image. The small children happily sat on Vali's knee – he was clearly a regular and trusted visitor. I was beginning to feel a bit unsure about eating most of a poor family's supply of biscuits and snacks but Vali thoughtfully resolved any potential awkwardness by suggesting an amount for a tip that I should leave that seemed neither too little nor too much (it would have spoilt the whole experience to have been subjected to the whole 'whatever you like' routine).

On our way out, with some reservations, I asked if I could use their toilet. I was directed down a narrow, curving, dried mud stairway below their lounge room, and towards a tiny dried mud pit toilet in the basement. The ceiling was far too low for me to stand up straight so I had to bend over awkwardly while trying to take out my willy and point it towards the hole. As I struggled over the surprisingly hygienic-looking mud pit I was startled by a bleating noise from behind. I twisted around as best as I could to be faced down by a rather grubby-looking sheep. I guessed that this is where they kept their winter's meat supply until it was time to be slaughtered and salted for the season ahead. My bladder was now uncomfortably full but I really couldn't go while the sheep was staring at me. It was giving me stage fright. I was feeling more than a little uncomfortable both with my awkward position and the sheep's unflinching glare. When I eventually managed to unleash a torrent of piss into the pit below, and could finally escape to the stair well so as to stand up straight again, I caught a final glimpse of that poor, lonely sheep returning to the shadows. It didn't seem like much of a life.

We carried on up through the village of Kang and continued on up the gravelly hill to the top from where we could look down over small villages dotted across the valley. After a considerable amount of wooden stick-aided traipsing and sliding down the other side of the shingled peak, we approached another more developed village. A number of restaurants and small hotels spread out along the small river than ran through its centre – apparently, many of the pilgrims to Mashhad would like to combine their holy quest with a few days stay in some of the scenic mountain villages. On seeing one of the local women, Vali went over to her and gave her some money – he always liked to help her out when visiting as she had been left in dire straits after her husband had been imprisoned for drug smuggling. In any of the rural areas in Iran that run close to the Afghan border there is little well-paid legitimate work so many are prepared to take the risks involved for the profits that can be made from distributing Afghan heroin. With strict bans on alcohol in place, there may not be many alcoholics, but there are over 3.5 million heroin addicts – the highest rate of any country in the world. One in three of these users is estimated to have HIV/Aids and around 90 per cent have become infected with Hepatitis C. For years, Iran used to cultivate its own drugs but following the revolution in 1979 the cultivation of opium poppies was quickly eradicated. Unfortunately, nothing could be done to stop the profitable production of heroin in Afghanistan and its inevitable smuggling across Iran on the way to the lucrative European markets. Drug-related offences account for more than 80,000 of Iran's prison population of 170,000 and large numbers continue to be killed as the government attempts to control the situation. As well as the public hangings and shootings of the smugglers themselves, over 3,300 members of the security forces have been killed in related skirmishes (an average of around three a day). Vali was concerned that, as Reza was due to do his compulsory military service next year, he may well be posted to one of the volatile regions along the Afghan border where so many young soldiers have lost their lives.

Vali next led me into a small café and ordered the standard working man's dish of *dizi*. Named after the earthenware pot that it is served in, *dizi* is a popular and filling soup/stew that is always eaten with the heavy local bread. There is something of an art to eating it: first, the bread is torn into chunks; these chunks are thrown into a bowl with the liquid from the stew; then the chunkier remains of the *dizi* are pummelled into a kind of paste using a pestle or masher. I was feeling full after just a small amount, but Vali kept urging me to eat more. The food was clearly too good to waste and I didn't want to offend him so I carried on eating. Unfortunately this wasn't such a good idea – the rough peasant's food didn't upset my stomach but the ridiculously heavy bread did leave me constipated for a couple of days (apparently it quite often has this effect on Westerners).

We rushed to catch the bus – while trying not to drop a newly purchased tray of village eggs – and just about made it as it was leaving. One of the locals got on the bus so that he could talk to me but then had to get off at a later stop and walked back home. While I continued to gaze out the grubby windows and admire the passing countryside, Vali lay down for a bit of a sleep – after all the *dizi* and the strenuous hiking, he felt like he deserved a nap.

It seemed much quieter back at Vali's once most of the others had moved on to either Tehran or Yazd. Mathias and two of the Japanese guys had to leave earlier than me to get the night bus but I still had some time to kill before catching my slightly more expensive but more comfortable sleeper train, so asked if I could use Reza's PC to book my flights back from Istanbul to England. I would have booked my flight earlier but I really didn't trust any of the PCs in China or Central Asia enough to enter in my visa card details – they all seemed to be riddled with viruses (that had already infected my Hotmail account) and I was concerned that I could risk having my bank account emptied. Fortunately, the Internet was now working again for

Mashhad and Reza's PC was properly protected so I could finally book up my ticket on easyJet. It now really felt like I was running out of time as it began to sink in that I was due to return to the world of work in just a few weeks (after nearly eight months of travelling the whole idea of settling back down to a life of wage slavery seemed almost too bizarre to be depressing). When it was time to leave, I said my farewells to the others, and Vali took me out to make sure that I got the right bus to the train station. He even told the bus driver where I was going and paid for my ticket with one of his tokens.

The train was clean and comfortable and the other passengers were disarmingly friendly and welcoming. As well as going out of their way to make sure that I was all right, many also brought me small presents of food or drink. Just as I was getting into my bunk bed to settle down with my headphones for the night, one guy came over and presented me with two cans of lager (fruit flavoured and non-alcoholic). I settled down to the rhythms of the train as we rolled on through the night across the desert to Yazd.

Yazd

Thus Spake Zarathustra • Fire and Divinity • Heaven and Hell
The Next Best Thing

I woke to find myself trundling through a huge, bleached white desert stretching out as far as I could see on both sides of the train. Only the occasional spectacular rock formation broke up the ocean of sand as it jutted up towards a sky that even this early in the morning, still appeared to be almost surreally blue and bright. Yazd lies in the middle of Iran between the northern Dasht-e Kavir and southern Dash-e Lut deserts and many believe it to be one of the oldest cities in the world (it is believed that the site has been continually inhabited for more than 7,000 years). Despite its status as a major Silk Road trading city, its relative isolation and lack of political power meant that it avoided the worst of many Persian wars and remained relatively unscathed by the invasions of both Genghis Khan and Timur.

By the time we arrived in the city it was getting on for mid-morning. It was easy enough to catch a minibus from the train station to a roundabout in the middle of the city that I could easily locate on my map. Unfortunately I then went off the wrong way before heading back to the roundabout again and eventually managing to track down the popular Silk Road hotel in the back alleys of the old town. At a table in the attractively restored old courtyard I again met up with Mathias and the two Japanese guys who had arrived earlier that morning on the bus. After being allocated a bed in the basement dormitory and making use of the decent shared bathrooms, I set out with Mathias to explore the city.

The blue-domed twelfth-century Jameh Mosque, just around the corner from the Silk Road Hotel, had been built on top of an existing Zoroastrian fire temple. Zoroastrianism had been the dominant religion across Persia and much of Central Asia until Islam was introduced along with the Arab Conquest in the seventh century, and Yazd remains something of a centre for the followers of Zarathustra (generally believed to have been born somewhere in Persia or Central Asia between 1000 and 1500 BC). Contrary to popular belief, Zoroastrians don't actually worship fire itself, but direct their prayers to the light as a focus towards Ahura Mazda, the divine being. It was arguably the first religion to popularize the notion of a single, omnipotent deity, and can be seen to have had a significant influence upon Judaism, Islam and Christianity. The concepts of resurrection, final judgement, and heaven and hell, were all taught in Zoroastrianism before Islam or Christianity even existed. Perhaps its greatest influence upon Western thought, however, can be seen in the concept of dualism and the constant struggle between good and evil, right and wrong, and us and them (Zoroastrianism had a major influence upon both Roman and Greek philosophy – Plato's Republic is said to be heavily influenced by the writings of Zarathustra). This dualistic way of looking at the world, which is so alien to much of Eastern thought, remains integral to Western dialectic concepts of history, economics and psychology, in which all progress is founded through the resolution of direct conflict. The dualistic nature of Zoroastrianism is thought to have come about after the civilized and settled people of Zarathustra came into sudden conflict with invading nomads; the others were cast into the role of foreign devils as Zarathustra came to see the world as a great struggle between good and evil.

We carried on towards the elaborate facade of the Zoroastrian Complex of Amir Chakmak. There is supposed to be a club in a nearby converted reservoir that is dedicated to the particularly Iranian form of body building, but we couldn't find it. As it is surrounded by desert, the storage and distribution of water is of particular importance to Yazd. Just across from the square with the Amir Chakmak Complex was the Yazd Water Museum, featuring exhibits on the *qanats* (the underground water channels used to irrigate crops and provide drinking water) that are still relied upon in many surrounding towns and villages, even today. The other big problem with living in the middle of the desert is that in the summer it would get very hot! To help deal with the summer heat, a forest of *badgirs* (wind towers) reach up to the sky from roofs all over the city. The wind catchers use wind shelves and often cool pools of water to help push out hot air from the houses and cool down the new air being caught – like a more eco friendly air conditioning unit. Thankfully I had actually managed to arrive in Yazd in the perfect time of spring, which made wandering through the narrow, winding alleys between mud brick houses, markets and mosques perfectly pleasant. Having said that, it was still a relief to walk down into the cool subterranean teahouse under the domed school known as Alexander's Prison (there is a story that the deep well in the courtyard was built by Alexander the Great, who used it as a dungeon). After getting suitably lost among the atmospheric lanes throughout the old city, we eventually climbed up onto some accessible rooftops to gaze down across the domed and *badgired* skyline of this ancient desert city as the sun began to set.

We returned to the courtyard of the Silk Road Hotel and ordered camel with celery and saffron rice. As I still hadn't paid for either my meal or my bed in the dormitory, and was planning to leave early the next morning for Shiraz, I went over to the desk to settle up. The man in charge asked me to come through to the back room on the pretence of getting some change. Once the door was shut he asked me if he could ask me a personal question. I didn't like the sound of this. When he asked me if I was gay and I said no, he looked as awkward as I felt and explained that it was just that the Silk Road Hotel liked to offer a discount to its gay guests. This seemed like an odd thing to say in a country where homosexuality is punishable by death. With more than a hint of desperation in his voice he attempted to explain that many foreigners thought that Iranians didn't like gays but that this wasn't true at all. In fact, historically speaking, certain types of homosexuality used to be widely accepted within Persian and Arab cultures, and healthy young boys were often seen as the next best thing to available women. This seemed in strong contrast to the ancient Zoroastrian belief that all homosexuals are inherently demonic and deserved to be punished with death.

Attitudes to sexuality still seemed confused, to say the least, in modern Iran. In 2007, President Ahmadinejad publicly stated that there was no such thing as homosexuality – this is probably just as well because, under Sharia law, homosexuality is punishable by beheading or burning alive. Rather bizarrely, following a fatwa issued by Ayatollah Khomeini, the religious establishment is actually willing to authorise sex change operations – this has led to many gay men being pressurized to have their willies cut off in order to avoid both persecution and prosecution.

I have only ever received this kind of attention in Islamic countries, where rather unsophisticated and sexually frustrated men seem to be confused by my long hair and general appearance. My theory is that they weren't even really gay – as genuinely gay men seem to be fitted with surprisingly effective 'gaydar' – and that they were just sexually frustrated perverts who didn't want to pay for a woman and thought that I might do as the next best thing (if you were to suggest they were gay then they would almost certainly have been offended). I quickly paid my bill and left the room.

Esfahan

Muhajababes • The Great Escape • Evangelical Ambitions • Never Alone
Love of a Stranger • Layers of Design • A Bridge Too Far
One True God • Freak Show • Brain Drain

I quickly turned off my alarm so as not to wake the others in the basement dormitory. I needed to get up early to catch the 8am bus to Shiraz from where I intended to visit the ancient ruins of Persepolis. The clock was now ticking and I was really going to have to rush along the Silk Road if I was going to make it to Istanbul in time to catch my flight and still see everything I'd wanted to see before it all came to an end.

Despite what I'd been told the evening before, there was still no breakfast to be had before I had to wait outside for the taxi that had been ordered for me. After it still hadn't turned up, ten or fifteen minutes later, I was beginning to worry that I'd fail to get to the bus station on time. I was torn as to whether or not to go back to the hotel and say that it hadn't turned up or to carry on waiting outside – if it turned up and then left without me I would miss the bus and then have to miss out on some of the places I had waited so long to see. I decided to rush back down the narrow, mud brick alleys and back into the hotel courtyard to let them know that it still hadn't turned up. The breakfast guy led me out to a different part of the street, where I'd been told to wait, only to see a taxi pulling away. Just as I sighed and lowered my bag to the pavement, another terrible Iranian driver pulled out in front of the taxi without signalling, forcing him to suddenly brake. This allowed us to catch the taxi driver's attention and, to my relief, I was soon in the car and speeding in and out of yet more appalling drivers on the way to the bus station on the outskirts of the city.

I managed to get there dead on 8am just as the only coach at the station was pulling away. It wasn't going to Shiraz. When I got to the ticket counter I found that there wasn't a bus to Shiraz for another six hours and the one that left at 8am – according to both the Lonely Planet and the Silk Road Hotel – had stopped running months before. As I really didn't want to wait another six hours for the bus only to spend another six hours travelling before travelling almost all the way back again on the way to Esfahan, I decided to simply cut my losses and go directly to Esfahan on the next bus. For the first time on this trip, so far, I really wished that I had just had a few more days.

I sat in the coach station café, drinking instant coffee and eating some greasy fried eggs, while one young guy stared at me. I stared directly back in an attempt to break his gaze but this made no difference. He seemed fascinated by me and my breakfast. I still had a few hours to kill before my coach to Esfahan left, so I took out my book and attempted to ignore him. When the coach to Esfahan eventually turned up I found myself sat next to a friendly old guy in a worn tweed jacket. He couldn't speak a word of English but had clearly intuited that I really didn't know what I was doing and needed to be looked after. After a few hours on the coach, as we began to approach the outskirts of Esfahan, he searched around the passengers for somebody who could speak better English and managed to find an attractive young woman who was willing to adopt me (despite being covered up under a black bag you could still clearly see that she was slim and pretty). She patted the seat next to her to gesture for me to come and sit there. This surprised me a little as burka-wearing young women I had come across in other Islamic countries had always seemed a little inapproachable (in Pakistan I spoke to hardly any women who weren't first introduced to me as some man's wife, mother or daughter, and people would go out of their way to make sure that you never ended up sitting next to a woman you weren't related to). In Iran – especially outside of the more conservative Mashhad and Yazd – I was to find young, conservatively dressed women to be surprisingly friendly. I sat down next to my new friend who went out of her way to help me. She was a twenty-year-old university student who was already married. It seemed like a bit of a waste to be married at such a young age but I doubt if she was really missing out on a lot of wild times at the student parties. When we pulled into the bus station, she found me a local bus that was going in the right direction, and made sure that the driver knew exactly where I was going – he dropped me right outside the front door of the Amir Kabir Hostel. In a gloomy dorm room, crowded with single beds, I met Peter from France and Tanya from Germany. I had at first assumed that they were travelling together but it turned out they had only just bumped into each other again after first meeting at a hostel in Columbia two years previously. Having claimed a bed and dumped my bags on it I headed out to look around.

Esfahan is generally considered to be Iran's most attractive city. Nobody seems entirely sure about how old it is but remains – such as that of a fire temple – seem to suggest an ancient history. By the end of the tenth century Esfahan was already a prosperous city with dozens of mosques and in 1047 the Seljuks made Esfahan their capital. For the next 180 years or so the city developed into something of an architectural showcase for the Seljuk Turks but this prosperity came to a sudden and brutal end with the arrival of Genghis Khan's Mongol hordes in 1228. The Mongols managed to resist the temptation to completely trash the city but the residents fared rather less well when Timur finally made it into town in 1388; they decided to rebel rather than pay tribute to the conqueror and were therefore promptly massacred. It took Esfahan a long time to fully recover from this disaster and it wasn't until Shah Abbas the Great (1571–1629) moved the capital of the Safavid Persian Empire to Esfahan that the city became what it is today; the Shah effectively rerouted the Silk Road through the city in an attempt to gain a monopoly on the profitable trade that came to fund much of Esfahan's outstanding architecture.

The atmosphere in Esfahan was quite different from either Yazd or Mashhad. It seemed like something of a tourist city for both domestic tourists and affluent middle-aged Western tourists on organized 'cultural' tours. Although all the women wore headscarves, many wore them pushed back far on their heads to reveal bleached or coloured hair. Popular among many young women was a kind of Amy Winehouse look, with dark bouffant hair bulging out of the front of their head coverings, and heavy, pointed eye liner. Many of their all-in-one *hijab* outfits had also been tailored to highlight slim waists and firm, pert breasts while still covering up all skin apart from the hands and face. Many would stop me as I passed by to ask me where I was from and to help me with directions. Despite Esfahan's status as arguably Iran's most popular tourist destination, there seemed to be surprisingly few places around to eat out. I eventually found an unremarkable burger and kebab bar that was almost identical to the other local cafés that I had found in Mashhad and Yazd, and munched down a passable kebab with a can of fruit-flavoured Iranian non-alcoholic beer. Afterwards, I cut across some pleasant parks – which seemed to be full of Iranian visitors eating their own elaborate picnics – and headed towards Imam Square.

The square was begun in 1602 as a showcase for Shah Abbas the Great's architectural ambitions. The square is second in size only to the bleak Tiananmen Square in Beijing but is infinitely more attractive; surrounding the ornate gardens and fountains at the centre, and between the colonnaded shopping arcades, are the architecturally outstanding Imam Mosque, Sheikh Lotfollah Mosque and Ali Qapu Palace. From the Qeysarieh Portal at the northern end of the square, you can enter into the maze of the Bazar-e Bozorg. Having wandered in and out of the mosques, and past a selection of not very busy shops flogging reproductions of Persian miniatures, I decided to check out the popular Qeysarieh Tea Shop. I hauled myself up a steep and rather well-hidden staircase to find myself in this thriving haunt with great views across the square from the balcony. Peter and Tanya were sitting on the edge of the wall, taking it in turns to puff away at a bubbling *qalyan* and sharing a plate of small cakes that had come with their pot of tea. I ordered the same. The Qeysarieh Tea Shop seemed to be the place where everybody ended up at the end of the day as the sun set over Imam Square. Peter had also managed to meet up again with a couple of German guys he had met a few weeks ago in Pakistan and, once the sun had descended and the last of the cakes had been guzzled, we all set off in search of something more substantial to satisfy our hunger.

Again, for what is a major tourist area by Iranian standards, there seemed to be few decent affordable places to eat. We ended up in a backstreet café, but as nothing on offer appealed Tanya and I set off for a basement restaurant that we had both noticed not far from the hostel. Having recently taken voluntary redundancy after ten years in an unrewarding administrative position, Tanya was now free to travel the world and have a good time. Unfortunately, she was finding some of the restrictions for women in Iran rather tedious; she hated having to keep her hair covered all the time, you couldn't buy beer anywhere, and she wasn't overly impressed by a lot of the men's attitude towards a single woman travelling on her own. Even at our hostel, which was used to international guests, she had felt that the staff had been far less welcoming to her than to male travellers. Strangely, although they insisted that she always wear *hijab* dress, even when just going down the hall to the shared bathroom, they seemed to have no problem at all with her sharing a dormitory room with a load of men she didn't know. She suspected that they thought she was something like a prostitute but I am more inclined to think that, as a genuinely independent Western woman, they really weren't quite sure what to make of her. All the other Western women I met in Iran were accompanied by men and seemed rather too keen to appear 'respectful' (in contrast to most young Iranian women who couldn't wait to get out the country and enjoy the same kind of personal freedoms that most women in the West take as a given).

While we sat in the surprisingly bright basement restaurant and picked out our dishes from the photos on the menu, Tanya told me how pleased she had been to receive the redundancy payout. She had rented out her flat to a friend and intended to keep travelling for as long as possible on the money that she now had in the bank. She knew it would be hard to go back home and start again once the money had run out, but she would have to deal with it when the time came. As she pushed back long hennaed locks that kept falling forward from her headscarf – as if even her hair itself was struggling to break free – she told me about how hard it had been when she had had to return to her job after a year's sabbatical in South America. While emailing a friend to let her know of her imminent return, she noticed water dripping on to her keyboard and had only then realized that she had been crying. I only had a couple of weeks left until I, myself, would also have to return to the world of work.

When we returned to the dormitory, we found that Peter was already back, along with a guy from Azerbaijan who very closely resembled, and acted like, a slightly swarthier Mr Bean. He was visiting Esfahan on some kind of business and clearly felt a bit left out of the conversation in the room as he couldn't speak any English. When he found out that there was a Polish woman staying at the hostel who could speak Russian, he was delighted. He quickly tracked her down and set about trying to convert her to Islam; it would be some time before she could find a way to respectfully break free from him and his evangelical ambitions. As the conversation returned to the Iranians' rather inconsistent attitudes towards sex and sexuality, it turned out that Peter had also been approached by 'gay' Iranian men who would have been mortified if anybody had actually considered them to be homosexual. They had suggested that he try anal sex with them just to see if he would like it but he had politely declined their offer and insisted that he wasn't gay. Apparently they weren't gay either – they just liked having sex with each other and thought that he might enjoy it as well if only he would give it a chance (it was also cheaper that paying for a wife or a prostitute).

We stayed up late into the night, swapping stories of inappropriate sexual advances and public stoning. We had only been asleep for a few hours when a ridiculously piercing ringtone, belonging to the Azeri Mr Bean's phone, wrenched everyone in the room from their slumber. As his phone relentlessly shrieked out, he obsessively laid out his prayer mats across the dormitory floor and began loudly chanting. By now everybody was ready to strangle him. He seemed to go on with this for at least half an hour. I looked at my watch and it was five in the morning. Everyone was only just beginning to return to sleep when his phone went off again and he began a long impassioned conversation about something that was no doubt of great interest to him. This went on for so long that everybody had now resigned themselves to an early start to the day. Apparently his company paid him expenses to stay in a proper hotel but he preferred to pocket the difference and take the cheaper option of staying in the hostel – he also thought it was more sociable.

* * *

The next morning I set off on a recommended 'half the world' walking tour (I'm still not sure why Esfahan is known as 'half the world' just because it has some nice buildings). I had barely had time to get properly lost among the dusty back street lanes before somehow finding that a grey-haired 'guide' in a tatty tweed jacket had somehow attached himself to me. Apparently he was a retired schoolteacher. He pointed out a few *medressas* and mosques to me and encouraged me to walk around in them when I might otherwise have been more cautious. Nobody seemed to be particularly bothered about me poking my nose into their schools or places of worship. He then led me through some more lanes towards the Mausoleum of Harun Vilayet, whose courtyard featured two large frescoes of Khomeini and Khamenei. The Ayatollahs glared down at me while I raised my camera to capture their imposing likenesses. They seemed closer to stars than to clerics; they had the look of those too accustomed to reverence.

When I suggested getting a drink, my 'guide' led me through some more gloomy back streets and down a basement into a 'real' locals' teahouse. I still wasn't sure what my 'guide' was expecting from me but I got the impression that he took all his tourists there (whether they wanted to go or not). As we sat in the gloom, sipping tea among an exclusively male and rather elderly clientele, I struggled to keep up the conversation before being presented with the bill. By the time we had worked our way further through the narrow, winding lanes of the bazaar to the entrance to Imam Square, he seemed to have lost interest all together. After asking me if I had any foreign money – which I said I didn't – he said his farewells and wandered off on his own.

I had only been free from his clutches for a minute or two before my next 'guide' presented himself. This one was apparently a student who wanted to practise his English. There was clearly no need to ever feel lonely while in Esfahan. When I attempted to ditch him by telling him that I was going to visit the Ali Qapu Palace, he insisted on paying for both of our entrance tickets, as he clung to my side. We climbed up towards the elevated terrace, side by side with an excitable school group, and admired the views over the square and Imam Mosque. My new 'friend' kept telling me how much he didn't want to bother me or be a nuisance while never standing more than about six inches away. I didn't want to seem rude or hurt his feelings, and I was happy to help him with his English, but this was getting to be a bit too much. He eventually took the hint, and we shook hands and parted as I left to visit the Sheikh Lotfollah Mosque on the other side of Imam Square. As I left the palace, I passed by my original 'guide' for the day who had already attached himself to a hapless Japanese tourist. We nodded and smiled.

After another poor-quality kebab, I set off back through the crowded alleys of the bazaar towards Jameh Mosque. As I grew closer to the ancient site, the roads on my map started to disappear. In their place were mud, gravel and wire fencing. Everything was being dug up and demolished to make way for a new underpass. I diverted through a series of run-down back streets that would normally attract few tourists and a tall, young blacksmith paused from his battering to wave and say 'I love you'. Unsure of how to reply, I thanked him. He didn't seem to understand. As I carried on past, he smiled again and cheerily called out 'Fuck you'.

Jameh Mosque is the biggest in Iran. Like many of the mosques in this part of the world, it was built upon the site of what used to be a Zoroastrian temple. I picked my way across a building site towards what appeared to be the main entrance but nobody seemed to be about. I looked through the gates in search of somebody. Despite the size of the whole complex there seemed to be only a couple of Iranian tourists wandering around, half-heartedly gazing at the occasional inscription. Suddenly the shutter at the ticket booth sprung open and a man poked his head through in the hope of selling me a ticket. I had only been walking around for a couple of minutes, when he jumped up behind me again. He seemed surprised although not offended that I couldn't remember who he was when I had only met him at the ticket booth a few minutes ago. As he was probably more than a little bored with manning the ticket booth – I suspect that he might have been asleep when I first arrived – he had decided to emerge to have a bit of a chat and act as my unofficial guide. As we meandered past the pillars and strolled under the domes, he pointed out the various layers and stages of over 800 years of Islamic design. On entering the Timurid-era Winter Hall, he turned off the strip light so I could be treated to the full effect of the light pouring in through the alabaster skylights. While we strode from the north to the south *iwan*, he pointed up proudly towards the Mongol-era stalactite mouldings. When it was time for me to leave he seemed a little sad. It seemed like too big a place for him to stay on his own.

Later in the afternoon, I walked down towards the Zayendeh River Bridges. As the sun began to set, this proved to be a popular place to take a stroll along the riverbank and enjoy an ice-cream. Friendly teenagers hung out among the arches of the scenic Si-oh-Seh Bridge (dating back to around 1600) and came over to chat as I walked past. All along the riverbanks, families laid out yet more elaborate picnics while keeping an eye on young children as they raced in and out of the sculptured park land along the river. The bridges used to be famous for their teahouses but few now remain. It was claimed that the smoke from the qalyan (water pipes) was damaging the bridges but it seems more likely that such open displays of pleasure seeking and sociability – particularly between the sexes – were increasingly discouraged under the rule of the Ayatollahs. As I crossed backwards and forwards across the bridges, licking a fake Cornetto, I was approached by more curious youngsters (there are a lot of young people in Iran and most seemed drawn to the West). One of them stated that I must be a Christian and when I said that I wasn't he seemed confused. He couldn't quite get his head around the idea that I didn't believe in God; according to his logic all religions believed in God so God must exist. Pointing out that Hindus and Buddhists don't really believe in a single god, as such, only seemed to confuse him further. He paused for a few seconds to think about this before a light went on his head. 'Which came first,' he stated triumphantly, 'the chicken or the egg?' I wasn't quite sure what to say to this. He walked off, head held high, confident in his own abilities to riposte with a devastating theological critique.

* * *

The next morning was a bit quiet. I kept forgetting that Islamic countries were like that on a Friday. As I still had most of the day to spend in Esfahan, I decided to check out some of the palaces and museums that I had yet to visit. I just wasn't sure how to get into them or whether they would even be open on a Friday. All around the general area was a metal fence covered in large yellow placards featuring quotes from the Koran. While some of the quotations seemed to be promoting common sense or good manners ('and do not be sarcastic to each other and do not insult each other by unpleasant nicknames'), the meaning of others seemed less clear ('[are those whom you consider partners for Allah better] or he who answers supplication when one calls him desperately and removes the disaster from him'). I traversed the perimeter, attempting to heed all the good advice from the evenly spaced yellow placards, until I found an entrance to the grounds of Chehel Sotun Palace. The palace was originally completed by Shah Abbas II in 1647 but was rebuilt after a fire in 1706. Chehel Sotun means 'forty pillars' – there are twenty actual pillars but they are reflected in the long pool in front of the palace. The Great Hall (Throne Room) of the palace is known for its grand frescoes depicting life from the Safavid era and the *talar* (verandah) is said to elegantly bridge the transition between the ornate interiors and the sculpted gardens. It also has a nice teahouse. I sat there nursing a warm pot and a biscuit while a group of young women nervously sat down close to me. They kept looking up and seemed to want to say something. By the time that I had finished the last of my tea, nobody had yet plucked up the courage to break the ice. As I got up leave, they all smiled and waved goodbye.

My next stop was the Natural History Museum. The rather unconvincing set of model dinosaurs set about the forecourt didn't promote particularly high expectations. It did, however, feature a stuffed animal freak show that I thought might amuse me for a while. The usual exhibits were pretty dull but I soon located the real attractions by heading for the densest part of a crowd of teenagers on a school trip. Like me, they were only really interested in the collection of two-headed monsters, five-legged freaks and mutant-like embryos staring out of bottles of formaldehyde. This may have been the high point of the museum but my interest couldn't be sustained for long; I was soon back out in the forecourt, having my picture taken in front of a plastic stegosaurus.

The only other thing to see in the area was the Decorative Arts Museum of Iran, which appeared to be closed. I met some young Iranian day trippers from a nearby town who were also waiting for it to open and they invited me to join their picnic at the roadside. Some of the girls had bleached hair poking out from beneath their headscarves and wore studded belts. The boys wore tight denim jeans and one of them even had a t-shirt with 'emo' written on it (although he didn't know what it meant). There didn't seem to be a lot to do in the town that they came from so they were always keen to make a day trip to the big city attractions of Esfahan. Judging by the sheer number of picnicking families and other domestic tourists, they were far from the only ones. I got the feeling that life in a small provincial town in Iran could be pretty dull. There were a lot of young people around who all seemed to wish they were somewhere else. Unfortunately for Iran, a lot of the best educated and most motivated of their young adults appeared to be doing their best to make this happen; Iran was being exposed to something of a 'brain drain' as many of the people who could most benefit their country were leaving for better opportunities not only outside of their local areas, but outside of Iran all together. Though young Iranians such as these weren't going out of their way to disassociate themselves from their political system, they seemed to be pumping me for information on how they could get to study or work in the West. I tried to lower their expectations to more realistic levels but nothing I could say would make a difference; their hearts and their minds had already been won. They were the future.

Tabriz

Under Cover of Darkness • Losing a Voice • Down to Earth
Darkness and Light • Dissident Exiles • Cyber Wars
Going Underground • An Illegal Alien

The night bus from Esfahan to Tabriz took less time than I had expected. At a service station stop on the way, I had been approached by a woman in a full black chador who turned out to be a lecturer in animation. Without even realizing it, I had begun to almost blank out women in the full chador as they hardly ever spoke to me. They just seemed to blend into the background. It seems ridiculous but when she first spoke to me I had been quite taken aback. I had gotten used to plenty of girls talking to me on the streets of Esfahan but these approachable young women were still very much just girls and none wore the full Islamic tent. Although the lecturer was still clearly younger than me, it still seemed strange that a fully chadored-up woman in her late twenties would even bother talking to me, and seemed stranger still that I should feel that it was strange. As a middle-class academic in a creative field, it seemed surprising that she should choose to adopt the full chador when presumably she could have gotten away with a simple headscarf. Maybe she felt that her conservative dress would help her to be taken more seriously? Maybe her family simply expected it? If she had been using the chador to hide behind – as I expect many women in the Islamic world do – then I doubt she would have come over to talk to me in the first place. I now wish that I had asked her these questions but the very chador that seemed so incongruous to her friendliness seemed to cast a long black cloak over the prospect of any really personal revelation.

As well as having been a major Silk Road city, Tabriz is also the fourth largest city in Iran, and the capital of East Azerbaijan

Province. Tabriz first came to prominence as a major trade hub under the Mongol Ilkhanid as their capital of Azerbaijan. It recovered fairly rapidly from the usual trashing by Timur in 1392 and went on to become a local capital for a Turkmen dynasty known as the Black Sheep (while the rest of Iran remained a vassal to the Timurids). Unfortunately it all went a bit wrong after that – the city was devastated by disease and a series of earthquakes culminating in the disastrous quake of 1727 that resulted in the deaths of 77,000 Tabrizis. By the nineteenth century Tabriz had managed to recover some of its prosperity but the provincial Azeri government was crushed soon after the end of the Second World War as the Shah attempted to further integrate Tabriz into the rest of Iran. The Azeri population in Tabriz so greatly resented this curtailing of their freedoms (particularly the restrictions placed upon the use of their mother tongue), that they were at the forefront of the 1979 revolution.

Having staggered off from the night bus, somewhere close to the maze-like and still waking bazaar, I eventually found my way to the Darya Guest House. The friendly owner, who had lived in England back in the 1970s, suggested that I visited the tourist information centre near the bazaar to check on the times for the night bus to Armenia, and that while I was over there I should pop into the nearby Rahnama Dairy Café to try out their *must-asal* (yoghurt and honey) for breakfast. This proved to be good advice. Every time that I was starting to think that most of the food in Iran was rubbish, I would come across something so good that it would completely change my mind. While the locals bothered at all with such dire burgers, kebabs and pizzas, when they must have known where to get far better food remained something of a mystery. It may well be that most of the locals simply chose to eat at home and that most of the customers at such cafés were actually visitors from other Iranian cities (as in China, domestic tourism is big business in Iran).

Before I even got to the bazaar, a head poked out of a window above the main arched entrance way, and asked me if I was looking for tourist information. When I said that I was, he looked delighted and rushed down the stairs at the side to welcome me up to his office. After going through the usual pleasantries of pouring out tea and enquiring as to my background, he handed me a map where he had helpfully marked the bus ticket office, and suggested that I visited the nearby troglodyte village of Kandovan during the day tomorrow, before getting my night bus to Yerevan in the evening. He already had a Danish couple who were looking for others to share a taxi with them (I got the impression that he was aware of every single foreign tourist in the entire city of nearly 1.5 million). I agreed to return the next morning.

After a small amount of inevitable confusion, I eventually managed to purchase my bus tickets for the following evening, and could then set out to explore the city. Not far from the bus company's office were the remains of Tabriz's citadel, the Ark. The whole structure is now quite unstable as the foundations have been undermined by the construction of the enormous new Mossalah Mosque just next door. They used to get rid of criminals by lobbing them off the top of the now crumbling Ark. A local legend tells of how one such woman was saved by the parachute-like effects of her chador. I knew they must be useful for something. Maybe the animation lecturer bore a deep ancestral fear of being thrown to her death and insisted on always wearing the full chador just in case?

Not much further along is the Blue (Kabud) Mosque. Originally constructed in 1465, the Blue Mosque was badly damaged by the murderous 1727 earthquake but didn't actually collapse until hit by another quake in 1773. It wasn't until after the Second World War that anybody even attempted any kind of real restoration and this work is still going on today. Rather inconveniently, in 2002 an ancient graveyard was discovered just to the north of the Blue Mosque. The planned construction work was inevitably held up, when one of the workers grassed to the authorities, but the 3,800-year-old remains were eventually incorporated into the buildings museum. Despite being one of Tabriz's biggest attractions, there really wasn't much to see. To the untrained eye it looked just like another in a long line of laboriously restored vanity projects.

Almost next door to the Blue Mosque is the Azarbaijan Museum. The exhibits on the top two floors featured all the usual old pots, coins and one-armed statues, but down in the basement I found something far more interesting: the 'Misery of the World' sculptures by Ahad Hosseini. These fearsome bronze masterpieces radiate a power and intensity that seems entirely alien within the confines of a small provincial museum. The twelve episodes that make up the collection are entitled 'Ignorance', 'War', 'Chains of Misery', 'The Miserable', 'Hunger', 'Political Prisoner', 'A Crystal Ball', 'Population Growth', 'Racial Discrimination', 'Five Monsters of Death', 'Anxiety' and 'Autumn of Life'. Each of these striking metal constructions exude a depth of darkness and despair that can only be found in the kind of great art that dares to reach through to the underworld and illuminate. Hosseini believes that 'all our misfortune is from our ignorance' and seems almost morally obliged to lead us on towards greater knowledge and understanding. At the same time, he seems to acknowledge that this same creative force has often only led to greater misery, hunger and anxiety: 'people are scared of the world they have made with their own hands'. Having filled my mind with Hosseini's apocalyptic visions of a world of misery, I emerged from the neon-lit, but darkness-filled, basement and walked into the museum's cafeteria for a nice cup of tea. I couldn't be bothered with the gift shop.

After a stroll through the large covered bazaar, and some rather nice cake that I bought from a gregarious baker, I returned to my room to crash out in front of an old portable TV. I was still tired from yet another overnight bus trip and could do with some decent telly. Unfortunately I wasn't going to get it here. From what little television I managed to catch in Iran, I got the distinct impression that what was freely available was of poor quality and extremely dull. Most of the more affluent Iranians seemed to subscribe to satellite services so that they could catch the higher quality Western shows, along with a surprisingly large number of Farsi language programmes beamed in by dissident expatriates. Unfortunately the government doesn't seem too keen on 'degenerate' and uncensored Western television being broadcast to their citizens through satellite dishes. Every now and again they would have a bit of a crackdown and start bothering to enforce the 1994 law banning the possession and use of satellite dishes. As nearly all the wealthier Iranians – along with around 4 million others – do, in fact, possess satellite dishes, this law seems to be rather selectively enforced.

It wasn't long until I grew tired of the 'entertainment' on public television, and headed off to a nearby Internet café. Despite most of the government attempts to censor it, it is the Internet that seems to be the most popular way for the young to gain access to international news, art and entertainment. The friendly young guys who worked there proudly showed off to me an arsenal of software they had acquired to get around any censorship or restrictions that the government might try to enforce on them – you just had to ask and Facebook and YouTube could soon be downloading to your chosen PC. It seemed that as soon as some government hack tried to block access to an unapproved site, some benevolent techie would make available a workaround. The authorities might have won a few of the battles in cyberspace but they were never going to win the war.

* * *

After another breakfast of yoghurt and honey at Rahnama Dairy Café, I headed up the stairs to the tourist information centre and was offered some tea while I waited for the Danish couple to arrive so that I could share a taxi with them to the troglodyte village of Kandovan, around 60 kilometres from Tabriz. Two hours and several cups of tea later, I was still waiting. When it became clear that they weren't going to turn up, I agreed to pay the driver US$20 to take me there and back on my own.

After a scenic drive through the Osku Chai valley, towards Mount Sahand, we pulled into the side of the only real road through the village and my driver pulled his cap down over his eyes to get some sleep. Down below were a few deserted tourist stalls and restaurants on either side of a dirty brown stream gurgling through the bottom of the valley, and up above was a hillside stacked with oddly shaped rock formations fashioned into homes. Kandovan is similar in many ways to Cappadocia in Central Turkey but it's smaller, dirtier and less homogenized. The villagers live in cone-shaped caves that were formed from volcanic ash spewed out by Mount Sahand over thousands of years. Their homes can be up to four stories high, often with a dedicated area for their animals on the lowest level. Some believe that the name 'Kandovan' derives from the plural of '*kando*', meaning 'bee's hive', while others believe that the name means 'land of unknown carvers'. The layers of hollowed-out cones stacked up against the hillside are actually closer in appearance to termite mounds than to bee's hives (termite mounds with washing hanging out the windows and donkeys crapping down the pathways). If it wasn't for the Iranian tourists wandering around with their digital cameras and mobile phones, you could almost believe you had emerged in some strange medieval time warp. The present villagers actually believe that Kandovan is around 700 years old and that it was formed by people fleeing from the advancing Mongol armies who used the caves as a refuge and a place of hiding. More recent evidence, however, seems to suggest that the caves may have been inhabited for up to 3,000 years – this would mean that the troglodytes' ancestors would have been contemporaries of the first known Zoroastrians in the region.

I traipsed up and down the hillside, admiring the wonderfully shaped houses, while trying not to slip on the crumbling mountain paths or tread in any donkey shit. I was the only Western tourist in the village but the whole area was clearly quite an attraction for Iranians from all around the country. On climbing up around one steep corner I found myself surrounded by dozens of excitable schoolgirls, all of whom seemed to want to have their picture taken with me. They seemed a lot more interested in me than in Kandovan. I had felt a little uncomfortable about invading the villagers' privacy too much by taking pictures of them going about their daily business, but saw no reason not to photograph the schoolgirls now that my image had been captured on seemingly dozens of teenagers' mobile phones. I wondered what they would think when they looked back at their snaps from the school trip and saw me staring back. I walked further along the hillside past morose-looking donkeys being dragged along by small boys, and past dumpy matriarchs hanging out their washing from one rock peak to another. Every time I met some other (Iranian) tourists they would seem delighted to see me and we would all have our picture taken together with our arms around each other. I was going to be appearing in a lot of pictures of Kandovan. The sound of drumming drew me down to the bottom of the valley, where locals sat around together, beating out their rhythms into the hills. There were plenty of stalls around that were clearly intended for the tourists but few had bothered to open. A few of the locals half-heartedly tried to interest me in their wares but soon lost interest. There was still some snow and ice visible on the peaks of the mountains. Maybe it would all soon change?

After waking my driver and returning to Tabriz, I had to be careful not to spend too much as I only had a few Iranian Rials left. I rationed myself to half an hour more at the Internet café and a large chicken sandwich with another lemon-flavoured non-alcoholic beer (I don't like alcoholic beer, but I was beginning to acquire a taste for these). On the way back to the hotel to pick up my backpack, I am pretty sure that I noticed my first Iranian transvestite in a chador. I couldn't really see the point of this. Maybe he was wearing a nice dress underneath but didn't want to draw attention to himself? If some men in Iran really do choose to wear the chador, then this would seem to suggest something rather more complex about the nature of transvestitism than is generally acknowledged. I shrugged and carried on. It was definitely a man.

After picking up my backpack I made my way over to the bus station office and met up with a young Korean guy who was also planning to catch the same bus. Neither of us was entirely sure about what was happening but it looked as if the man from the office was going to take us out to the outskirts of the city where we would have to wave down the bus that had already left Tehran on the way to Yerevan. He made us give him all the money that we still had left to pay for a taxi to the edge of the motorway, and then made us stand around at the side of the road. The young Korean guy seemed quite upset about this. Nobody had explained this to either of us and it seemed like a bit of a cheek that we were expected to pay for our escort to get another taxi back to his office. After a lot of waiting around in the dark, the coach eventually rolled up and we were bundled aboard onto the two remaining seats by a bus steward who looked remarkably like Ben Stiller. We would soon start nodding off as we settled down into the drive through the night towards yet another border.

After only a few hours we were all ushered off the coach by 'Ben' and led to the border post. The Armenian visa was cheap and straightforward to get but we still seemed to be stuck for ages after walking over to the Armenian side. I think they were searching the coach. All of the women on the coach had now removed their headscarves and were busy with brushing their unleashed hair and generally tidying themselves up. Now that they were free, their own styles and personalities started to shine through – they no longer just merged into a herd of covered women. On the walk across the no-man's land between what was technically Asia and Europe, I met Reza, an Iranian Christian who seemed even more determined than most to leave his own country. He had previously been jailed in Canada as an illegal immigrant and had only been back in Iran for a few months. As several attempts to gain political asylum on the grounds of his Christian faith had failed, he was now attempting to try his luck in Armenia as a first entry point into Europe. His father had already paid for a number of illegal documents and passports but, so far, each time that he had attempted to make it outside of his home country, he had failed. He seemed tired and desperate but not yet broken. I hoped that he could get to where he wanted to be – and find that it was what he had hoped for.

Armenia

Yerevan and Lake Sevan

Sowing the Seeds of Conflict • Stairway to Heaven • Attracting Evangelism The Crossing Point • Home of the Gods • Youth in Revolt • Natural Death Warrior Monks • Drowning the Sorrow • Cursed to Wander the Earth Torn Between Two Worlds • Saving Souls • Twin Spires Emerging Markets • Screamers • National Identity

One of the main routes of the Silk Road led up through Armenia and Georgia to the port of Batumi on the Black Sea, and then on towards the Mediterranean. As the coach continued on from the Iranian border towards Yerevan, I wasn't sure exactly where I was going – it was still dark and I kept falling in and out of consciousness. As the sun began to rise, I woke as the rhythm of the bus was broken while we passed through ancient-looking stone-built towns and villages. I had at least wanted to catch a glimpse of the supposedly attractive southern town of Goris as we passed through it, but even if I had been awake it would probably have been too dark to make out much. As the sun rose so did we, through the stone-littered, cloud-topped mountains. To the left was Naxcivan, the isolated enclave of Azerbaijan, and to the right was Nagorno Karabakh (*nagorno* means 'mountainous') – formerly a part of Azerbaijan but now struggling to be recognized as an independent country. As in Central Asia, the Soviet Union's policy of divide and rule inevitably led to tension across the Caucasus – as well as tearing up Azerbaijan into two parts by awarding the province of Zangezour to Armenia, Lenin also handed the mainly Armenian-populated region of Karabakh to Azerbaijan, thus sowing the seeds of future conflict. Needless to say, all borders between Armenia and Azerbaijan are still currently closed and relations are more than a little strained. Ever since some Ottoman Armenians decided to side with the Russians during the First World War

– as they thought this would give them a better chance of re-establishing an independent Armenia – relations with Turkey have also been rather difficult (the term 'genocide' was actually coined to describe the systematic murder of around 1.5 million Armenians by the Ottoman Turks). It doesn't help that modern-day Turkey still fails to acknowledge that the genocide ever took place and seems determined to punish any nation that does. As you might have guessed, the border between Armenia and Turkey is also closed. Fortunately, Armenia was still just about muddling along with Iran and Georgia, which meant that I would be able to carry on up this particular Silk Road through Armenia to Georgia, from where I could cross into Turkey and continue on to my final destination of Istanbul.

By the time that we pulled into the bus station in Yerevan, it was getting on for the middle of the day. The young Korean guy was set on staying at a hostel he had heard of that only cost US$3 a night. As his 'hostel' was just one room without actual beds or even a communal shower, I opted to spend a little more so that I could stay at the much nicer sounding Envoy Hostel. We hopped on a *marshrutka* together, which was heading over the bridge across the gorge and into the city. I got off far too early, and ended up having to trudge for far too long through the drizzle, while trying to figure out where I was on my badly photocopied street map. After months in Asia it seemed somewhat disconcerting to have fallen asleep in the Middle East and to have woken up in what is generally considered to be not only a part of Europe but also the oldest Christian nation in the world (it was declared the state religion in AD 301). I had also gotten so used to seeing women in *hijab* that they now seemed strangely exposed without it. It didn't, however, seem as if I was necessarily stepping forward into a more modern world – as in Kazakhstan, many of the styles and fashions seemed strangely dated and vulgar, as if they were almost trying too hard to be what they thought of as sexy and liberated.

When I eventually managed to find the Envoy Hostel, I was warmly welcomed in. It cost more for a bunk bed in a dormitory than I had been used to paying for my own room with a bathroom, but it seemed like an exceptionally clean and well-run hostel with friendly staff and a good range of organized day trips. I signed up for their 'Essential Armenia' tour for the next day. Having had some good places to eat and a few sights recommended to me, I set out again with the advice that I couldn't possibly get lost. I walked up towards Opera Square and sat down at one of the attractive outside restaurants that surrounded the Opera House. The menu turned out to be far more limited than I had expected and the burger that I eventually settled for turned out to be just as bad as the ones in Iran. I then set off down the grandest of the avenues towards what I thought was going to be the entrance to the Cascade but turned out to be the Matenedara, Armenia's library of ancient manuscripts. It looked as if I could get lost after all.

As the Matenedara was closed I retraced my steps back towards Opera Square and eventually located the right branch leading out towards Yerevan's most famous site, the Cascade. It's basically a very big and expensive marble staircase that looks like a skyscraper set into the side of a hill. Some interesting statues, such as Fernando Botero's chubby 'Cat', line the boulevard leading up to the Cascade, and a number of grand fountains are recessed into the megalithic structure as it crawls up towards the sky. The whole project ground to a halt when independence arrived in 1991 and it wasn't until 2001 that construction continued under the backing of American-Armenian businessman and art lover, Gerard Cafesjian. The US$30 million Cafesjian Museum, incorporated into the Cascades, was almost finished but huge idle cranes still stood at the very top of the cascades, waiting to finish off the final stretch towards the Fiftieth Anniversary of Soviet Armenia Monument that lords it over the city.

Cafesjian is far from the only Armenian to have made it big abroad and then to have returned to help his home country. The genocide led to something of a diaspora for the Armenians and there are now somewhere in the region of 8 million Armenians living abroad but only just over 3 million in Armenia and Karabakh. As with the Jews, many Armenians have done very well for themselves in their adopted countries and have made large financial contributions towards Armenia (about US$5 billion a year is sent to Armenia in remittances). Most notable of all of Armenia's beneficiaries is Kirk Kerkorian, the American-Armenian billionaire who has channelled more than US$180 million into Armenia through his Lincy Foundation (Kerkorian was head of MGM in the 1970s when it produced *Midnight Express,* a film that didn't exactly cast the Turkish in a flattering light).

By now, the museum complex at the top was already starting to close down for the day, but I carried on up the internal escalator to take in the views from the top. I stood there on my own looking down over a strange mixture of grand European-style avenues and monuments, and dull, grey Soviet concrete blocks. The main strip through the centre of the city seemed as affluent as any other capital in Eastern Europe, but only a few blocks back from the designer clothes shop and marble statues were the kind of run-down back streets and dilapidated houses that seemed to belong more in the Third World than in what was ostensibly, at least, Europe. The Middle East might not have been that far from the Westernized surface but one very apparent cultural difference was the Armenians' attitude towards personal space. While still being very friendly and welcoming, it seemed quite refreshing to have managed to have walked this far around the city without actually attracting a 'guide'. In fact, the only people who had approached me so far had been a couple of Jehovah's Witnesses who had let me off with accepting a copy of *The Watchtower*.

As I walked further up from the top of the unfinished Cascades, around a building zone, and towards the Monument at the very peak of the hill, I was greeted by another couple whom I assumed to be tourists. It soon became clear that they were actually Jehovah's Witnesses as well. It seemed unlikely that these were the only people outside of the hostel that had actually talked to me, but I guessed they must have been hanging around Yerevan's attractions in the hope of converting any visitors. (I later found out there were around 9,000 Jehovah's Witnesses in Armenia and that they were less than popular with the Armenian Apostolic Church – of which 90 per cent of Armenians are at least nominally members.) The odds of them just happening to convert any independent travellers seemed pretty remote but I suppose that they were obliged by their faith to at least try, and it was better than risking a beating or abuse by the kind of Armenians who consider them to be anti-Christian. They soon gave up on any attempt to convert me and seemed happy to chat. It didn't look like they were saving a lot of souls in Armenia but apparently it was still better than in Iran, from where they had fled. When I mentioned something about there still being a death sentence in Iran for converting from Islam, they conceded that this had been something of an obstacle.

There seems to be something about Armenia that attracts evangelism. It first attracted Christian missionaries as early as AD 40 and Armenia seems always to have been positioned at the centre of a 'clash of civilizations'. Both physically and culturally, it seems always to have been a 'crossing point'. Over the centuries, dozens of civilizations – from the Mongols and Timurids, to the Romans and Persians – have attempted to impose their culture upon this land, but against the odds the Armenians seem always to have retained their own identity. As I made my way to the highest point, I could just about see through the mist to the twin peaks of Mount Ararat: the great symbol of Armenia. Mount Ararat is currently located in modern-day Turkey but forms a near-quadripoint between Turkey, Armenia, Azerbaijan (Naxcivan) and Iran. Mount Ararat seems always to have been associated with religion and is thought in Western Christianity to be where Noah's ark landed after the great flood. In Armenian mythology, Mount Ararat is nothing less than the home of the gods. For most of the last century this holy mountain and its surrounds have been classed as a militarized zone.

On the way back to Envoy Hostel I stopped at an international supermarket. I didn't feel like eating at another restaurant on my own, so I picked up some food to eat at the hostel with the other travellers. Tonight it was movie night and they were showing the just released DVD of *Avatar* on their large new plasma screen. I sat there among the various nationalities at this 'crossing point' while munching away on my imported food and gazing up at the proud freedom fighters as they struggled to protect their land and their culture from the evil invaders.

* * *

After breakfast at the hostel I joined the group for our day trip led by Gevorg and Marina. For a youth hostel trip, none of the guests looked very youthful. Almost everyone was over forty. Maybe all the younger backpackers were staying at the other really cheap hostel? When I commented on this to a dour sixty-year-old Yorkshire man (whom Marina had dubbed Mr Bob), he agreed that the average age of the guests at the 'youth' hostel was quite surprising, but commented that he had recently been to Syria where most of the other travellers had made him feel like a teenager. This seemed like a relatively recent phenomenon that we theorized had been fuelled by a growing familiarity with 'exotic' locations and the near-systematic transfer of wealth in developed Western countries from the young to the old; as the recently retired had made huge profits from the fetishization of property, the youth had become increasingly crippled by debt in order to pay off both the debts the baby-boomers had racked up for their countries, and to finance their own education and the continuing obsession with home ownership. Mr Bob reckoned that hardly any young people would be able to afford to travel in the future and that the youth hostels would soon start to look more like old people's homes.

Our first stop of the day was at Lake Sevan and Sevanavank (Sevan Monastery). As the lake sits up in the cool mountains at 1,900 metres above sea level, it is a popular summer resort during the stiflingly hot summer months in Yerevan. Outside of the peak of summer, however, it's like a morgue. The peninsular on which the two rough-hewn churches of Sevanavank stand used to be an island until a lot of the water was drained off by the Soviet Union to use for irrigation and hydroelectricity. In 1910, one of the same civil engineers that were behind the disastrous draining of the Aral Sea suggested lowering the water level by 45 metres. This plan was modified to 55 metres during the Stalin era and approved by the Armenian Supreme Soviet without any consultation with the local people. Fortunately, these plans took longer than expected to put into place and, by the time that the environment had started to noticeably deteriorate and the fish had begun to die, the Stalin era was at end. Various projects since then have helped to raise the level of the lake and improve the water quality but it is still 20 metres lower than it used to be. Monks lived on what used to be the island from the end of the eighth century and almost continuously seemed to be fighting in battles to protect the monastery from a series of invasions from Arabs, Persians and Ottomans. The last monk didn't leave the monastery until 1930 and today it is run by the Church as a summer retreat for seminarians.

Not far from Lake Sevan was Noratus Cemetery, known for its *khachkars,* the distinctively Armenian carved gravestones.

The often large and intricately carved headstones regularly featured complex stories relating to the life of the deceased and often gave clues as to what caused their death. They were clearly something of a status symbol and poor local families would often borrow thousands of dollars in order to commission such works of art (according to Gevorg, some of the more elaborate *khachkars* cost over US$8,000). The level of craftsmanship did, however, appear to be in decline. Gevorg reckoned that there wasn't much to do in this part of rural Armenia apart from fishing, growing potatoes and drinking vodka, and, since most of the fish had died, the locals had killed off far too many of their brain cells through their habitual heavy drinking.

As we wandered around the cemetery admiring the graves, elderly peasant women tried to sell us knitted hats and gloves. Their ankle-length skirts, knitted cardigans and flowery headscarves gave the impression that they'd have been more at home in rural Iran than in cosmopolitan Yerevan. When we asked if there was a toilet in the area, we were proudly directed to a brand new block of two sparkling clean Western toilets at the edge of the cemetery. They seemed to belong in a different world altogether to the kind of public pit toilets I had come to expect in Soviet Central Asia. Presumably, the toilets had been donated by yet more affluent Armenians from abroad and the ladies received a small salary for keeping them in tip-top condition. As we stepped back over the graves they asked us what we thought and were delighted by our approval.

For lunch we were taken to eat with a local family. We were enthusiastically ushered through into an old-fashioned looking dining room and spread out around a large wooden table. As we made our way through plates of heavy local peasant food, our glasses were constantly replenished with a scouring local spirit that we were encouraged to knock back in one go. Apparently it was made in the bathtub. And it tasted like it. It wasn't until we stood up to leave, however, that we realized its full potency. If this is what the locals drank every day then it was hardly surprising that the quality of the local workmanship had gone downhill. In fact, it was surprising that any of the stone carvers still had any fingers left.

After a rather drowsy after-dinner drive, we arrived at the monastery of Geghard, a UNESCO World Heritage Site. The name 'Geghard' derives from 'The Spear of Destiny' – the lance used to pierce the side of Christ as he hung on the cross. This particular Holy Lance – others are in Austria, Poland and the Vatican – was supposedly brought to Armenia by Apostle Jude (Thaddeus?), one of the patron saints of the Armenian Apostolic Church. The spear of destiny is often thought to have potent mystical powers and to bring victory to whoever possesses it (Hitler's lust for the spear of destiny has become a staple of popular mythology). We couldn't actually see the spear as it was moved to the Echmiadzin treasury but I have seen pictures of it and it doesn't look like it could pierce a wet paper bag. Some have even argued that the spear of destiny wasn't really a spear at all but a sharpened pruning hook (an agricultural tool) that was used by Cain, the original settler, to slay Abel, the archetypal nomad (for his sins, God cursed Cain to be a 'restless wanderer of the earth').

The original Geghard Monastery was first founded in the fourth century on the site of a spring in a cave that was held to be holy in pre-Christian times (it used to be called 'Ayrivank' meaning 'Monastery of the Cave'). This version was destroyed in the ninth century by the invading Arabs and it wasn't until 1215 that the architecturally outstanding rock-cut main chapel was built under the auspices of Queen Tamar of Georgia (her empire dominated the Caucasus until its collapse under the Mongol attacks less than two decades after her death).

As we wandered out of the cave church and into the drizzle, we bought sheets of *lavash* (dried fruit) from an old man in the stone-paved parking area, before making the short drive to the Greco-Roman-style Garni Temple. Recent architectural evidence suggests that this complex on the bend of the Azat River dates back as far as the third century BC, but it is thought that the main peripteros temple (one that's surrounded by columns) on the edge of the cliff, was constructed in the first century BC as a declaration of Armenia as a Roman province. We were actually looking at a restoration by the Soviets as the temple was destroyed by an earthquake in 1679. Rather than having been constructed with marble and mortar, the temple had been made of harder basalt blocks that were tied together by lead-sealed iron cramps. Unfortunately, these iron clamps had often been stolen and melted down, which made the temple rather vulnerable to seismic activity (Armenia is particularly vulnerable to such disasters as it lies between the Arabian and European tectonic plates – around 60,000 were killed in the Spitak earthquake in 1988).

Later in the evening, at the hostel, I started talking to a young American guy about my initial impressions of Armenia. I commented on how strange I thought it was that so many Jehovah's Witnesses seemed to be coming from abroad to look for converts in Armenia when the Armenian Apostolic Church was so well established and so central to Armenia's Christian identity. He listened attentively and nodded his head in all the right places. He seemed sympathetic and sane. When I asked him what he was doing in Armenia, he told me that he was a missionary. He had come to Armenia and Georgia two years before, when he was only nineteen, to work as a missionary for The Church of Jesus Christ of Latter Day Saints (the Mormons). He pointed out an older couple on the other side of the room who were actually his mum and dad. They had come over from the States to visit him and he was taking them on a bit of a tour of the region. His Mormon parents were insistent that this was 'The Middle East' and were clearly very proud of their son's dedication to saving souls. From what I could gather, these 'born again' and mainly American sects targeted the poorest and most deprived areas of such regions and then tried to win new followers through various forms of financial support (they always try to get you when you're down). When I asked if they had attracted many new converts, he seemed a little vague. It seemed most unlikely that many Armenians, after all that they had been through, would ever choose to surrender any part of their identity to these latest, and least convincing, of foreign invaders.

* * *

The Envoy Hostel ran a free city walking tour every morning. I was the only one who had signed up for it but Gevorg said that it was fine and he was still happy to take me on my own. As soon as we got outside he launched into a well-rehearsed spiel about how the tour was free but that tips were always welcome. This immediately made me feel uncomfortable, as I had no idea how much I should be tipping on a free tour. If there was a group of ten, then you would only have to chip in a small amount each for the tour guide to get a worthwhile amount of cash, but if there was only the one on it, then this could be awkward and embarrassing. What would be fine as part of an overall tip from the group could seem insultingly low on its own, but I wouldn't have signed up for a 'free' tour if I had felt that I had to pay up enough to make it worth his while to take just me.

Eventually I managed to relax and just enjoy the walk as Gevorg led me around his city. We walked down past the large indoor food market, towards the gorge, and on to Republic Square. In the distance, in the hills above the football stadium – where Armenia had recently lost to Turkey in what must have been quite an emotion-fuelled match – towered the Genocide Memorial. Almost everywhere you went in the city, the 40-metre-high spire acted as a reminder of the Turkish-led massacres. Gevorg told me that they preferred not to get maudlin and dwell on the past. I believed him. Further on from the old embassy buildings around Parliament Square were the Yerevan Brandy Company (that runs tours for tourists), a statue of a famous drunk who always used to sell flowers in the city, and another statue of a popular film character who was famously always drunk. I seemed to have stumbled on something of a theme. All over the former Soviet Union, heavy drinking seemed to be revered as an almost heroic activity. (Soviet army conscripts used to be forced to consume their daily rations of vodka, as senior officers found that it made the men more compliant.) When we returned to the hostel, I found that the only notes I had on me to give as a tip were either so small as to seem borderline insulting or far too much. I explained the situation to Gevorg and offered to go and get some change but he told me not to worry about it. I offered to buy him a drink later on.

In the afternoon I had intended to walk up towards the Genocide Museum and Monument but had underestimated the distance and the difficulty in getting there. I found myself wandering in and out of the kind of run-down back streets that you would more expect to find in a country village than just a short walk from an apparently thriving capital city. Like the young of Yerevan, I eventually turned my back on the twin spires of the Genocide Monument – echoing the twin spires of the mystical Mount Ararat – and headed back towards the designer shops and nightclubs of the city. While the rock scene in Iran was kept firmly underground, in Yerevan it appeared to be openly thriving along with other forms of popular culture. As well as a rock club just up the road from Envoy Hostel, there was also a nearby 'Beatles' club, a jazz club and even a thriving dance club that ran from inside the Opera House. It still, however, all seemed a little dated. The international rock groups that Yerevan was now starting to attract appear to have peaked in the seventies; the most popular acts to be visiting Armenia were 'veteran' British rockers Deep Purple and Uriah Heep. I doubt if many rock fans in the UK know that Uriah Heep are still going, but presumably they can still scrape a living from touring such 'emerging markets' as Armenia. At the Yerevan Puppet Theatre I also saw a poster advertising a show being put on by a local heavy metal act. I couldn't help wondering if – Spinal Tap-style – the act would be opening up for the puppet show. The stars of the forthcoming rock show actually more closely resembled Bad News, the British equivalent to the better-known Spinal Tap; with their stripy spandex, big hair and bullet belts, they could easily have passed for obscure early eighties UK rock wannabes.

Outside of Armenia itself, however, Armenians have made far more of an impact on cutting-edge rock and roll. The American Armenian 'Nu Metal' stars, System of a Down, exploded out of California in the late nineties, to become one of the biggest and most politicized rock groups in the world. Their second album, *Toxicity*, became a modern-day classic and went on to sell more than 5 million copies. According to Gevorg, System of a Down is virtually a household name throughout Armenia and, when Serj Tankian, the band's lead singer, recently visited Armenia, he was greeted as a returning hero. Like many Armenians who have found international success, they haven't forgotten their roots; they named their song 'Holy Mountain' after Mount Ararat and also financed a documentary about the Armenian Genocide in an attempt to gain international recognition of Armenia's tragic recent past.

As I now had to rush to get back to Istanbul in time for my flight, this evening would be my last in Armenia. Tomorrow morning I would leave for Georgia, my last new country for this trip and the one that I had hoped would be my hundredth. Being refused entry into Kyrgyzstan because of the uprising had messed that up. While being fully aware that keeping count of the number of countries you had visited was kind of ridiculous, I still kind of liked the idea of having visited so many places. It made me feel like I had something to show for my wanderlust. Everything that I had ever wanted to achieve might have ended in pitiful failure but at least I had seen a lot of the world and still wasn't dead. I decided to look up a list of all the countries in the world on the Internet to check on where I'd actually been. This wasn't as simple as you might think, as nobody seemed to agree on exactly how many countries there are. Some lists didn't include countries that aren't fully independent, which excluded countries such as Scotland or Hong Kong, but I don't think many Scottish people would be too happy if you told them that their country didn't exist. Also, Hong Kong may technically be under the control of China, but it has its own money, its own borders and visa regulations, and effectively its own government – that sounds like a country to me! Other countries with their own money, army, borders and government – such as Nagorno Karabakh and the breakaway Georgian states of Abkhazia and South Ossetia – aren't recognized as countries by some other countries simply as it wouldn't be politically expedient to do so, and yet some EU member states with no currency of their own, no enforceable borders and little real independence have no trouble at all in being recognized as a county in their own right. I decided to include non-independent countries in my list; if Scotland and Wales aren't countries, then what are they? I also noticed that there were a couple on the United Nations list of countries that I hadn't initially considered: Palestine and the Vatican. It seemed a little odd that Palestine was included when Hong Kong, Scotland and Taiwan weren't, but then every pub-quizzer in the world knows that the Vatican is the world's smallest country. According to my new list of countries I'd been to, I would now be in my hundredth country by tomorrow!

Georgia

Tbilisi

Consuming Experiences • Soviet Scheming • All Hail to the New Lords Begging for Approval • Drunk and Defiant

I had been told that *marshrutkas* would leave for Georgia's capital Tbilisi every hour or so. I caught the city bus down to the station that I had arrived at and easily found a small run-down minibus that would apparently soon be on its way. An hour later nothing much had changed. I had spent nearly all of my remaining Armenian *drams* on a few snacks and some water but fortunately I had held on to enough change to pay for the use of the smelly bus station toilets. Another hour later and still nothing had changed. When I asked when it might be leaving I was told that it would be soon. That was what I'd been told two hours ago. Over the next hour or so a few old women in long skirts and old men in tatty old jackets began to loiter around the idle *marshrutka*. When a few of them got in, I joined them. After another hour or so, we eventually got on our way – but only after a Scandinavian-looking young woman with a short skirt and hair down to her waist had eventually managed to part from her more Mediterranean-looking boyfriend. They had spoken English to each other, but he had spoken to the bus driver and the other passengers in Armenian.

After a couple of hours of trundling up through the lush mountain scenery, we stopped near some small waterfalls for a break, and the young, fair-skinned woman introduced herself as Inger. She had come from Lithuania to work as a volunteer on aid projects in Armenia and was due to catch her flight home from Tbilisi in the evening. The Baltic countries had gained their independence from the Soviet Union at almost the same time as the countries in the Caucasus, but were faring considerably better. I had been through the Baltic region less than a year ago and had been amazed at how quickly these former Soviet outposts appeared to be catching up with neighbouring Scandinavia. In contrast, much of the Caucasus, at the other end of Eastern Europe, was still dilapidated, poverty stricken and corrupt. It wasn't so much that there wasn't any money around as that most of it ended up in the hands of a small elite who would generally prefer to spend it on luxury high-status imported goods than invest it in their own countries. When I asked Inger how much good she thought her volunteering work had actually done, she seemed a little unsure. Apparently she had enjoyed her gap year 'experience' but it hadn't come cheap (it looked like it would be a while until affluent young Georgians and Armenians moved on from consuming 'name brand' commodities to 'experience' commodities).

Crossing over into Georgia was simple enough and was the only country along the Silk Road that didn't require a visa. After arriving at a run-down bus station at the edge of Tbilisi, we made our way to the start of Tbilisi's underground system, where Inger carried on to the airport and I made my way towards Dodo's Homestay. As I ascended the underground's escalators towards the bustling crossroads of Marjanishvili, I could make out something familiar among the shining lights and neon that were all competing for my attention as the light of day began to fade. Out of the crumbling streets emerged a shining icon of the Westernized, neo-liberal, free market values that Georgia had been so keen to buy into: McDonald's. The first one I'd seen since the ones in China at the other end of the Silk Road. It seemed to be doing a lot more business than the surrounding kebab shops.

After eventually locating the gate into Dodo's Homestay, I was enthusiastically allocated to one of the dilapidated shared rooms and told that it was my lucky day. The only other guests had arranged to hire a taxi for the following day to visit the Davit Gareja Monastery and were looking for another person. Dodo took me through to the kitchen to make me some strong

Georgian coffee (similar to the bitter Turkish sludge) and introduced me to William and Tom from Belgium. It actually was my lucky day, as I had wanted to visit this Georgian landmark – which was partly in Azerbaijan – but hadn't been sure if it would have been a viable trip on my own.

As the other guys had already made plans to meet up with a friend at a nightclub in the old city, I unpacked my bag, made use of the incongruously newly installed bathroom (still with some of the plastic sheeting left around the fittings), and wandered back onto the pot-holed pavements to find something to eat. Although plenty of shops were still open, they nearly all seemed to be pharmacies, money exchanges or cake shops (this may well have said something about Georgian culture). As I couldn't find anywhere more appealing to eat, I eventually gave in and surrendered to the familiar. At least McDonald's wouldn't make me sick (in small enough doses).

* * *

After a breakfast of Nescafé instant coffee and cake, we set off with the driver and car that we had hired for the day towards the Davit Gareja Monastery. William and Tom had been friends since school in Belgium and were just on a two- or three-week holiday to Georgia and Armenia. They had fancied going somewhere different that wasn't too far from home, and, like Inger, had managed to pick up reasonably cheap flights through the budget airline airBaltic.

The monastery complex had originally been founded in the sixth century by St David Garejeli, one of the thirteen Assyrian monks who had come to Georgia from Mesopotamia to promote their own particular brand of Christianity (Christianity first arrived in Georgia in the fourth century, not long after it was adopted in Armenia). The monasteries were destroyed by the Mongols in 1265 and later sacked by Timur, but it was the Persian Shah Abbas who caused most harm: he ordered his soldiers to kill 6,000 monks and destroyed nearly all of their artistic treasures. The monasteries had been restored in the seventeenth century and remain in use today, but have never recovered their former importance.

On arriving at the gateway of the Lavra monastery (on the Georgian side), we were welcomed in by a monk with a full beard and long hair. He suggested that we visit his gift shop when we had finished looking around. As we wandered in and around the rock-hewn chapels in the hillside, we ran into a Georgian school outing. When two teenage girls timidly approached the entrance to one of the poorly lit caves they were startled by the site of the exceptionally tall and ginger William emerging from the darkness. Their screams soon turned to giggles and an overriding curiosity. We ended up joining up with the school group on the hike to the top of the hill that marked the border between Georgia and Azerbaijan. Just over the peak, in what is officially Azerbaijan, was a series of small cave monasteries decorated with renowned frescoes. Theses 'monasteries' were rather smaller than I had expected, and could easily have been missed as they were little more than decorated caves, but the views across the plains of Azerbaijan and the surrounding countryside were among the best in the world. According to the GPS on William's mobile phone we were now officially in Azerbaijani territory. There has been pressure from the Azerbaijan government to make the Davit Gareja Monastery an official tourist site for both Georgia and Azerbaijan but the only way to make it up there from the Azerbaijan side would be to hike over what appeared to be miles and miles of open plains and hillside. Fortunately, Georgia and Azerbaijan have managed to maintain a basically good relationship and are unlikely to resort to anything worse than bickering over the disputed territory. According to the Georgian monks at the monastery, the dispute is 'the result of Soviet scheming to undermine relations between Christian Georgians and Muslim Azerbaijanis'. None of the Georgians I met seemed to have particularly strong opinions about Azerbaijan but the same couldn't be said for Russia. 'We hate Russians,' chorused the schoolgirls. I thought that this sounded a bit strong so they went on to clarify it wasn't so much the ordinary Russians they hated as the Russian government. Georgia's pro-Western stance and desire to join NATO hasn't exactly gone down well with their neighbouring superpower. Russia's backing of the separatist regimes in both Abkhazia and South Ossetia and a ban on most Georgian imports seems to have damaged their relationship beyond repair. In 2008, Georgia broke off all diplomatic relations with Russia.

On the way back, we were invited to a picnic with the friendly school group. We didn't have anything to bring along but they didn't mind. They had plenty of food and vodka for everybody. We followed their school bus back down through the countryside until it pulled over seemingly randomly at the edge of a field. I think they must have been looking for somewhere a little more scenic but had eventually given in to their hunger and decided that this would have to do. While the girls laid out checked cloths across the grass and brought out wicker picnic baskets full of bread, salads, fruit and vodka, the boys pulled off branches from the trees in a surrounding orchard in order to make a camp fire on which to cook great big hunks of meat. They promised that it would be good, and it was. A selection of vodkas and spirits was passed around to everybody, including the eleven-year-old son of one of the teachers (he looked like he was going to get a bit rowdy later on but then simply fell asleep).

After encouraging us to drink and eat as much as possible, the teachers let us know that the girls would like to play a drinking game with us. Whoever was chosen by a spinning vodka bottle would get to ask whoever they liked to perform a dare. This could be to sing a song, or perform an amusing dance, or to generally make a fool of themselves in front of all the other participants. The first drunk schoolgirl to be selected dared me to kiss her. I gave her a peck on the cheek. (She was later rather taken back to find out that I was the same age as her dad – this was a little sobering for both of us). After we'd all taken turns at drunken acts of foolishness, we exchanged email addresses, and staggered back towards our car and the school bus. The two young Belgian guys promised to visit the girls at the school before they went home. They were glad they'd chosen Georgia for their holiday.

* * *

I made my down past the McDonald's near the crossroads at Marjanishvili and over the bridge crossing the Mtkvari River. As I trudged up the winding, cobbled road, yet another shining edifice came into view: standing proud above the medieval streets of Tbilisi was another, even larger, McDonald's, lording it over the city like a glittering temple to globalization. I looked down over thousands of years of history, through the gleaming plate glass windows, while consuming donuts and cappuccino. Suitably indulged, I carried on down Rustaveli Avenue, the main thoroughfare of the city, past the country's best-known museums and theatres, and the trampoline outside of the Georgian Parliament. It was outside of this building that the Soviets massacred twenty Georgian hunger strikers in 1989, leading on to Georgia's declaration of independence exactly two years later. Following on from a notoriously dodgy election, it was also the focus of a bloodless coup, the Rose Revolution, in 1993, in which a cluster of malignant elites was effectively expelled from the system. Such actions have set something of a precedent in a region where real democracy is a rarity and where those in power are often closer to parasites than to servants of the state.

The piss-smelling subterranean walkways used to cross the busy thoroughfare of Rustaveli were plastered with a series of peeling posters promoting, alternatively, ageing Western rock groups – Tbilisi had been added to the Eastern European tour dates for both Deep Purple and Uriah Heep – and some rather undignified-looking politicians. Looking incongruous in their suits, they had their arms around each other and held their thumbs up high while jeering for the camera. They looked more like drunken insurance salesman on a company karaoke night than aspiring statesmen. While, in nearby Iran, huge paintings of the severely sober and bearded Ayatollahs were displayed for all to see on the nation's grandest public buildings, in Georgia the politicians had to make do with small, cheap posters of their cheery, unshaven selves begging for approval in poorly lit tunnels.

Further on lies arguably the most interesting part of Tbilisi, the old town. Although Tbilisi has been the capital of Georgia almost continuously since the fifth century, most of what was in the old town was actually destroyed by the Persians in 1795. It looks as if they are still waiting to start work on the reconstruction. The narrow, winding stone alleys, decaying wooden balconies and general decrepitude may add to the atmosphere, but the discarded rubbish, graffiti and general disrepair make it seem more like a genuine medieval shithole than the sanitized versions of 'old towns' you might expect to find in most Eastern European capitals. If it had been in Turkmenistan, then I'm sure that Turkmenbashi would have wasted no time in razing it to the ground and replacing it with some garish, marble-clad tower blocks. To be fair, it was a nice enough area to wander around in and, outside of the grimiest parts of the old city, there were a number of atmospheric, smoke-stained old churches, some curious statues and a few overpriced tourist restaurants that thankfully provided some shelter when the drizzle turned to full-on rain. This small section of more affluent shops and restaurants in the old town gave some indication of what Tbilisi could be like in a few years' time if the country continues to grow economically at the current rate and it starts to attract the numbers of tourists that it deserves.

At the moment, Georgia is still slightly too inconvenient to get to, has a reputation for political stability, and few even know of its outstanding historical and natural attractions. With promised new routes from budget airlines, increased stability and a growing reputation among independent travellers, this could all change very quickly.

When the rain slowed from a downpour to a drizzle, I carried on up the hill, past the Armenian Cathedral, towards Narikala Fortress. The fortress dates back to the fourth century when it was first built as a Persian citadel but most of the existing towers and walls were built by the Arabs in the eighth century, to be variously patched up and added to by the Georgians, Turks and Persians over the following centuries until the Russians accidently blew it up in 1827. The Church of St Nicholas has since been rebuilt but the fortress itself is still largely a ruin. From the surviving walls, through the mist of the remaining rain, there were still some great views over the rooftops and churches and the Mtkvari River as it wound its way through the city. Between the church domes and spires there was also a series of smaller beehive-shaped domes that were home to Tbilisi's famed sulphur baths ('*tbili*' means warm). On top of the cliffs, on the other side of the river, stood Metekhi Church and the equestrian statue of King Vakhtang Gorgasali. This was where Gorgasali built his palace when he made it his capital in the fifth century. It was also the palace of King David the Builder (1089–1125), who led Georgia on to a golden age that reached its zenith under his great-granddaughter Queen Tamar (1184–1213). As with a lot of Tbilisi, it got trashed by the Mongols in 1235 and then completely destroyed by the Persians in 1795. A few hundred metres further along the crumbling fortified walls of Narikala stood a 20-metre high aluminium statue of Kartlis Deda (Mother Georgia), thought to perfectly represent the Georgian virtues of hospitality and courage. With a sword in one hand and a glass of wine in another, this symbol of the city is seen as a perfect metaphor for the Georgian character: drunk and up for a fight.

Batumi

Black Gold and White Slaves • A Touch of Class
Comfort in Desolation

After descending into the deep, dark metro to emerge into yet another chaotic bus station, I caught one more *marshrutka* heading down to the Black Sea. Batumi was first developed as a fortified port in Roman times under Hadrian (r. AD 117–138). It later passed through the hands of a series of empires including both Arab and Georgian. Under Ottoman Turkish rule, in the seventeenth century, Batumi became famous for its slave market, but it wasn't until the late nineteenth century, when it became the terminus of the oil pipeline from Baku, and Russia declared it as a free port, that Batumi truly began to prosper. Following a gradual decline over the last century, Georgia is now attempting to promote Batumi as an international holiday resort.

After five or six hours of a gradual descent through the mountains, I arrived at the harbour and was immediately surrounded by enthusiastic taxi drivers. Being unable to locate myself on my badly photocopied map and not wanting to traipse around for ages with my backpack, I negotiated what I thought was a reasonable cross-city fare, only to be dropped off a few hundred metres up the road. At first, I was a bit annoyed with myself, but then I realized that I would never have been able to find the small Hotel Iliko on my own, as any identifying signs or markers seemed to have been removed, along with most of the roads and pavements. The whole of the city looked a cross between a war zone and a building site. I guessed that some drastic 'improvements' must have been taking place, as part of Georgia's attempt to promote Batumi as a Black Sea beach resort, but for the moment, at least, the whole place was an absolute mess; all of the pavements were broken or missing, everything was covered in dust and mud, and the whole place looked more like a recent disaster area than somewhere you would visit for a fortnight in the sun.

Having settled into my surprisingly comfortable budget hotel room (which was cheaper than the popular shared and dormitory rooms in Yerevan and Tbilisi), I decided to visit the seaside. I managed to negotiate my way along about half a mile of mud, rubble and pot holes, then found myself walking through the main, central square, Evropas Moedani, and into the lush, well-maintained gardens surrounding the beach. Overlooking the square was a huge monument to the Greek mythological figure of Medea, of Jason and the Argonauts fame (Jason came to Colchis, the ancient name for Batumi, to find the Golden Fleece). Nobody seems to have a very convincing reason as to why the Georgian government spent such a huge amount of money on erecting a statue of a sorceress who murdered her children, Maybe they thought it would add a touch of class. I can only assume that was why they added a line of Greek-style colonnades on either side of the walk down to the stony beach. If it hadn't been outside, I'm sure they would have fitted in some chandeliers as well. Around the beachfront area were a number of theatres, some expensive-looking restaurants and a huge Ferris wheel. Outside of the central building zone it seemed nice enough, but strangely subdued. Having seen all there was to see, I made my way back through the desolation to my own, small, comfortable room.

Turkey

Trabzon

The Great Modernizer • Resurrected Islam • The Balance of Power
Nationalism and Modernity • Mosques and McDonald's
In Search of Divine Wisdom • Cast out into the Wilderness

After picking my way through more rubble and wreckage to indulge in a pastry and a cappuccino at the Café Literati, I attempted to find out where the bus left from Batumi to Trabzon in Turkey. As I was having no luck, I caught a minibus to the nearby border. I eventually found out where to pay for my Turkish visa, then walked back over into what is technically Asia (Anatolian Turkey) from what, despite being further east is generally considered to be Europe. In a small parking space, next to the Black Sea, were a few taxis but none of the expected minibuses that I had hoped to get onwards to Trabzon. Instead, I found myself as part of a small group of Turks involved in some intense negotiation with a taxi driver. Having eventually agreed on a reasonable fare to the nearby town of Hopa, where coaches apparently left regularly to Trabzon, I was bundled into the back of the taxi, only to find all my fellow passengers storming back out onto the road again. There appeared to have been a hitch in the negotiations. The driver looked like he was about to cry. I just sat there, feeling a bit awkward, and wondering if I ought to get out of the taxi as well. A few minutes later the driver seemed to give in to what he clearly thought were the other passenger's unreasonable demands, and we were soon speeding along an unexpectedly smooth road, running parallel to the dark, rippling waters of the Black Sea.

I was dropped off at a modern-looking bus station, just outside of Hopa, where it was easy enough to buy a ticket for one of the nice new coaches that would be leaving for Trabzon in just over an hour. After only a few hours on a comfortable coach, and a short ride on another local minibus, I found myself being nudged to get out at the top of Ataturk Alani, the thriving square at the heart of Trabzon. Everywhere you go in Turkey, you seem to find plenty of buildings, monuments and public spaces named after Turkey's great modernizer. Mustafa Kemal (he adopted the name 'Ataturk' meaning Father Turk) is venerated as a great champion of Turkish culture but in many ways seemed opposed to traditional Turkish culture: he adopted the Roman alphabet (in place of Arabic script), switched to the Gregorian calendar (in line with the West), outlawed traditional Turkish dress such as the Fez, and established a Western-style secular state. The success of one dominant figure in leading Turkey so far towards becoming one of the 'developed' countries could only really have happened in a country that was a long way from being either Westernized or European. Ataturk was closer in many respects to a Middle Eastern despot than to an elected statesman in a developed democracy, and, without being in possession of such power or authority, it is inconceivable that he could have pushed forward such great change. Whereas in the West any politician is considered fair game for criticism, any perceived insult to Ataturk, even today, would not only be seen as near heretical but would also be illegal. Such unquestioning attitudes towards authority would seem very foreign indeed to most of the young in the West, and a very long way from the developed, democratic values that Ataturk strove to establish in modern-day Turkey.

In recent years, Trabzon has emerged as a stronghold of nationalist politics and Turkey as a whole seems to have moved back from secularism towards a more traditional Islamic identity. As many Turks returned after working in low status jobs abroad – especially in West Germany – they reverted to their Islamic beliefs as a way of preserving their self-respect (if you consistently receive less status or recognition than some-one with the same values as yourself, then you will need to adopt a different set of values if you are not to feel inferior). This shift back to an Islamic identity was inevitably advanced by opportunistic politicians and demagogues. More than seventy years after Ataturk had banned the fez as a symbol of backwardness, schoolgirls were now returning to the Muslim headscarf.

I walked through Ataturk Alani and then down towards the cheaper hotels where I checked in to the surprisingly comfortable Hotel Anil. From my room on the side of the steep hill, I could look down over the Black Sea's busiest port where goods are shipped to and received from Georgia, Armenia, Azerbaijan and Russia. For decades, Turkey received substantial amounts of aid from the developed world in recognition of its allegiance with the West and its proximity to the former Soviet Union. Turkey seemed always to have hoped that its siding with NATO and the West would further its membership into the European Community but, when the Soviet Union collapsed and dreams of integration into Europe failed to materialize, it turned instead towards the Middle East. For centuries, the Trapezuntine leaders managed to skilfully balance alliances among such groups as the Seljuk, Mongol and Genoese, and Trabzon prospered as a Silk Road crossroads for commerce between Europe, Russia, Iran and the Caucasus. The thriving port was also known for its diverse range of ethnicities and cultures: Muslims and Christians lived happily side by side, and Turks, Greeks, Armenians and Georgians all seemed to muddle along together well enough. It wasn't until the European concept of nationalism was fully absorbed into Turkish consciousness that the former Ottoman Empire fragmented into separate states, and minority ethnicities began to be expelled or persecuted. It was this same surge in nationalism – a phenomenon that regularly seems to raise its ugly head during times of crisis and insecurity – that Ataturk exploited to gain the popular support of the Turkish majority needed to establish the modern state of Turkey (to the cost of the resident Greeks, Armenians and Kurds).

While the smaller Turkish towns and villages that the coach had passed through on the way along the Black Sea coast had seemed run down and sleepy, Trabzon shone out with an energy that was generated through a clash between the East and the West. Headscarves and baseball caps seemed to be almost equally distributed among the teenagers to be found in either the mosques or the McDonald's. The usual, aspirational, large plasma television screen had been suspended at the shopping street end of Ataturk Alani, flashing out MTV idols over the heads of burka-clad pram-pushing mothers. The heaving shopping streets and covered lanes around the square seemed to belong somewhere between an American mall and a Middle Eastern bazaar. Anything that was bright and shiny was welcomed in – anything that aided commerce. I bought my ticket for my last long overnight bus trip along the Silk Road, to Safranbolu, and walked back across Ataturk Alani and towards the bright lights of Burger King.

* * *

I was woken by the sun shining in through the curtainless windows. It seemed too soon to rise but the bright early morning sunshine and the arbitrary time difference between here and Georgia meant that I couldn't get back to sleep. I turned on the television and found an advertisement-heavy channel dedicated to the kind of second division US imports that are given away almost for nothing in an attempt to spread the American dream (the only other channel that I could find in English was dedicated to porn). After breakfast on my own, I checked out of the hotel (leaving my backpack at reception), and set off past the statue of Ataturk, the rows of opening clothes shops and the occasional mosque to find my way to Trabzon's best-known attraction, the Aya Sofia (Church of the Divine Wisdom) Museum. I couldn't figure out where to get the bus from so just kept walking in the general direction. I was a bit disappointed when I first found what I thought was the Aya Sofia but then I realized that it was just another mosque I'd never heard of, and continued my pilgrimage.

The Aya Sofia was originally a pagan temple dedicated to Apollo (associated with dominion over colonists). The original Greek Orthodox Church was first built on the site during the Byzantine period in the thirteenth century but was converted into a mosque by the Ottomans in 1461. For a brief period in the twentieth century, the Russians took it over to use as a hospital and ammunitions depot but it was later restored in the 1960s to become the tourist attraction of today. I walked around with yet another group of schoolchildren, gazing out over the Black Sea from the ancient stone walls, and staring up at the Georgian-style dome and the faded frescoes. The most photographed of these restored frescoes depicted Adam and Eve's expulsion from paradise – banishment from your tribal group was among the most feared punishments in pagan times – but the most popular attraction was the onsite teahouse. I abandoned the hordes of marauding Turkish school children to join a few elderly European tourists for a nice cup of tea (not many Western tourists made it this far into eastern Turkey and most of those that did seemed to be coffin dodgers).

Later in the afternoon, I was picked up from the bus company's ticket office in town to be driven on to the coach station and my night bus to Safranbolu. I settled down for the journey, with my book and my headphones, relieved that this would be my last long overnight bus ride. After a few hours I was bursting to use the toilet. I asked the steward when the bus might be stopping but he just shrugged and said 'maybe an hour'. Two hours later I was still crossing my legs. I asked again and this time he said that they would stop at 10pm. That was still another two hours. There was no way I could hold it in that long! I was starting to get desperate. I figured that if I could drink the rest of my water then I might be able to piss into the bottle – it would be hard to get away with this without it being noticed but it would still be better than wetting myself (I was having visions of oceans of piss washing up and down the aisles of the bus, every time we turned the corner). I had just managed to finish the last of the water and was unzipping my flies when we pulled into a service station. He must have meant ten minutes.

SAFRANBOLU

Greener on the Other Side • Blind Faith • Alien Annihilation

We pulled into the bus station as the sun was rising and I stepped out into the drizzle. Not wanting to get caught in the rain while searching for a bus into town, I got a taxi to take me to Bastoncu Pansiyon in the old town of Safranbolu. After waking the owners to let me in, I quickly washed and brushed my teeth before finding a bed in the unoccupied dormitory room to crawl into. Lying exhausted between the crisp white sheets in the wood-beamed, Ottoman-style room, I could finally lie down to catch some much-needed sleep.

I wasn't woken until a couple of hours later when Awa, from Hong Kong, walked into the dormitory, soaking wet. He had turned up at the bus station around the same time as I had but had tried to catch the local buses into the old town and inevitably gotten lost.

After breakfast downstairs, I set off to explore the UNESCO World Heritage Site that is Safranbolu. The exceptional old Ottoman buildings were originally financed by wealthy merchants, grown rich on the lucrative Silk Road trade along the Black Sea coast, but the modern-day town relies heavily on tourism. As well as a number of attractive family houses that have been turned into museums or guest houses, there is a working trader's caravanserai that has been converted into a posh hotel, and an old public bath house that now trades as a luxury spa. Safranbolu's name derives from the former abundance of the rare flower Saffron in the surrounding area but there no longer appears to be much Saffron growing wild; instead, there are gift shops, purveyors of Turkish delight (*lokum*), and expensive tourist restaurants sprouting up all over the old, cobbled streets.

On my way back from the castle at the top of the hill – where I was obliged to wear blue plastic bags over my shoes – I was approached by two tourism students called Farouk and Ahmed. They had been looking for tourists to 'interview' as part of a project, and Farouk had picked me out as he thought I looked 'different' (they probably say that to all the tourists). It may simply have been that I didn't turn away when he started to talk to me. Having only just come from the exceptionally friendly and genuine countries of the Caucasus and Iran, I had yet to fall into the kind of defensiveness that it is all too easy to revert to in some of the most heavily touristed but under-developed parts of the world. Farouk seemed genuinely hurt that so many of his country's visitors would choose to just blank him, but I explained that they had probably become defensive in response to a constant barrage of harassment from hawkers and hustlers. They were both keen to experience the kind of travel that many of those they would go on to serve simply take for granted. The nearest either of them had so far come to experiencing life outside of Turkey was when the teenage Farouk had become engaged to a Russian girl who was visiting on holiday, and she had tried to bring him back home with her. I'm really not sure that he would prefer to live in Russia than Turkey but he was keen to try. When they asked me how many countries I'd visited, for the first time I could say that it was over a hundred. 'Fist me,' said Farouk. I assumed that this was a local variant of 'Fuck me' and was meant as an expression of surprise. At least I hoped it was. We said our farewells and I walked back down the hill to find something to eat.

Not far down from my guest house I found a cheap restaurant that was popular with the locals but also had a menu with some English on it. I ordered a popular local dish that consisted of a kind of Turkish macaroni with a walnut-type topping, and sat down with them to watch the television. They appeared to be watching a Turkish version of *Blind Date*. To add an extra element of surprise, the women to be chosen were wearing veils. It must have been particularly hard to feign delight with your choice when each of the women that was presented to you still had a bag on her head (to be fair to the selected ladies they seemed to have made an effort to pick out some particularly colourful headscarves and some seemed even to be wearing mascara).

After an hour or so at the local Internet café – where, like anywhere else in Asia, I was surrounding by alien annihilating teenagers – I walked back up through the cobbled streets to try to buy some fresh fruit and bumped into Awa, my dormitory room mate, who was chatting with Farouk and Ahmed. In a town like Safranbolu, everybody seemed to meet up with everybody else, often sooner than later. After only a day there, I was already starting to recognize and be recognized by the locals (in the town where I live in England I don't even know who my neighbours are). Having purchased a banana I returned to the dormitory room in the lovely old Ottoman house and succumbed to a full night's sleep.

ISTANBUL

Crossing the Bridge • The Fall of the East • Holier than Thou
Running out of Memory • End of the Road

The owner of Bastoncu Pansiyon dropped me off at the bus station office, on his way into the new town, from where I joined the onward coach to Istanbul. Six or seven hours later, I was crossing the Bosphorus, literally on a bridge between the Istanbul of Asia and the Istanbul of Europe – one of the world's great cities, lying torn between the East and the West. Whether as Byzantine, or Constantinople, or as the 15-million-strong metropolis of today, Istanbul has always been both a cornerstone and a crossroads of civilizations. As the capital of the Ottoman Empire, Istanbul lay at the very centre of a civilization that, as well as spanning large parts of the Near and Middle East, also, at its peak, included around half of Eastern Europe. It wasn't until their failure at the Siege of Vienna in 1683 that the Ottomans' expansion into Europe ground to a painful halt. While Western Europe continued to make huge advances – scientifically, culturally and militarily – the Ottoman Empire fell into a slow decline (perhaps the single greatest reason for this was the Ottoman Clergy's banning of the printing press). Today, Turkey seems desperate to once more be accepted into Europe, but many 'developed' European countries are reluctant to grant Turkey membership into the EU. Human rights violations, widespread corruption and repression of minorities (especially of the Kurds) have all been cited as valid reasons for other EU member states' rejection of Turkey, but perhaps the biggest reason is simply that they don't really think that the Turks are European.

I got off the coach at the large bus station complex and quickly realized I had no idea where to go. I had been at this bus station just seven months earlier while travelling around Turkey and Eastern Europe with my wife, so I hadn't even brought a map of Istanbul with me. Unfortunately, my memory was fading faster than I'd thought. There seemed to be a lot of people walking over a bridge towards another group of buildings so I decided to follow them. After a few false starts and some awkward questioning I eventually found myself on one of the underground trains heading towards the centre, from where I followed more locals walking the five minutes or so across to the tram stop. Some of it was starting to come back to me but I was still slightly alarmed at how much I had forgotten so quickly.

I knew that we were almost at Sultanahmet, the main tourist zone of Istanbul, when the tram passed the large McDonald's. I stepped out into Sultanahmet Park and merged into the hordes of invading tourists. To my left stood the monumental Aya Sofya, completed under the Roman Emperor Justinian in 537, and considered to be the greatest church in Christendom until the Conquest in 1453. Mehmet the Conqueror then had it converted to a mosque, until Ataturk set it up as a museum in 1935. When I last visited it, it was full of scaffolding. To the right stood the Blue Mosque, constructed under Sultan Ahmet 1 (r. 1603–1617) in an attempt to outdo the grandeur and beauty of the nearby Aya Sofya. I hauled myself and my backpack through the coachloads of camera-wielding tourists and downhill towards the location of most of the budget accommodation. I thought I'd try to get a room in a dormitory that I'd stayed at previously, but couldn't remember where it was. There were hostels and hotels everywhere and a lot of them looked the same. After traipsing around in circles a couple of times I walked into what I thought was the right one only to realize that it wasn't once I'd already checked in. It didn't matter – they all seemed more or less the same, anyway. Everyone was packed full of twenty-something 'gap year' travellers, fiddling with their digital cameras and laptops. For the first time since Chengdu in China, I really felt like I was back on the well-trodden backpackers' circuit.

I walked into my allocated dormitory where a podgy Australian was showing off an extensive collection of images he'd captured as proof of all the experiences he'd consumed. He proudly boasted of the organized tour of Vietnam that he'd been on where he'd got to go to every single place that they'd shown on the *Top Gear* Vietnam special. He didn't worry about getting his expensive digital camera and laptop stolen as he kept them strapped to his body at all times. In a few days he would be returning to Australia, having 'done' his gap year.

As the light began to fade, I walked back up past Aya Sofya and the Blue Mosque, across the Grand Bazaar and then down towards the Golden Horn and the Galata Bridge. It seemed strange and kind of lonely to be wandering these streets on my own when just seven months before I had been exploring them with my wife. As well as being at the end of the Silk Road, and at the end of Asia, Istanbul, with all its renowned melancholy and faded grandeur, would also be my own final destination. In a few days I would be reunited with my wife and in a few days more I would be back at work. In some ways I was looking forward to the comfort and warmth of home but I knew that it wouldn't be long until that part of myself that desired to be settled would soon come under siege from my nomadic soul. I looked out over the Bosphorus and, like Istanbul, was torn between one world and the next.

* * *

I rose early, like a man condemned, and waited on the rooftop terrace for the buffet breakfast to be laid out. As the sun began to rise, I looked down over this crossroads of civilizations for the last time. Not long after, I was being picked up from outside the hostel by a minivan heading for the airport (the one that's 50 kilometres outside of Istanbul that easyJet uses). I sat at the back with a slim, young woman and an older, fatter one. They were mother and daughter. They had only been away for a few days on a city break but the daughter had spent nearly all the time holed up in her hotel room with a stomach bug. They were amazed that I had been through all those 'uncivilized' places to get here without really getting ill. I stayed silent about the lump on my throat. The mother thought that Istanbul was a beautiful city but wasn't keen on all the Muslims. She worried about them being terrorists. Her daughter looked embarrassed and told her mother not to be so silly.

In the queue to the easyJet check-in we were joined by a veiled English woman who struck up a conversation with the mother and daughter. She patiently explained to them why she had chosen to wear the veil even though she didn't have to. I wasn't very convinced by her arguments but they all seemed to be getting on like a house on fire. They all carried on happily chatting away as we strolled through to security where we were abruptly asked to step back. There was a problem with one of the carry-on bags in front: it was ticking. A middle-aged Turkish man stepped forward with his hands raised in a conciliatory gesture and slowly pulled out the offending object. It was an alarm clock. It was just the sound of time passing by.

Selected Bibliography

Alexander, Christopher Aslan, *A Carpet Ride to Khiva: Seven Years on the Silk Road* (Icon Books Ltd, 2010)

Aziz, Shahzad, *In the Land of the Ayatollahs Tupac Shakur is King: Reflections from Iran and the Arab World* (Amal Press, 2007)

Fukuyama, Francis, *The End of History and the Last Man* (Penguin, 1993)

Huntingdon, Samuel P., *The Clash of Civilizations and the Remaking of World Order* (The Free Press, 2002)

Leonard, Mark, *What Does China Think?* (Fourth Estate, 2008)

LeVine, Mark, *Heavy Metal Islam: Rock, Resistance, and the Struggle for the Soul of Islam* (Three Rivers Press, 2009)

Marozzi, Justin, *Tamerlane: Sword of Islam, Conqueror of the World* (HarperCollins, 2004)

Marsden, Philip, *The Crossing Place: A Journey among the Armenians* (Flamingo, 1994)

Murray, Craig, *Murder in Samarkand: A British Ambassador's Controversial Defiance of Tyranny in the War on Terror* (Mainstream Publishing, 2007)

Polo, Marco, *The Travels of Marco Polo* (Wordsworth Editions Ltd, 1997)

Rall, Ted, *Silk Road to Ruin: Is Central Asia the new Middle East?* (NBM Publishing Company, 2006)

Robbins, Christopher, *In Search of Kazakhstan: The Land that Disappeared* (Profile Books, 2008)

Satrapi, Marjane, *Persepolis: The Story of a Childhood and The Story of a Return* (Jonathan Cape, 2006)

Thubron, Colin, *Shadow of the Silk Road* (Vintage, 2007)

Thubron, Colin, *The Lost Heart of Asia* (Vintage, 2007)
Weatherford, Jack, *Genghis Khan and the Making of the Modern World* (Three Rivers Press, 2004)

Index